BETTER LIVING BY THEIR OWN BOOTSTRAPS

Arkansas History

JEANNIE WHAYNE, GENERAL EDITOR

BETTER LIVING BY THEIR OWN BOOTSTRAPS

Black Women's Activism in Rural Arkansas, 1914–1965

CHERISSE JONES-BRANCH

The University of Arkansas Press
Fayetteville
2021

978-1-68226-166-8 (cloth)
978-1-68226-167-5 (paperback)
978-1-61075-744-7 (ebook)

Manufactured in the United States of America

25 24 23 22 21   5 4 3 2 1

Designer: Liz Lester
Cover image: Assistant home demonstration agents from Arkansas, 1950.
Courtesy of Dorris Vick Collection, University of Arkansas Libraries Special Collections.
Cover Design: Erin Kirk

♾ The paper used in this publication meets the minimum requirements of the American National Standard for Permanence of Paper for Printed Library Materials Z39.48-1984.

Library of Congress Cataloging-in-Publication Data

Names: Jones-Branch, Cherisse, author.
Title: Better living by their own bootstraps: Black women's activism in
    rural Arkansas, 1914–1965 / Cherisse Jones-Branch.
Other titles: Arkansas history (Fayetteville, Ark.)
Description: Fayetteville: University of Arkansas Press, 2021. | Series: Arkansas history |
    Includes bibliographical references and index. | Summary: "Better Living by Their Own
    Bootstraps is the first major study to consider Black women's activism in rural Arkansas.
    The text explores Arkansas's rural history to foreground Black women's navigation of racial
    and gender politics as a means to uplift African Americans, develop opportunities for social
    mobility, and subvert the formidable structures of white supremacy during the Jim Crow
    years"—Provided by publisher.
Identifiers: LCCN 2020042353 (print) | LCCN 2020042354 (ebook) | ISBN 9781682261668
    (cloth) | ISBN 9781682261675 (paperback) | ISBN 9781610757447 (ebook)
Subjects: LCSH: African American women political activists—Arkansas—History—
    20th century. | Rural African Americans—Arkansas—History—20th century. | Rural
    women—Arkansas—History—20th century. | Arkansas—Rural conditions. | Arkansas—
    Race relations.
Classification: LCC E185.93.A8 J655 2021 (print) | LCC E185.93.A8 (ebook) |
    DDC 305.896/07301734—dc23
LC record available at https://lccn.loc.gov/2020042353
LC ebook record available at https://lccn.loc.gov/2020042354

CONTENTS

ACKNOWLEDGMENTS

I would never have been able to write this book without the help and advice of friends, colleagues, and family. Elizabeth Griffin Hill's scholarship was among the first I read about Arkansas home extension clubs that piqued my interest in rural Black women members. She very generously shared her digitized research from the Department of Agriculture Extension Service records housed at the National Archives in Fort Worth, Texas. John Kirk at the University of Arkansas at Little Rock unknowingly provided me with the first forum to talk about African American home demonstration agents employed by the Arkansas Agricultural Cooperative Extension Service. Further, I am extremely grateful that I was able to "find my tribe" when giving my first and subsequent papers at the Agricultural History Society and Rural Women's Studies Association meetings.

Soon after those early meetings, I realized that my research was going to become a book. I so appreciate the staff at Special Collections of the University of Arkansas Libraries (Fayetteville), the Butler Center for Arkansas Studies in Little Rock, University of Central Arkansas Archives, Conway, and the Arts and Sciences Center for Southeast Arkansas, Pine Bluff, for helping me locate little-known information about Black women's activism in rural Arkansas. The help I received from the Arkansas State Archives and the Archives Research Center, Atlanta University Center Robert W. Woodruff Library in Atlanta, Georgia, proved critical to helping me flesh out my analysis of Jeanes Supervising Industrial Teachers, as did scholarship by Valinda Littlefield.

Melissa Walker read an early draft of the manuscript and provided substantial feedback. Her scholarship, along with that of Lu Ann Jones, Linda Ambrose, Joan Jensen, Carmen Harris, Debra Reid, and others, profoundly influenced my understanding of the rich layers and textures embedded in rural women's history. Thank you, Michael Pierce, for the information on Ethel B. Dawson. Because of the very large zip file of information you sent me, I was able to present her life as an agrarian activist at the 2019 European Rural History Organisation meeting in Paris, France. I send a special shout-out to the Delta women writers who read my essay on Dawson. Your sharp eyes and brains helped me think deeply about the many ways to frame her life and convinced me that I am establishing a new way of exploring Black women's experiences in the rural Jim Crow South.

I certainly could not have finished this book without the staff at Arkansas State University's Archives and Special Collections and the Dean B. Ellis Library. They have been wonderfully patient with my many interlibrary loan requests, as well as the large volume of books I have checked out over the years. I promise to return everything as soon as this book is published!

My thanks to the readers, who labored over a very rough draft of my manuscript. I appreciate you tolerating my many mistakes and oversights. Your substantial feedback makes this a much better book.

David Scott Cunningham, I so appreciate your support of this project from the very beginning and your urging me to get it done so it could be published in 2021. I have done that. I thank you and the University of Arkansas Press for providing me with the opportunity to write about this overlooked aspect of Arkansas history.

Dr. Anes Wiley Abraham, thank you for sharing your home archives with me. Your generosity and that of my sisters in the Blytheville Social Arts Club have enriched my knowledge of Black women's activism in Mississippi County and Arkansas. To my Sorors in Sigma Gamma Rho Sorority Incorporated, thank you for welcoming me back into the fold after such a long absence. You truly represent "Greater Service, Greater Progress." My family and friends, of course, are more important to me than anything else in the world. Thank you for your love and support throughout this process. You inspire me more than you will ever know, and I always strive to represent you well. I hope I have made you proud.

Finally, I dedicate this book to Annie Zachary Pike, who welcomed me into her home in Marvell and into her heart. Thank you for sharing your story with me. You are a phenomenal woman, and the world should know that.

BETTER LIVING BY THEIR OWN BOOTSTRAPS

Introduction

THE IDEA FOR this book came to me as I was finishing my first monograph on women's interracial activism in South Carolina. Sara Z. Daniel, one of the women I chronicled, was a home demonstration agent whose civil rights activism as president of the Manning NAACP in Clarendon County resulted in her losing her job with the South Carolina Agricultural Extension Service.[1] I must admit that it never occurred to me to ask what a home demonstration agent was until I had completed my book. Furthermore, I had no previous training as a rural women's historian, and up until that point I did not know that such a field even existed. But after reading the very fine work of such US scholars as Joan Jensen, Melissa Walker, Katherine Jellison, Grey Osterud, Nancy Berlage, Debra Reid, Carmen Harris, Valerie Grims, Rebecca Sharpless, Jenny Barker Devine, and Canadian historians Linda Ambrose and Margaret Kechnie, I discovered a rich and flourishing field that intentionally centered rural women's experiences.

My interest in rural Black women's activism was subsequently piqued when I read Valerie Grim's stellar article "From the Yazoo Mississippi Delta to the Urban Communities of the Midwest: Conversations with Rural African American Women," and Carmen Harris's poignant "'Well, I Just Generally Bes the President of Everything': Rural Black Women's Empowerment through South Carolina Home Demonstration Activities."[2] These two studies helped me begin to better conceptualize what Black women's activism looked like in rural southern spaces and how they created all-female spaces to discuss and engage in health, education, and family activism free from southern white regulation and interference. Jenny Barker Devine has written most eloquently about how white farm women "adapted their rhetoric and politicized aspects of their daily work, responded to female leadership at the state level, related to male leaders, coped with limited resources, and claimed a presence in male-dominated spaces in order to work toward favorable agricultural policies."[3] Using this analytical framework, I questioned how rural Black women accomplished the same while facing the additional challenge of combating southern white racism.

Rural southern Black women have most often been studied as enslaved laborers or in the context of their movement out of the South to northern and western locales. Such studies have also emphasized how they transferred culture, language, foodways, and organizational strategies to urban Black communities. I understand well the reasons why rural African American women migrated to urban communities and even southern ones; as Grim wrote, they "left the fields and farms by the hundreds of thousands" to escape southern white terrorism.[4] In so doing, they sought increased social, cultural, and educational opportunities for themselves and their families. They were often freer and safer to engage in political, economic, educational, and community activism. As Black women, they also left the South because they knew they could not expect protection from physical and sexual abuse from either white or Black men. And so they salvaged their womanhood and migrated to urban spaces that offered increased protection and opportunity, though these were limited due to their race and gender.[5]

But many rural Black women remained in the South either by choice or circumstance. I wanted to know how they evaluated their lives and communities. What forms did their activism assume in rural Black communities? What state, federal, and philanthropic apparatuses did they utilize? I wanted to write about how all of this occurred in Arkansas in particular because most scholarship on rural Arkansas has privileged men's experiences, particularly those of white men.[6] Even when African Americans are the focus, with the exception of Daisy Bates's role in the 1957 Little Rock Central High School Crisis, Black women are largely invisible. When they do appear, it is briefly and in a one-dimensional fashion as agricultural laborers. Their lives and activism have received little notice and even less critical examination. Furthermore, most studies on rural Black activism have focused primarily on men in such organizations as the Arkansas-founded Progressive Farmers Household Union of America and the Southern Tenant Farmers Union. For these reasons, I deemed it necessary, even critical, to unearth and productively complicate rural Black women's lives and activism, to rectify their marginalization by exploring the many ways they individually, collectively, and diligently augmented African Americans' quality of life in rural Arkansas.

Better Living by Their Own Bootstraps centers Black women's activism in Arkansas communities and examines their particularly crafted and honed form of rural uplift. Not all of these women were agricultural laborers, or at least not for all of their lives. And not all of them resided in rural Arkansas or even in the Delta. Mame Stewart Josenberger, for instance, was born and raised in upstate New York, along Lake Ontario, and spent her entire adult life in Fort Smith in Sebastian County, where she was a business and property owner, and a prominent clubwoman.

Rural Black women activists were a mixture of educated profession-als and agricultural laborers, home demonstration agents employed by the Arkansas Agricultural Cooperative Extension Service (AACES), Jeanes Supervising Industrial Teachers, and Arkansas Association of Colored Women (AACW) club members. Some of them were landowners: Phillips County's Annie Zachary Pike and her first husband employed African American sharecroppers. Their independence often buffered them from the worst vicissitudes of white racism. This economic privilege, along with her relationship with Governor Winthrop Rockefeller in the 1960s, provided Pike with political access that enabled her to run as a Republican candidate for the Arkansas State Senate in 1972.

All of the women considered in this book had an acute understanding of the difficulties African Americans endured as they enacted change in rural spaces. In many instances, they were compelled to couch their efforts in terms that did not alienate or infuriate white landowners or the larger white community. But individual Black women activists such as Elveria Heard and Annie Zachary Pike had few reservations about challenging existing racial and gender hierarchies. Collectively and individually, these women assumed responsibility for improving food insecurity, health and sanitary conditions, and political and educational access in rural Black communi-ties, because they understood that hungry, sick, illiterate, and uninformed people could not very well focus on being politically viable.

Yet they did not merely project their reform agenda onto the commu-nities where they worked. Poor uneducated rural Black women naturally understood their communities better than anyone else possibly could and were best positioned to speak to the changes their communities needed and to demand the help they required. This book lifts these women from the obscurity of Arkansas's rural history. It examines them through a complex and nuanced analytical lens that reveals how they harnessed their organiza-tional and intellectual skills to implement change in their communities. It also highlights how Black women agricultural laborers' deep understanding of their environment led them to become activists in ways that have not been fully explored. They did not merely learn about better living from

outsiders. Rural Black women's power was derived from an intimate understanding and development of their own leadership capabilities.

Better Living by Their Own Bootstraps excavates the little-known but
deeply textured contours of Black women's activism in rural Arkansas by first
examining Jeanes Supervising Industrial Teachers (or Jeanes Supervisors)
who worked in the state from 1909 until 1950, educating African Americans
in the rudimentary skills white landowners deemed most appropriate to
keep them on the land as agricultural laborers. While they aided African
American educators, Jeanes Supervisors stealthily helped rural communities
challenge the economic and political marginalization they endured in Jim
Crow Arkansas. Chapter 2 follows by highlighting the labor of African
American home demonstration agents employed by the AACES. Segregated
from their white colleagues and discriminated against in their pay and access
to resources, Black home demonstration agents nonetheless helped African
Americans mitigate myriad health concerns within their communities, in
conjunction with local, predominantly Black organizations with national
connections, like the AACW. Chapters 3 and 4 augment the discussion
about Black home demonstration agents' activism in rural Arkansas communities during and after World War I by considering Black women's experiences during and after the racialized terrorism of the 1919 Elaine Massacre
and their role in helping destitute African Americans during the Mississippi
River flood of 1927.

My exploration includes local rural Black women's activism through
the segregated State Council of Home Demonstration Clubs (SCHDC)
and fleshes out their roles as community activists in ways that challenge
assumptions about their experiences as agricultural laborers. This theme
continues with a specific focus on the AACW, an organization of which
many rural Black women were members, and their campaign to obtain
support from Arkansas's governors to establish industrial schools for African
American youth. World War II and the postwar years are prominently featured in chapter 7, as rural Black women made their communities' concerns
public through their affiliations with statewide and national forums and
organizations. In the late 1940s, this included the Arkansas Farm Bureau
Federation's Negro Division, the subject of chapter 8. The chapter begins
with a vignette of Leoda Gammon and goes on to discuss Black women
leaders who addressed concerns about African Americans' roles in Arkansas's
agricultural future. Chapter 9 details Black home demonstration agents'
activism among African American agricultural producers and political activists, and chapter 10 spotlights former extension service employee Ethel B.

Dawson's pivotal role as a rural religious extension agent and civil rights activist in Pine Bluff in the 1950s and 1960s. Dawson's work underscores the importance of long-standing and locally cultivated activism at time when such national organizations as the Student Nonviolent Coordinating Committee increased their presence in rural Black communities.

As the 1950s came to a close, new opportunities arose for rural Black women to organize and discuss their rural uplift experiences with colleagues from around the South. Black agricultural extension agents, some of whom were Arkansas based, founded the National Negro Home Demonstration Agents' Association, the subject of chapter 11, in reaction to their exclusion from its predominantly white counterpart. Because it is important to recognize the rural Black women who still live and labor in Arkansas in the twenty-first century, chapter 12 concludes this monograph with the fascinating yet little-known story of Phillips County farmer, activist, and politician Annie Zachary Pike. Her story brings into greater relief rural Black women's activism throughout the twentieth and twenty-first centuries, and it is particularly instructive about the ways that sources beyond the archives can illuminate and give texture to the complexities and nuances of Black women's lives in rural spaces.

African American women's rural uplift activism throughout Arkansas resulted from the groundswell of grassroots networks they cultivated and utilized within and beyond their communities. Whether they were professional, educated landowners or poor, illiterate agricultural laborers, Black women developed strategies, that informed their activism in the rural communities where they worked, lived, and loved, to realize impactful change. This exploration recovers their stories from the margins of rural, women's, African American, and Arkansas history and provides them with the visibility in the historical record that they so rightly deserve. I hope my work here does them justice.

— 1 —

Arkansas Jeanes Supervising Industrial Teachers

BUENA VISTA, MISSISSIPPI, native Ila Upchurch was a well-known Arkansas Jeanes Supervisor. A graduate of Shorter College in Little Rock, with a master's degree from Tennessee State College, she had lived and worked in Nevada County in southwestern Arkansas since 1925. Upchurch was a member of the Arkansas Congress of Colored Parents and Teachers (ACCPT), founded in 1928, and was elected its vice president in 1936 and 1940 and president in 1942.[1] The Upchurch Training School in Prescott was named in her honor.[2] Indeed, Upchurch was so greatly esteemed in Prescott that she was described thusly in a 1942 *Arkansas State Press* article: "Nevada County, with Miss Ila Upchurch as Jeanes Supervisor, as always, has been a 'pace-setter.'"[3] Also a civil rights advocate, Upchurch became a Prescott and Nevada County NAACP member when the chapter was established in 1945.[4] She attended the NAACP district council meeting in 1946 and was also the NAACP Youth Council state chairperson.[5] Upchurch clearly understood the importance of teaching African American children about their civil rights. Informed by the democratic rhetoric of World War II, she was intimately involved in raising children's political consciousness. In 1946, she hosted the youth council's "lawn social" at her home in Prescott to underscore her efforts.[6] Upchurch remained a Nevada County Jeanes Supervisor until she was fired in 1949 for failing to "discharge her duties properly." It is more likely, however, that she was terminated because of her membership in the Prescott branch of the NAACP.[7]

Ila Upchurch's story reveals much about what has been overlooked in the silences surrounding Black women's labor and leadership in rural communities. Their overt, and more often covert, activism is symbolic of what bell hooks called "homeplace," a praxis through which Black women leaders like Jeanes Supervisors navigated and at times created spaces that not only provided a temporary refuge from southern racism but also allowed African Americans to care for their communities.[8]

Jeanes Supervising Industrial Teachers, or Jeanes Supervisors, active in Arkansas from approximately 1909 until 1950, were valued and revered for their educational and community activism.[9] Despite this or perhaps because of it, they provided much-needed guidance and educational assistance to impoverished rural Black communities throughout the state. They, like the people they assisted, were concerned about obtaining basic educational skills, but they also deliberately engaged in rural community health work and political activism through such organizations as the NAACP in the years before the modern civil rights movement. Like their counterparts throughout the South, Arkansas Jeanes Supervisors improved educational quality and access and reformed domestic habits. They accomplished this despite having to navigate a fraught racial terrain that was intentionally engineered to ensure African Americans' educational, political, and economic subordination.

In the late nineteenth century, southern states often lacked the resources to provide adequate education for what one scholar called the "sophisticated work and civic demands of the twentieth century."[10] State governments spent pathetically little on public education. By 1900, 15 percent of southern whites and 50 percent of southern African Americans were functionally illiterate. Southern educational efforts were supported by funding from the General Education Board (GEB), chartered in 1903 by the Rockefeller family. With a public mission to help "the needs of the people of our Southern states," the GEB, initially endowed with $1 million which grew to $53 million by 1909, was led by New York Baptist ministers Frederick T. Gates and Wallace Buttrick, both of whom were descended from families with abolitionist roots. Gates and Wallace were particularly, though paternalistically, concerned about southern African Americans because their condition presented a "peculiar and special obligation." Yet, while they recognized that exploitative economic conditions and unyielding racism marginalized the South, they were unwilling to challenge deeply rooted Jim Crow laws and the region's commitment to maintaining white supremacy.[11]

During the early years of the twentieth century, the GEB's efforts largely centered on supporting schools and universities throughout the South. Its leaders were particularly focused on African American educational and economic opportunities, even as they increasingly turned their attention to the region's agricultural devastation.[12] By 1929, the Rockefeller family had contributed over $129 million to the GEB to establish rural one-room county training, urban, and public high schools throughout the South.[13]

These efforts in rural African American communities were also assisted by the Jeanes Fund teacher supervision program (1907), the Slater Fund (1910), and the Julius Rosenwald Fund (1914). As a result of these funding sources and educators' efforts, between 1900 and 1920 illiteracy rates in the South dropped to 5.9 percent for whites and 25.8 percent for African Americans.[14] Despite this dramatic improvement, southern educational rates continued to lag behind those nationwide. And, unfortunately, the situation remained far worse for African Americans. As one historian has argued, "great economic expenditures and reform crusades for black industrial education" resulted in educational "underdevelopment" because these rarely provided African Americans with a quality education.[15] That is, the education they received was largely designed to keep them from migrating out of rural areas and to force them to accept their subordinate status.[16]

Educational and school reform was most often women's domain in the late nineteenth and early twentieth centuries. Women, regardless of race, recognized that their activism was critical, because they were frequently and dramatically impacted by the disadvantages of poor educational access. But educational activism was particularly important to African American women who experienced firsthand chronically and deliberately under-funded community schools, teacher shortages, and some southern whites' reluctance to provide Blacks with even basic education.[17] Educational activism was largely the province of Black women in the twentieth-century South and was supported by increased advocacy for more university and teacher training opportunities that allowed them to go into and, in some cases, return to rural southern communities to ameliorate the problems they found there. Helping African Americans was more often than not a cooperative venture. Arkansas home demonstration agents—employed by the Arkansas Agricultural Cooperative Extension Service (AACES) and the Arkansas Association of Colored Women (AACW), and about whom more will be said later—were often assisted by local Jeanes Supervisors.

Jeanes Supervising Industrial Teachers were funded by an endowment known as the Negro Rural School Fund, which had been created in 1907 by Pennsylvania Quaker Anna T. Jeanes to support rural Black education in cooperation with white state and county school officials. White county superintendents hired industrial supervising teachers to work in rural Black schools. Most Black educators were appointed by and depended upon financial support from southern white school boards.[18] This was the case for Jeanes Supervisors, at least in part. While the Jeanes Fund initially provided all the monies for industrial teachers' activities, county school boards and quorum courts eventually paid at least part of their salaries and traveling expenses for the resources they required to perform their jobs.[19] For instance, in 1916 the Hempstead County quorum court appropriated $150 to pay its Jeanes Supervisor—a $100 increase from the previous year. In 1935, it appropriated $300 for a salary, although it did not list any such appropriations for 1934 or 1936, largely because funds were unavailable during the Depression years.[20]

Jeanes Supervisors assisted Black teachers in rural communities throughout the South who were often untrained in addition to being poorly paid. Black educators in Arkansas were responsible for improving the quality of education in rural schools and reforming domestic habits in the community. Their efforts were supported by the Arkansas Department of Education (ADE), which in the early years of the twentieth century organized five industrial summer normal schools for Black teachers in Little Rock, Pine Bluff, and other locations in Arkansas with significant African American populations. White officials, however, were only interested in providing teachers with "such training as will fit them for their work." That is, their mandate was to educate rural Blacks to become a more "industrious," "sanitary," "moral," and tractable agricultural labor force. The summer institutes' special objectives then were to train Black teachers to "teach children to use their hands as well as their brains," "spread knowledge of how to avoid disease," and "to raise standards among the Negroes."[21] This was also as part of Jeanes Supervisors' responsibilities in rural Black Arkansas schools and communities.

At other times, training was available to Jeanes Supervisors at ADE-sponsored "Negro Education Conferences." In December 1909 for instance, rural schools supervisor Leo Favrot organized a conference for "negro teachers and county agents" employed by the Jeanes Fund, the extension service, and the Arkansas Colored Teachers Association (ACTA) at Pine Bluff's Arkansas Agricultural, Mechanical, and Normal (AM&N) College.[22] Indeed, even Favrot's wife benefited from the Jeanes Fund's resources. In 1915, her work was highlighted at a Little Rock Art League meeting during which she was commended for providing "domestic sciences training among the Negroes in the rural districts, this work being made possible through the Anne Jeanes Fund."[23] Despite white school officials' objectives, Black educators assumed the lead in creating better education opportunities for the African Americans among whom they lived and worked. During

1915, Jeanes Supervisors gathered at a meeting with the ACTA and Slater industrial teachers to discuss such important issues as creating a "school improvement league," "better schoolhouses and grounds," and obtaining school equipment.[24]

While Black educators were invested in quality education for African Americans, white school officials wanted rural Black youth educated to perform agricultural labor. This occurred through the establishment of corn clubs, which were the precursor of the more commonly known 4-H club, a rural youth program established in the early twentieth century and operated by the US Department of Agriculture.[25] Corn clubs were the most effective way to reach rural youth, who then influenced adult farmers to embrace innovative agricultural methods.[26] In southern Black communities, Jeanes Supervisors were tasked with providing agricultural education before the passage of the Smith-Lever Act of 1914, which led to the establishment of state agricultural extension services. In fact, Jeanes Supervisors were required to be trained in domestic arts that they were then expected to teach in rural communities. This included sewing, cooking, and gardening for females, and repairing harnesses, furniture, and fences for males. This list was not exhaustive, and the gender norms mapped on these activities did not always hold up in real life. Most members of agricultural families were expected to labor in whatever capacity was necessary for their farm's optimal operation.

Jeanes Supervisors were further tasked with engaging rural Black communities and encouraging them to adopt better health, home, and farming practices.[27] Much of this work began with young people, who were more easily influenced. In 1913, Jeanes Supervisor Samuel Johnson obtained the names of "200 negro boys and girls who desire to plant corn and tomatoes under government instruction." Arkansas Jeanes Fund agent C. W. Watson then enrolled them in agricultural clubs and provided them with information from the United States Department of Agriculture (USDA). Arkansas rural school supervisor Leo M. Favrot also cooperated with the USDA to encourage the cultivation of corn and tomatoes among rural Black Arkansas youth.[28]

By 1913, Jeanes Supervisors were present in Arkansas, Ashley, Chicot, Dallas, Desha, Jefferson, Lafayette, and Pulaski Counties.[29] They were so successful that in this same year Favrot received permission to secure additional Jeanes Supervisors for Hempstead, Jackson, and Monroe Counties.[30] Jeanes Supervisors had also been employed as local agricultural club agents and promoted rural reform before the Smith-Lever Act's passage. Jeanes Supervisors Mary D. Sims (for Lafayette County) and Della Edith Vance (for Monroe and Clark Counties), for instance, were hired as club agents in April and December 1913 to promote agricultural and domestic training among girls and boys.[31] Della Vance, who had been born in South Carolina in 1885, was a farm laborer before she became a Jeanes Supervisor in Monroe County in 1913. The fact that she was born in South Carolina but was living in Arkansas was not unusual. Between 1870 and 1910, one in every ten Black southerners migrated to another southern locale. Vance and her family were among the 200,000 African Americans who migrated to Arkansas in search of increased economic opportunities in the late nineteenth century.[32] Their concentration, particularly in the Arkansas Delta, contributed to heightened demands for Jeanes Supervisors' services.

Because they were so desperate for the training Jeanes Supervisors provided, white school superintendents scrambled to secure yearly funding to hire them in their districts. In 1915, the Jefferson County superintendent directly contacted Favrot to ensure that monies were available to retain Jeanes Supervisor Genie Curtis, who taught domestic science. He was assured that $350 would be donated from the Jeanes Fund if the school district supplied the balance. This was added to the $40 monthly pay Curtis was already earning.[33] It was not at all unusual that Curtis taught domestic-science education. Indeed, it was particularly welcomed among white southerners as the most suitable education for African Americans, particularly young women, and was usually part of the curriculum taught in county training schools, many of which were built through a combination of community efforts and monies from the Julius Rosenwald Fund.

Officially established in 1917, the Rosenwald Fund helped African Americans access equal educational opportunities in rural communities throughout the South. In the same year, Congress passed the Smith-Hughes Act, which appropriated federal funds to promote agricultural education in rural schools.[34] Julius Rosenwald, president of Sears, Roebuck, and Company, created the fund as a result of his personal relationship with Booker T. Washington, head of Alabama's Tuskegee Institute. The fund's partnership with local southern Black communities, which were responsible for raising a portion of the necessary monies, enabled the construction of rural schools to educate African Americans.[35] In 1916, Rosenwald Schools operated in Hope, Camden, Marianna, and Edmondson. They were under construction in Dalark (Clark County) and near Mason (Cleveland County), and the Doss School near Emerson (Columbia County) was being replaced with a Rosenwald building. This was in addition to plans to build schools in Emerson and Madison (St Francis County).[36] By 1924, Arkansas had 107 Rosenwald Schools, five of which had been constructed in Saint Francis County.[37] During this same year, more than $28,000 from the fund had been allotted to rural schools. By 1927, more than 200 schools had been built in Arkansas to educate African American children.[38] The fund also provided grants and fellowships for teachers to further their educational training.[39]

Southern whites tolerated Rosenwald Schools because they did not prepare African Americans for higher education but rather reinforced the Hampton and Tuskegee Institutes' model of "industrial" training advocated by Booker T. Washington.[40] Whites could not imagine and certainly did not want Black people to consider seeking more fulfilling opportunities within or beyond the South.[41] Jeanes Fund representatives at times reinforced these ideas. In 1914, Jeanes Fund representative B. C. Coldwell addressed a joint gathering of Black industrial and agricultural agents in Pine Bluff; he asserted that the greatest work before them was to "teach the negro to think and ask for a 'square deal' for the black man." Yet some African American leaders rejected this line of thinking, which clearly stigmatized Black people and held that their aspirations were limited to agricultural labor. V. M. Townsend, presiding elder of the Little Rock district of the African Methodist Episcopal Church, criticized Jeanes Supervisors for devoting too much time to talking about farming at the expense of discussing teaching methods.[42]

Jeanes Supervisors often worked with extension-service agents in training schools to filter information to African Americans from the AACES and to organize rural community activism. Moreover, training schools were spaces where extension-service agents and local leaders could engage rural inhabitants in greater numbers than they could on their own.[43] Jeanes Supervisors and extension service agents used domestic-science courses taught at training schools as a form of outreach to rural Black communities to establish connections between home and educational facilities by teaching parents and children about proper personal hygiene and nutrition.[44] This also included sexual-health education. In 1923, Mississippi County Jeanes Supervisor Annie H. Currie, recently returned from the ACTA annual meeting in Little Rock, lamented in a report that "the lecture on sexual hygiene should have been heard by every teacher of the county."[45]

Training schools were often sponsored by the AACES and served as spaces to promote rural uplift agendas. In 1926, Mississippi County farm agent C. C. Haraway and home demonstration agent Mary McCain met with local Blacks at schools in Sandy Bayou and Frenchmans Bayou. In this same year in Crittenden County, Smith-Hughes vocational educator B. T. Burkett and county agent R. T. Butler taught agricultural, sanitation, and domestic-science courses at the Marion County Training School, a Rosenwald institution.[46]

Domestic science made "previously private spaces a matter of public debate."[47] Southern whites hoped that Jeanes Supervisors, like home demonstration agents, would lead rural African Americans, both because they were readily recognizable community leaders and because Black people, presumably, could not be trusted with their family's health or education without guidance.[48] But Jeanes Supervisors were also among the earliest civil rights activists in rural communities. They, along with home demonstration agents and Black club women, stealthily commandeered public and private Black spaces to organize communally and develop local leaders who then became part of a statewide network of activists dedicated to enacting changes for rural African Americans and combatting white supremacy.

Much of this work was organized and led by women Jeanes Supervisors. Fund administrators preferred women because they believed women possessed a stronger work ethic and a greater ability to navigate the always dangerous social and racial terrain in which they travailed.[49] In Arkansas, however, some of the earliest Jeanes Supervisors were men who had been hired before World War I.[50] Jeanes Supervisor Samuel A. Johnson was hired in Pulaski County in 1909 and was followed by P. A. Garrison in Arkansas County in 1910, Samuel A. Mosely in Jefferson County in 1912, and Oscar Douglas in Monroe County in 1914.[51] Later male Jeanes Supervisors included Rufus Charles (R. C.) Childress in Pulaski County, C. S. Smith in Ashley County, and R. C. Caesar in Chicot County.

Some of these men went on to careers as school administrators. R. C. Caesar, for instance, became principal of McRae High School in Prescott and Lake Village High School in Chicot County. He was also president of the ACTA from 1940 to 1942.[52] R. C. Childress was born in 1867 to formerly enslaved parents in Laurens, South Carolina. One of the first graduates of Philander Smith College in Little Rock, he began his career as a Jeanes Supervisor in Jackson and Monroe Counties. From 1921 to 1932, he was the Arkansas Rosenwald Schools state building agent and supervised the construction of close to four hundred schools. In 1932, Childress was appointed the Black public schools' assistant supervisor, a position he held until 1946. He remained involved with Jeanes Supervisors and assisted the teacher training programs funded by the Anna T. Jeanes Foundation.[53] Childress was also one of the founders of the ACTA, established in 1898 in Pine Bluff, and was its president from 1920 to 1923.[54] His second wife, Oklahoma native Inola McIntosh Childress, had been a Jeanes Supervisor first in Colquit County, Georgia, and later in Howard, Pike, and Ouachita Counties. She retired in 1944, later becoming the first Black licensed social worker in Arkansas.[55]

Early female Arkansas Jeanes Supervisors included Georgia-born Mattie J. Johnson, who worked in Desha County. Because she operated during a time of increased racial tension throughout the nation and particularly the rural South, Johnson carefully cultivated relationships with white landowners to teach African Americans sewing, basketry, cooking, and domestic arts in McGehee and Arkansas City in Desha County and Bayou Mason in Chicot County. The high quality of her work in these communities was particularly important in 1911 when Jeanes and Slater Fund agents toured the area to assess the impact of the funds on African Americans.[56] It additionally allowed Johnson to utilize a teaching praxis that counteracted white stereotypes about Black inferiority that were so prevalent during these years.

Jeanes Supervisors, then, traveled in rural areas teaching domestic arts and helping teachers and entire communities improve the qualities of their schools, which were often woefully underfunded and ill-equipped. Rural roads were often treacherous and dangerous, particularly for Black women, and transportation was severely limited, but Jeanes Supervisors were dedicated and enthusiastically imparted important skills to African Americans in order to demonstrate that, while they may have been impoverished and uninformed, they were neither ignorant nor inferior. In 1913, for example, Chicot County Jeanes Supervisor Edmonia A. Parker walked four miles to take lessons from a basket maker who constructed her wares with split oak. Parker later taught other Black women this potentially marketable skill. And, although she was not employed by the USDA, she and Mattie J. Johnson attended canning club meetings in Little Rock at their own expense, in order to better educate the rural Blacks about food preservation methods.[57]

Jeanes Supervisors understood that placating local whites was critical not only for their safety but also to ensure that programs and the resources they procured to help rural Black communities continued. In doing so, they cleverly employed both accommodationist and emancipatory strategies.[58] At times, whites were so impressed by Jeanes Supervisors' results that, ironically, they questioned African Americans near-exclusive access to them. A young white girl, for instance, complained and "bitterly reproached a school director for giving the colored children advantages that white children did not have."[59] In another example, whites who were deeply enthusiastic about

Jeanes Supervisor Mary L. Robinson, who from 1912 to 1915 worked in Dallas County, ensured that she had access to generous resources and even paid for her travels in other parts of the county, provided she maintain her base of operation in Fordyce.[60]

Jeanes Supervisors smartly used community connections to highlight their students' accomplishments as agricultural producers and as yet another opportunity to augment African Americans' achievements. In 1915, Lizzie Ryles and Della Vance directed rural industrial school students' and Negro Girls Homemaker Clubs' canning, sewing, cooking, basket-making, and mat-making demonstrations at the Little Rock City Arcade and Market. Arkansas's first African American farm agent H. C. Ray was present at the exhibition, which was directed by the state's Black school supervisor Leo M. Favrot.[61]

For Jeanes Supervisors, strengthening the connection between education and the home was key to ameliorating adverse conditions in rural Black communities.[62] They taught basic educational skills but were additionally responsible for extension-service work among rural Blacks before the first African American farm and home demonstration agents were appointed in Arkansas. In fact, white state and local school officials hired Jeanes Supervisors with the understanding that they would form homemakers and agricultural clubs in rural Black communities. In 1914 for example, just after the passage of the Smith-Lever Act, Jeanes Supervisors met with white farm agents in Pine Bluff to learn about "corn culture, raising vegetables, and the art of canning." The "state Negro club organizer" was inundated with letters from all over Arkansas requesting membership in agricultural clubs. This included a letter from the Hughes sisters from Dallas County, who quite likely knew and may have even been encouraged by Jeanes Supervisor Mary L. Robinson. The sisters became homemakers' club members and, later, prizewinners at the state fair.[63]

Although the number of Arkansas Jeanes Supervisors decreased during World War I, there was enough need for their services that Leo M. Favrot reported that Calhoun, Crittenden, and White Counties were hiring them for the first time in the fall of 1916. He further noted with optimism that quorum courts in Chicot, Hempstead, Desha, and Clark Counties had appropriated funds to help pay Jeanes Supervisors' salaries. This development, according to Favrot, was "encouraging, as it has been a hard matter to get the quorum courts to take such action."[64] By the fall of 1916, Jeanes Supervisors were working in Calhoun, Chicot, Clark, Columbia, Conway, Crittenden, Dallas, Desha, Drew, Hempstead, and Mississippi Counties.[65]

Jeanes Supervisors' work in rural Black Arkansas communities during World War I was so effective that a 1917 report filed with the ADE highlighted their accomplishments around the state. Fourteen labored in Arkansas in 1917. They traveled over 11,251 miles, visited 156 schools, invested 10,288 hours, and enrolled 6,588 Black students in industrial classes. Arkansas Jeanes Supervisors also raised $3,500 to support rural Black communities through their connections to school improvement associations.[66] As the war years came to a close, their numbers only increased, and by 1918–19, twenty-one Jeanes Supervisors were employed in Arkansas. In 1920, their oversight was transferred from the counties where they were employed to the AACES because the state lacked county school funds. During that same year, Dr. James H. Dillard, president of the Jeanes board, agreed to provide salaries for teachers in Dallas, Desha, Hempstead, Lonoke, and Union Counties until May 31. After that point, the GEB advanced the funds to extend their terms until December 31, 1920.[67] White school officials recognized Jeanes Supervisors' important roles in rural Black communities. Black rural school supervisor Fred McCuiston, who replaced Leo Favrot in September 1924, readily admitted how critical their activism was. He emphasized that Jeanes Supervisors provided an important link between African American homes and educational facilities.[68] Also during 1924, there were only twelve Jeanes Supervisors collectively in Crittenden, Jefferson, Mississippi, Ouachita, and Union Counties, and they were paid in part by monies from the Slater Fund. Funding from the GEB also allowed Jeanes Supervisors to attend summer training programs to further hone their skills.[69]

According to McCuiston, Jeanes Supervisors were primarily responsible for "unusual progress in a county."[70] By 1927, the Jeanes Fund had contributed $8,450 to Arkansas to pay supervisor teachers, which was matched by $8,470 from the state's counties. Though their numbers dwindled in the 1920s—almost certainly due to the onset of the Depression years when local funds were especially strained—there were nineteen Jeanes Supervisors in the state in 1927.[71] The need for their services was apparently more critical than the lack of available funds during the Depression. By 1931, thirty-eight Jeanes Supervisors were living and working in Arkansas.[72]

Black educators often worked in rural environments either where schools had not existed or where conditions were beyond unfortunate. In these instances, they helped rural Blacks build or improve educational facilities. Assistance from Jeanes Supervisors, for instance, sometimes meant providing Black teachers with basic classroom equipment. In 1930 in Blytheville, for instance, Jeanes Supervisor Annie Currie gave Mozelle Carter, a teacher at the Ekron School, a desk and chair for the one-room school she operated in a private home, where she taught fifty students daily.[73]

Annie Currie is an exemplar of the domestic-reform activism in which Jeanes Supervisors engaged in rural Arkansas from the 1920s through the 1940s. Born in rural Morrilton, Arkansas, in Conway County in 1885, Annie Elva Holland Currie knew well the struggles of Black agrarian life. Her father was a farmer and her mother, a dressmaker. She attended school in Morrilton and later completed a normal course at Shorter College in Little Rock, where she earned her teaching credentials. Currie returned to Morrilton to teach after graduation. In 1911, she married William L. Currie Sr. (also known as W. L.), a Mississippi County school system principal, farmer, and president of the segregated chapter of the Mississippi County Farm Bureau. W. L., whose parents had moved from Tennessee to Arkansas in 1894, had formerly been a schoolteacher in Marie, Arkansas, one of planter Robert "Lee" Wilson's towns in Mississippi County.[74] The couple had eleven children, most of whom attended the Carson Lake Rosenwald School in Mississippi County and one of whom, Geraldine Farrar Currie (1918–97), later became a home demonstration agent.

Annie Currie, also a homemaker, cared for the family farm. Both she and her husband stressed upon their children the importance of education and further ensured that they learned the necessary gender-segregated skills for agrarian life. Their daughters learned domestic skills, while their sons learned to farm. Currie became a Jeanes Supervisor in 1921.[75] Her name was synonymous with Black cooperative efforts in the county. In 1924, Currie and home demonstration agents Mary J. McCain and Fannie Mae Boone were on the planning committee for the segregated tenth annual Mississippi County Rally and Fair to demonstrate African Americans' agricultural skills.[76]

Currie was also well-known throughout Mississippi County for her educational advocacy. She and her husband were active ACTA members and officers in the Mississippi County Negro Teachers Association.[77] During the 1924 dedication of the new Wilson Colored School, attended by Tuskegee Institute principal and Booker T. Washington's successor Dr. Robert R. Moton, Currie highlighted the importance of educational access among African Americans in a talk titled "School Consolidation and Rural Life." Wilson was a plantation town and company established by Robert Lee Wilson, Mississippi County's richest planter until his death in 1933.[78] Also on the program was home demonstration agent Mary J. McCain, who discussed "the practical in education." R. C. Childress lectured on the "value of the Rosenwald Fund," which had partially funded the new school.[79]

Like many Black educators throughout the South and Jeanes Supervisors in particular, Annie Currie improved her education and her teaching skills by attending summer-school courses at Tuskegee and Hampton Institutes and Arkansas AM&N College.[80] In August 1938, an article in the *Chicago Defender* noted that she was "back on the job" after spending the summer studying at Hampton Institute.[81] She was additionally awarded the "Diploma of the School" from the Atlanta University School of Social Work in 1940.[82] Jeanes Supervisors were often able to attend summer school or workshops sponsored by or using scholarships funded by the Southern Education Foundation.[83] In 1939, at least one Arkansas Jeanes Supervisor attended a workshop at Hampton Institute on "educational problems of the southern states, including economic problems of the rural south."[84]

Jeanes Supervisors' workloads were often very heavy because Black community needs were so great. In 1932, Currie assisted twenty-three schools and taught eight demonstration courses. Community needs extended beyond the classroom and involved aiding Black people's quest to address acute health concerns in rural Arkansas. To this end, Currie cooperated with county health nurses to ensure that Black Mississippi County children and adults received much-needed vaccinations.[85] Currie was further involved in the annual Christmas seal drive since at least 1923 and disseminated stamps to help Black families fight tuberculosis, which disproportionately impacted their communities.[86] She also led Mississippi County's segregated tuberculosis seal drive.[87] Throughout rural communities, regardless of race, public health and school nurses assumed a central role in providing rural health-care access.[88]

But Jeanes Supervisors' top priority was ensuring African Americans' access to quality education. In 1934, assisted by the $22 donated by the Mississippi County Teachers Association, Currie attended the National Conference on Fundamental Problems in the Education of Negroes in Washington, DC, sponsored by the Department of the Interior, which provided her with critical information to address unequal educational opportunities back home.[89] Called together by Harold L. Ickes, the secretary of the interior, the conference brought together a wide range of professionals who were interested in Black education. In addition to Currie, representatives from Arkansas included Nevada County Jeanes Supervisor Ila Upchurch, ACCPT state president and Lee County educator Anna M. P. Strong, and former Chicot County Jeanes Supervisor and then–state Rosenwald agent R. C. Childress.[90] President Franklin D. Roosevelt addressed a letter to the conference and First Lady Eleanor Roosevelt personally attended and spoke to delegates.[91] And for Currie, improved educational opportunities were not just for Black children. During the same year, she also spoke at a segregated 4-H club rally about the possibility of establishing a school for illiterate adults.[92]

Currie further sought to augment the activism of the local segregated parent-teacher association. In 1936, she issued copies of a pamphlet entitled *Helps* at the PTA's semiannual meeting. The pamphlet, distributed to Black schools throughout Mississippi County, was a study guide to improve parents and teachers' cooperative ventures. Anna M. P. Strong, who by this point was assistant supervisor of Black education, also attended this meeting.[93] Currie was so well regarded among African American parents that in 1937 she was elected ACCPT president, the same year she and her husband were elected reporter and treasurer of the Mississippi County Colored Teachers Association.[94]

Currie ensured that Black schools had adequate books and supplies and worked with school administrators to provide sports competitions and musical and oratorical events for African American students. In 1938, Currie organized the twenty-fourth annual field event for Black schools, held in Wilson.[95] Again, like most Black women working in the rural South, she carefully maneuvered within the confines of Robert Lee Wilson's delta empire. Even though Wilson was known for his benevolence toward African Americans, Currie knew well that his primary concern was placating and retaining his Black agricultural labor force. Lee Wilson and Company provided lemonade for the festivities, which included eight hundred African American students from thirty-three Mississippi County schools.[96] Among the winners of the oral English contest was Bernard Tollette from Blytheville, who won first place for his lecture "The Negro, a Factor in the Solution of the Race Problem."[97]

Unfortunately, Jeanes Supervisors' responsibilities were many and their work arduous. Their sense of what Stephanie Shaw has called "socially responsible individualism" demanded that they use their relatively privileged status to navigate a racial minefield and find common ground with powerful whites in order to obtain important resources for rural Black communities.[98] At times, this took a toll on their health. In December 1939, after seventeen years as Mississippi County's first Jeanes Supervisor, Currie resigned due to ill health. The local newspaper reported her resignation and underscored her service to the community and her role as a racial broker: "She has worked to create a better understanding between her people and the white race. Much has been done to promote better health conditions among the Negroes because of her efforts in the schools."[99] Annie H. Currie died in 1943.[100] As is evident from Annie Currie's example, Jeanes Supervisors usually had few resources available to them; but they used their creativity to impart important lessons to rural Blacks.

Equally, if not more, important, Jeanes Supervisor also attacked the health problems that affected rural Black schools and communities. They taught rural Black women how to improve sanitation in their homes and their families' health by planting vegetables and improving cooking methods.[101] In fact, Black leaders (midwives, teachers, home demonstration agents, sorority and club women, nurses, dentists, and physicians), who were most often but not always female, engaged in public health work in their communities.[102] In a joint effort during the Mississippi River flood of 1927, Jeanes Supervisors assisted home demonstration agents by compiling lists of children who had not been vaccinated against such illnesses as typhoid, diphtheria, and smallpox.[103] Tuberculosis also remained a concern. According to one report, in Arkansas in 1928, 155.6 of every 100,000 African Americans died of tuberculosis as compared to 46 of every 100,000 whites.[104] In 1934, Howard County Jeanes Supervisor Inola McIntosh Childress hosted Nashville's first tuberculosis clinic at the white First Methodist Church, a move which suggested a fluidity in race relations, particularly during health crises that seriously impacted rural communities regardless of race.[105] Jeanes Supervisors' efforts were aided by Arkansas AM&N College and the Arkansas Tuberculosis Association (ATA), which from 1925 to 1933 provided Black teachers with health education to help rural African Americans protect themselves against the disease.[106] Indeed, African American leaders were particularly important in this initiative. In the early 1930s, Florence C. Williams, a Columbia University graduate, was the ATA's Director of Health Education for Negroes. She worked with such white women as ATA executive secretary Erle Chambers and in 1930 represented Arkansas at the White House Conference on Child Health and Protection. By 1934, however, she had left Arkansas to become the first African American hired by the Chicago and Cook County Tuberculosis Institute.[107]

By the late 1930s, the number of Blacks dying from tuberculosis had declined by 40 percent, due to a combination of efforts and funds from Arkansas Jeanes Supervisors, the federal government, the Rockefeller

Foundation, and the American Red Cross. Health departments were also established in these areas to aid public health officers and sanitary "engineers" in facilitating the eradication of typhoid, malaria, hookworm, and diphtheria, which in turn contributed to the decline of tuberculosis.[108]

Jeanes Supervisors used their creativity to help rural Blacks help themselves. They could not immediately change the racial injustice that held African Americans captive, but they fully recognized that an illiterate and unhealthy people could not effectively challenge and subvert oppression.[109] Thus their activism most often occurred quietly and clandestinely.

Jeanes Supervisors were well respected among rural Blacks because of their daily presence in local schools and communities. In 1943, when the home economics department of the junior high school in College Station (a community in Little Rock) held its Christmas party, Jeanes Supervisor Viola Harris was invited as the school's special guest.[110]

They were further connected to other educators in the region as members of the Regional Jeanes Association (RJA), region two, which included Arkansas, Missouri, Kentucky, Tennessee, and the US Virgin Islands. The RJA, which was established in 1943, was affiliated with the National Jeanes Association (NJA), founded in 1942 by Kentucky Jeanes Supervisor Mayme Brooks Copeland.[111] The NJA was also a member organization of the National Council of Negro Women, established by Mary McLeod Bethune in 1935.[112]

The RJA held its first meeting at Lane College in Jackson, Tennessee, in 1943. Ila Upchurch served on the program committee, which chose "Living and Learning in Small Rural Communities" as its theme the next year. She assisted the Research and Guidance Committee and was chairperson of the health committee. When the RJA expressed concerns about illiteracy among young Black men during the World War II years, Upchurch was among those who encouraged educators to return to teaching basic literacy skills in their classrooms. Other Arkansas Jeanes Supervisors were active in the RJA as well. Mary Foster Jones, a Jefferson County Jeanes Supervisor since 1928, was on the nominating committee, and Alena Erby Wiley was a Classroom Instruction Committee member.[113] The 1945 annual meeting was held at Arkansas AM&N College, where Viola Harris, former Arkansas Teachers' Association assistant secretary as well as a Jeanes Supervisor, welcomed delegates. Anna M. P. Strong, the American Teachers Association vice president and National Congress of Colored Parents and Teachers (NCCPT) president, gave the keynote address.[114]

In October 1966, the NJA, which had changed its name to the National

Alena Wiley, Mississippi County Jeanes Teacher. *Image courtesy of Dr. Anes Wiley Abraham, Blytheville, Arkansas.*

Association of Supervisors and Consultants, held its last meeting in Atlanta, Georgia. Maeleen Clay Arrant, a former Dallas County Jeanes Supervisor, attended the meeting. Born in Fordyce in 1902, Arrant attended the Dallas County Training School and in 1939 graduated from Arkansas AM&N with an elementary-education degree. In 1946, she earned a master's degree in curriculum and instruction from the University of Minnesota.[115]

Between 1923 and 1937, Arrant taught in a special experimental school for African Americans established by the Southern Education Foundation. She recalled, "The purpose of the experiment was to see what could actually be done with a good teacher in rural low income areas." The school served five plantations in the Barnett Chapel area of Jefferson County. Like many rural educators, Arrant taught her pupils more than basic reading and writing; she taught domestic science, industrial arts, and music. Arrant further taught her students sexual-health education using a female dog who had birthed puppies. When she brought a local doctor out to the school to discuss venereal disease prevention with local adults, Arrant allowed children age ten and older to listen at the door. Additionally, like many African

American educators, Arrant stealthily engaged in political rights activism with her students and adults on the plantation when she asserted, "As my grandfather taught us, . . . you'd never be a citizen until you paid taxes."[116] For Arrant, full citizenship began with safe and sanitary homes, even on the plantation. She believed that location did not necessarily determine one's quality of life: "If you're gonna live here, make it livable. Clean yards. And· make the house in which you live decent."[117]

In 1944, Arrant became a student-teacher supervisor at Arkansas AM&N College. From 1950 to 1959, she was the first Black supervisor of elementary education for the ADE.[118] Arrant had begun her career as a home-economics teacher before going to work for the ADE. She had served on the governor's Committee for the Integration of Institutions of Higher Education and as assistant director of the National Retired Teachers Association. She was an active member of the ACTA until it merged with the Arkansas Education Association (AEA) in 1969 and the Pine Bluff elementary school supervisor until she retired the same year. In 1980, the organization named a scholarship in her honor.[119] Arrant died in Dallas, Texas, in January 2000.[120]

For Jeanes Supervisors like Maeleen Arrant, social welfare activism was intimately connected to educational activism. This quite logically extended to community activism. It was critical to cultivate working relationships across racial lines, yet Black activists understood well the condescension and patronization that African Americans could face in these interactions. Thus, African Americans, and Black women in particular, often founded parallel organizations and deployed their own leadership capabilities to serve their communities.[121]

As part of their political agenda, African American educators often opposed state efforts to limit Black education to industrial curricula.[122] But many still adhered to Booker T. Washington's philosophy of Black self-help and improvement, in which Black teachers were expected to be agents of rural progress.[123] Any assistance from white donors to Black schools had to come with the assurance that industrial education would be part of the curriculum.[124] Yet educators often subverted and enhanced industrial curricula by including liberal arts education, including African American history and literature.[125] It was these efforts that informed Upchurch and other Black Arkansan educators' membership in the RJA.

In September 1947, three years before the Jeanes Supervisor program ended in Arkansas, Ila Upchurch once again attended the RJA annual meeting at Tennessee Agricultural and Industrial State College (now

Maeleen Clay Arrant, 1976.
*Image courtesy of the University
of Central Arkansas Archives,
Conway, Arkansas.*

Tennessee State University) in Nashville.[126] The theme, "Education Through Community Cooperation," underscored the collaborative nature of African Americans' activism to increase their access to equal education, particularly at a time when southern institutions of higher learning were contending with Black challenges to segregation.[127] Upchurch was one of the Arkansas Jeanes Supervisors who participated in these conversations and engaged in local civil rights activism through the NAACP. This endeavor ultimately ended her employment as an Arkansas educator.

Civil rights activism and membership in such a controversial organization was unacceptable to school officials and others who were empowered to

Ila Dedia Upchurch,
1950s. *Image courtesy
of the Arkansas State
Archives, Little Rock,
Arkansas.*

make important decisions about Black education in rural communities. Yet
Jeanes Supervisors often defied racial conventions and joined the NAACP.
Back in 1932, Ouachita County Jeanes Supervisor Cleo McDonald had been
involved in the Camden NAACP.[128]

Upchurch may have lost her job in 1949, as mentioned at the beginning
of this chapter, but she remained an important and industrious figure in the
Prescott community. She opened a sewing and alterations shop, prepared
taxes, and served as a notary public. Upchurch also worked as an adult-
education instructor at Hempstead County's Blevins Training School.[129]
In 1969, Upchurch was elected chairperson of the Prescott Neighborhood
Council, an honor which she said was "truly progress in Prescott."[130] In 1971,
she became the district president of the Prescott District African American
Episcopal Church's layman's organization.[131] After a long life of community
service, Ila Upchurch died on September 4, 1989.[132]

By 1949, the number of Jeanes Supervisors in Arkansas had dwindled. In 1947–48, only six Jeanes Supervisors remained in Arkansas. By 1948–49, they could only be found in Ashley, Jefferson, Mississippi, Nevada, Ouachita, and Pulaski Counties. The Jeanes Supervisor program ended in Arkansas by 1950, although region-wide it lasted until 1968. For the time that they existed in the state, Jeanes Supervisors engaged in the important work of reforming Black schools and communities. Their critical services and responsibilities, while seemingly overwhelming, were always varied, and some of their obstacles—namely racism—were insurmountable. But Arkansas's Jeanes Supervising Industrial Teachers, like those throughout the South, working in tandem with all segments of the African American community and with white allies, brought much-needed help to rural Black schools at a time when few other resources were available. Many of their services had long been performed by Black home demonstration agents, the subject of the next chapter.

— 2 —

Home Demonstration Agents in Rural Black Arkansas Communities

IN 1916, MARY LEE MCCRARY RAY was appointed Arkansas's first Black home demonstration agent. Her husband, Harvey Cincinnatus (H. C.) Ray, was the state's first African American farm agent. The two met at Langston Institute in Oklahoma in 1914, where Mary had been a home economics instructor, and married in 1915.[1] Long involved in the struggle for African Americans' equal access to education, she was also an Oklahoma's Colored Teachers Association member. At the organization's annual meeting in 1904, she led a discussion titled "The Age Calls for Action as Well as Thinking."[2] However, Ray understood that she, like African American extension agents throughout the Jim Crow South, operated in dangerous terrain in Arkansas, where adherence to the racial status quo was strictly and often violently enforced. The caution required of Black home and farm agents when dealing with deeply entrenched racism sharpened their keen understanding of the racial and political landscape in Arkansas during World War I. Some agents were able to gain autonomy and earn promotions as a result of their presence and community-based work. In July 1918, Ray was promoted to district agent and was responsible for all Black home demonstration agents statewide. She, like all African American agents, focused her energies on the rural uplift initiatives that assumed increasing importance during and after the World War I years.

Home demonstration agents trained and employed by state agricultural extension services shared their domestic-science expertise with people in rural communities throughout the South and the nation. Grounded in the domestic economy movement, agents attempted to transform and modernize rural homes by teaching wives and mothers to be better homemakers or, more pragmatically, to behave like their middle-class and often urban counterparts. Concerns about agrarian moral degeneration led many home demonstration agents to believe that their paternalistic guidance could change rural dwellers' habits to positively impact their communities and alleviate the squalor in which many of them lived.

For many, if not most, reformers, rural uplift began and ended with improved homes. Better homemaking was informed by social, cultural, and political changes wrought by the Progressive Era, which impacted rural as well as urban dwellers. Domestic-science movement advocates desired increased economy in time, money, and work in rural communities, concepts that resonated with southern white landowners, most of whom employed Black agricultural laborers.[3]

Most reformers, regardless of race, understood women as the primary force for change in rural communities. Their activism was necessary to ensure social and economic development and was guided by middle-class, educated professionals who were employed by the state agricultural extension service. Increasingly, home demonstration agents were the vehicle through which rural women first engaged progressive domestic economy initiatives in their communities.[4]

The development of demonstration work was spearheaded by minister, educator, and farmer Seaman A. Knapp. Born in New York in 1833, Knapp was at first a preparatory school teacher. In 1865, he and his family moved to Iowa where he became a farmer, a superintendent of a school for the blind, and a farming newspaper editor. In 1879, he became an agriculture professor at Iowa Agricultural College (today's Iowa State University), where he also served a short term as the institution's president.[5]

Concerned that agricultural programs at land grant colleges lacked scientific knowledge, Knapp in 1882 drafted a bill that was introduced in Congress, later known as the 1887 Hatch Act, to establish federal experiment stations around the country. After a stint in Louisiana, Knapp embarked upon a new career with the USDA in 1898.[6]

Knapp believed that farming demonstrations could be used to convince poor and uneducated farmers to adopt new agricultural techniques and modernize their farms. These efforts were supported by male farm and female home demonstration agents who served as guides and sounding boards for rural people seeking to improve the quality of their lives and their farms.

The South, more than any other area of the country, desperately required rural rejuvenation. After his time in Louisiana, Knapp believed that this could best be obtained through community demonstration activities. By 1902, he was employed by the federal government to promote southern agriculture.[7] Farm and home demonstration efforts had been present in rural southern communities since the earliest years of the twentieth century. In 1904, Congress inaugurated the Farmers' Cooperative Demonstration Work conducted by the US Department of Agriculture (USDA) through the Bureau of Plant Industry. In the same year, the first white agricultural agents were hired to work with farmers. Farmers' Cooperative Demonstration Work was widely available in Arkansas by 1907. Ralph Amos, the first African American county farm agent hired in Arkansas in 1912, was responsible for Lee, Pulaski, Phillips, Lonoke, Arkansas, Crittenden, Monroe, Saint Francis, and Jefferson Counties.[8]

Farm agents were expected to possess scientific agricultural knowledge of and considerable experience with demonstration work.[9] These efforts were also influenced by the Country Life Commission (CLC). Convened in 1908 by President Theodore Roosevelt, the CLC was chaired by Liberty Hyde Bailey, cofounder of the American Society for Horticultural Science and an agricultural expert at Cornell University. The CLC determined that people from farming communities left rural life because of poor roads, lack of communication, and social isolation. For some reformers, farm people who were "economically and socially impoverished endangered the nation as a whole."[10] They believed the key to reversing this trend lay reforming rural life, improving education, and making farming more "efficient, productive, and profitable."[11] While this assessment largely pertained to rural whites, African American reformers shared similar concerns about rural Black communities and argued that poor Blacks' habits threatened and retarded the entire race. Georgia State Industrial College president Benjamin Franklin Hubert attempted to address concerns about rural African Americans through a community based, scientific approach to farming when he founded the CLC's segregated counterpart, the Association for the Advancement of Negro Life in 1928. The genesis of Hubert's ideas for rural Black communities had been influenced by his time at Massachusetts Agricultural College, where he had studied with Kenyon L. Butterfield, founder of the field of rural sociology and president of the Country Life Commission and, later, the American Country Life Association.[12]

In the early twentieth century, southern Progressive reformers also focused their attention on rural Black communities. They were particularly concerned about controlling African American laborers, prohibiting them from migrating to urban areas, and alleviating the challenges posed by single crop production. In 1909, for instance, the USDA and the Penn School (St. Helena Island, South Carolina), designated a demonstration farm site where farmers were strongly advised to embrace crop diversification even before the onslaught of the boll weevil infestation that devastated cotton crops throughout the South. Progressive reformers' strategy also included asserting the primacy of farm women's gender-specific roles as homemakers. Working with Penn School employees, rural Black women on St. Helena Island learned domestic skills, health, sanitary, and food security methods to alleviate the severe privation most of them experienced and to better care for themselves and their families.[13]

Before the passage of the 1914 Smith-Lever Act, farm and home demonstration work was available in rural communities throughout Arkansas, particularly after the boll weevil infestation.[14] In 1912, a $1,500 appropriation from the USDA, supported the beginning of home demonstration work in Arkansas. It is not clear how much of that money was designated to support work in rural Black communities, but African American home demonstration agents had been working in Arkansas since 1913 when the state legislature empowered quorum courts to provide funds to increase the resources provided by the federal government.[15] According to Dr. Charles Hillman Brough, a University of Arkansas economics professor and later state governor, their work was impactful. Writing in 1915 about the "southern race question" for the *Arkansas Gazette*, Brough noted that the "report of negro county agents' activities in homemakers club work for the 1913–14 session was particularly gratifying." Agents traveled 2,385 miles, visited 675 homes, gave 105 canning demonstrations at which 647 mothers and visitors were present, visited 23 schools, and provided 16 sanitation lessons. Of particular importance was the agents' emphasis on health. According to Brough, home demonstration agents emphasized "the use of individual drinking cups, care of the bodies, teeth, nails, hair, etc. . . . and have lectured on diseases of various kinds."[16]

The 1914 Smith-Lever Act and the creation of the USDA Cooperative Extension Service brought farm and home demonstration work in all states under the federal government's purview.[17] Named for South Carolina representative Asbury F. Lever and Georgia senator Hoke Smith and informed by Progressive reformers' concern about rural southern reform and development, the act authorized the use of federal, state, and local funds to support the creation of the agricultural extension services at state land grant colleges and universities that had been established under the 1862 Morrill Land Grant College Act.[18] Because African Americans had been excluded under the 1862 act, Black land grant colleges were created under a second Morrill Act in 1890, which adopted the oft-quoted language of "separate but equal"

in declaring that "the establishment and maintenance of such colleges sep-
arately for white and colored students" was legal as long as federal appropriations were equal. As scholar Carmen Harris has posited, this effectively
"normalized racial discrimination in educational policy and practice."[19]

The AACES was formed shortly after the passage of the Smith-Lever
Act. Because Jim Crow laws throughout the South mandated racial segregation, the agricultural extension service's headquarters were divided into
two locations: the University of Arkansas in Fayetteville (for whites), and
Arkansas AM&N College in Pine Bluff (for African Americans).[20] Before
the Smith-Lever Act's passage, southern governments had been recalcitrant
about providing financial support for African American extension agents.
But they quickly supported this initiative when they realized the value of
harnessing federal government resources to ensure a productive, predominantly Black agricultural labor force. Unfortunately, the respective funds
available for Black and white extension work rarely reached parity and were
carefully controlled by white administrators.[21] Extension activities were further supplemented by the 1917 Smith-Hughes Act, which funded vocational
agriculture and home economics education.[22] During the late nineteenth
and early twentieth centuries, home economics was increasingly structured
as a scientific and academic discipline—one in which professionally trained
and educated women wielded limited authority. Agricultural reformers
understood that women played a crucial role in the maintenance of family
farms and rural life and accordingly disseminated information to them to
help them form local home demonstration clubs. The professionalization of
home economics education further allowed women of all stripes to access
occupational opportunities that increased their credibility among rural
dwellers as they imparted scientific information to augment the quality of
life for rural families and communities.

African American home demonstration agents' activism, however, was
further complicated by the racially divisive times in which they lived. Like
other Black agents throughout the Jim Crow South, they had to navigate
deeply entrenched racism and segregation as they helped agrarian Black
Arkansans. Most rural African Americans were agricultural laborers trapped
in a vicious and unyielding cycle of debt. The work of Black home demonstration agents was hampered by the endemic poverty, malnutrition, chronic
illness, and unsanitary and unsafe conditions in which African Americans
lived. Their efforts were further circumscribed by unequal funding of extension services for Black communities. Yet they created what historian Pete
Daniel called "zones of autonomy."[23] That is, despite the constraints of

racism, segregation, and severe privation, home demonstration agents and club members subtly manipulated the AACES's agenda to meet their needs.

Furthermore, extension service policies did not challenge the gender norms of the early twentieth century. Extension service programs hired and supervised farm agents, who were almost exclusively male, to advise farmers on such practices as crop rotation and livestock breeding.[24] Although traditional understandings of the operation and maintenance of rural life viewed women's work as subordinate, such a gendered division was ironic and unrealistic, considering that women assisted their husbands in the fields and assumed their authority in emergencies. But their domestic production was considered the most important element in rural development.[25] Accordingly, the extension service employed female home demonstration agents, who were subordinate to male agricultural agents, to teach farmwomen about food production and preservation and home improvement techniques.[26]

Like most southern states, Arkansas was overwhelmingly rural and its economy was dependent on agricultural production. The state's African American population resided mostly in the Arkansas Delta, where cotton cultivation reigned. During the World War I years, however, African Americans migrated out of the South to escape racial violence, debt peonage, and in search of industrial jobs. For this reason, hiring Black extension services agents throughout the South assumed increasing importance. They helped white planters understand that in order to retain their labor force, they had to make some concessions to improve conditions for southern Blacks.[27] In 1915, H. C. Ray became the first federally appointed African American USDA Cooperative Extension Service agent in Arkansas.[28] By 1917, H. C. and Mary L. Ray were well respected for their work among agrarian Blacks around the state. According to white state extension agent C. W. Watson:

> H. C. Ray and Mary Ray, Negro agents supervising the work among the Negroes have turned in [the] most excellent reports throughout the year. Negro agents with education and training of the right kind can be made great asset(s) to a county and I would be glad to see commercial clubs, business men and farmers take more interest in this phase of demonstration work in Arkansas.[29]

White leaders were subsequently convinced that more, not fewer, Black agents were necessary.

Medora Louise Reed, a Black agent who had formerly labored in Dermott, Arkansas, was appointed assistant Negro district home agent in

May 1917. By 1920, Mary L. Ray had assumed the position and was responsible for Black agents in Forrest City (Saint Francis County), Clarendon (Monroe County), Texarkana (Miller County), Trenton (Phillips County), Fort Smith (Sebastian County), New Augusta (Woodruff County), Dermott (Chicot County), Monticello (Drew County), Marianna (Lee County), and Menifee (Conway County).[30] Because rural Black communities were devastatingly poor, Ray understood the importance of currying favor with and procuring resources from local whites to support extension service programs for African Americans. During the 1920 black farm conference at Branch Normal College (later Arkansas AM&N) in Pine Bluff, club girls, dressed in "complete canning girls' uniforms," participated in a canning contest and stood before an audience of two hundred, discussing "in clear cut sentences" how they had grown and canned tomatoes. Ray awarded prizes obtained through donations from Texarkana National Bank, Merchants and Planters Bank, State National Bank, and white merchants in Garland County.[31]

Black agents were unable to circumvent deeply entrenched racism and the AACES reinforced Jim Crow laws mandating racial segregation. Agent meetings at the University of Arkansas were rarely integrated. Yet Mary L. Ray and Saint Francis County agent Lugenia Bell (later Christmas) attended a three-day meeting at the University of Arkansas in 1921. They quite likely attended other meetings regularly, although they were probably among the few African Americans present.[32]

Black demonstration agents reported to white county agents and worked within communities shaped by almost impenetrable racial boundaries. Because it was socially and politically unthinkable for white women to even consider entering Black people's homes, employing Black home demonstration agents to serve Black homes was the only logical option.[33] In Arkansas, whites viewed these Black agents a threat because of their educational backgrounds. Educational attainment was an important qualification to become an agricultural extension agent, and it was especially so for home demonstration agents whose work among women was already marginalized, if not considered altogether suspect and unnecessary. Women's academic training allowed them to "reinforce assertions about the highly specialized and professional nature of home economics and demonstration work." It further cemented connections between rural women, the university, and home economics knowledge.[34]

For African American agents in the rural South, academic training could prove dangerous, as whites felt threatened when Blacks received even the most basic educational opportunities. White landowners were often suspicious of Black agents, because they feared they might encourage tenant farmers and sharecroppers to challenge the carefully crafted social and economic control the landowners held over them. Black agents' educational experience often far exceeded what many whites imagined possible for agrarian Blacks. At a time when few women and even fewer Black women could scarcely obtain educational opportunities beyond the elementary level, most African American extension agents in Arkansas had attended college, and some had earned degrees. Many were graduates of historically Black institutions such as the Tuskegee and Hampton Institutes.[35] Others had done some graduate work or even taught at a university.[36]

Mary L. Ray had been educated at Tuskegee Institute, from which she graduated in 1897.[37] During the weeklong commencement exercises in 1897, she was among the graduates selected to discuss and display samples of work in their trades. Ray's presentation, "Dressmaking in the Home," discussed the cost of materials and the economic benefits of making one's own clothing.[38] Ray went on to attend Hampton Institute, the University of Chicago, and the Vienna Ladies Tailoring Institute in New York.[39] The contacts she made at these institutions remained important throughout her career as an extension service agent. Her connection to fellow Tuskegee alumni led to her being elected one of the vice presidents of its national alumni association at its 1932 annual meeting in Hot Springs, Arkansas.[40] In 1911, Ray also was the home economics department head at Oklahoma Colored Agricultural and Normal University (later renamed Langston University).[41]

In the Arkansas Delta, Black agents were reluctant to sacrifice their programs by challenging white supremacy.[42] They were often disrespected and marginalized by their white counterparts. In a 1920 manual for boys' and girls' agricultural work, where white agents were listed by their title and specialization, H. C. and Mary Ray were merely listed as district agents under the category "Negro Workers," which belied their education and training as professionals.[43] Despite this slight, they understood well that they had to tread carefully in white-dominated spaces for their own personal safety and the well-being of their programs. The Rays traveled throughout Arkansas, demonstrating farming, canning, and home improvement techniques. As they did so, they cultivated the goodwill of planters and county officials. This allowed them to maintain a force of African American extension service agents in areas with large concentrations of Blacks, who desperately needed their services and exposed whites to the economic, health, and sanitation issues plaguing their communities.[44]

Many whites, such as Governor Brough, considered rural Blacks par-

ticularly inferior and developmentally backward. He understood agents'
work as "pioneer constructive service . . . greatly valued by the white people
of the South" and claimed that "morally and religiously the Negroes have
made substantial progress, but in both respects they are still lamentably
weak."[45] Brough's racist comments aside, Black extension service agents utilized their access to state and federal resources to engage in much-needed
community uplift. They skillfully and adeptly gauged the best moments to
procure resources for the communities they served. Arkansas's rural Black
activists found themselves employing these skills to a greater extent during
World War I.

African American Women's Activism in Rural Black Communities during and following World War I

AGRARIAN BLACK WOMEN'S bravery and activism during and after World War I in the face of racism and violence is a little-known story. As farm laborers, these women were routinely paid less than their Black male and white male and female counterparts. And though they were especially vulnerable during times of intensified racism, they continued to challenge southern white racism in all of its manifestations. For instance, Black women were members of the Progressive and Farmers and Household Union of America (PFHUA) in Phillips County, Arkansas, and were present when African Americans met at a church in Hoop Spur, Arkansas, in 1919 to discuss plans to demand for their fair share of that year's cotton crop. Emboldened by the democratic rhetoric and material gains of the World War I years, they defied racial conventions, challenged white planters who had cheated them out of wages, and asserted their right to sell their cotton crops directly to the market.[1]

Among the women present were Cleola Miller, wife of Hoop Spur Lodge PFHUA member Jim Miller, and PFHUA secretary Lulu Ware. Cleola, twenty-four years old and the mother of three children, had filled out the organization's membership and examination card. She affirmatively answered such questions as "Do you believe in the Almighty God?" "Do you give due respect to all humankind?" and "Do you obey the law at all times?" In response to a question about the state of her health, she wrote "unhealthy." Like many rural women and their families, she suffered ill health due to poor nutrition and food insecurity.[2]

Lulu Ware and her husband Ed, on the other hand, were prosperous landowners who employed Black farm laborers.[3] Lulu was also among the

African Americans arrested for allegedly taking part in what was errone-
ously termed a "riot" after a gunfight ensued between PFHUA members
and Phillips County law enforcement officers.[4] The men involved in the
event, who became known as the "Elaine Twelve," were initially imprisoned
but liberated between 1923 and 1925. The Black women involved lost their
few worldly possessions when whites ransacked their homes, yet they consciously challenged local white supremacist structures and socioeconomic
deprivation in rural Arkansas by virtue of their PFHUA membership.[5]

The United States' entry into World War I in April 1917 fundamentally
changed rural women's roles around the nation. As men went to war, the
government became concerned about the agricultural industry's ability to
ensure food security. In reaction, Congress passed the 1917 Lever Food Act
(also known as the Food and Fuel Control Act), to provide special funding
for increased numbers of farm and home extension agents in agricultural
communities. The USDA was also imbued with emergency powers to provide seed and fertilizer to communities who lacked these commodities.[6] In
addition, President Woodrow Wilson created the US Food Administration
(USFA) to control and conserve the nation's food supply and to increase
agricultural production and exports to decimated European countries.[7]
Increased food security, a battle fought and won on the American home
front under Hoover and the USFA, was designed to prevent internal col-
lapse due to insufficient food supplies, a point woefully understudied in
World War I scholarship.[8]

Hoover and the USFA looked to American housewives to assume
the lead in wartime food control efforts. Many women understood their
work in food conservation as part of their patriotic duty to feed and aid
American families and Allied troops in Europe. This message was especially impressed upon African American women, who were considered to
possess a "special aptitude for the conservation and production of food,"
a claim that reinforced racial stereotypes about Black women as domestic
laborers.[9] Arkansas women were further made keenly aware of the expectations placed upon them by state and county food administrators, who
encouraged them to participate in a "thrift program" as part of a plan for
Food Conservation for World Relief Week. The program employed patriotic language to underscore its urgency, encouraged women to buy food
"thoughtfully," to assess the needs of each family member and plan meals
accordingly, to only consume three meals per day, and to become involved
in the "home card and conservation" campaign. Hamp Williams, Arkansas's
food administrator, lauded women's efforts: "We are more than pleased with

the work that was done . . . and the women of Arkansas, judging by the inquiries that have been received, are anxious to learn just what is expected of them."[10] Although Williams's pronouncement probably did not refer to Black women, they took to heart the patriotic calling of his message as well as that of Milton Waymon Guy, chief of the USFA's Arkansas Negro Educational Division.[11]

Home demonstration agents, tasked with enforcing federal food conservation legislation, were concerned about cash-strapped homemakers who were often unable to prepare nutritious meals, let alone meals of any sort, for their families. African American men were often rejected for military service due to physical "deformities" resulting from poor diets. Cotton remained a primary crop for many farm families who were often unable to grow vegetables to supplement meager diets during the winter months and suffered from a wide range of health issues as a consequence.

Southern white landowners were particularly invested in keeping African Americans on the land, especially as labor demands increased and they migrated out of the South to urban areas and more lucrative job opportunities.[12] Throughout the war years, then, farm and home demonstration agents, working on behalf of landowners and therefore the federal government who employed them, encouraged Black Arkansans to remain in rural areas and increase food production and conservation by planting gardens and canning produce.[13] Mary L. Ray, for example, taught farm families how to turn the process of canning tomatoes into a community project. Using the facilities of a local Black school or church, to which African Americans typically had unfettered access, and possessing limited resources, Ray led them in the construction of a cannery made of zinc tubs, with a foundation, top, and the joints of two stovepipes. This crudely made but efficient contraption allowed them to can 500 quarts of tomatoes daily.[14]

Other community canneries resulted from similar cooperative efforts of home demonstration agents, who provided instruction, and rural Blacks, who provided the labor. Not only were canneries an important means to increase the quality and availability of food, but they were also relatively safe spaces in which to discuss ways to improve hygienic and sanitary conditions, lessons that no doubt informed how African Americans cared for their homes. Canneries also fostered community cohesion. Gathering to can permitted the cultivation of rural Black culture and provided opportunities for women to congregate for "canning parties," that is, much-needed social interaction. Within these cultural incubators, Black women shared stories, recipes, and entertained themselves and others.[15]

African Americans not only increased food security for their families and shared the surplus with others in their communities, but they also were able to sell what they did not consume. This locally based entrepreneurship helped them obtain a small measure of economic independence from local white officials and landowners, who were often one and the same, and increased their sense of racial solidarity as they challenged southern economic injustice.[16]

Although local funds were limited during and after World War I, white landowners supported agents' activities because they feared the outmigration of the Black labor force upon which they depended. They were often concerned about what Jeannie Whayne called the "possible subversive influence of federal programs" like the extension service.[17] But white landowners quickly realized the economic benefits of having their tenants and sharecroppers exposed to agricultural innovations as a means to pacify their workforce and augment their productivity. White and African American leaders and extension service agents in turn pressed for more resources. The Arkansas Women's Committee's department of food production and home economics, which was led by white state home demonstration agent Connie J. Bonslagel, and women's committee chairmen from various counties lobbied for increased funding for agents. In 1918, eighty-four white and twenty-nine Black home demonstration agents were hired.[18]

As African Americans left the South in droves during and after the war, planters looked to Black community leaders to appease those who remained. Like oppressed people the world over, rural Black Arkansans were never entirely powerless. When all else failed, the recalcitrance of southern racism left them little choice but to speak with their feet. Perceiving educated Black home and farm demonstration agents as a potential challenge to the plantation system, white landowners increasingly realized it was in their best interests to cooperate with them in order to alleviate intensified racial tensions and inculcate them with the AACES's rural reform efforts.[19] For example, Mississippi County planter Robert Lee Wilson relied on educator, farmer, and Negro County Farmers Organization president W. L. Currie to quell fears after Black laborer Henry Lowery was lynched in 1921 in Nodena, Arkansas, after demanding a settlement from and subsequently murdering a white landowner (he also killed the landowner's daughter).[20] Currie was lauded for opening the meeting after which attendees sang the hymn "Lord, I Want to Be a Christian." The gathering then proceeded with talks on such subjects as "The Farm and the Church," and "Cooperation of Farmer and Banker." The white county home demonstration agent lectured on "Better Trained Mothers" and the "Woman's Place on the Farm." Among those at the meeting were Black extension agents Mary J. McCain and H. C. and Mary L. Ray, who in "well-chosen words reviewed every phase of both farm and home activities." Mary Ray was further praised as one who always "brings sunshine and happiness." In other words, her ingratiating exterior did not threaten to undermine the racial order or white control over Mississippi County's Black agricultural labor force.[21]

Planters like Wilson supported Black extension agents' work as a means to help overcome "the poverty, dissatisfaction, and unrest among Negro farmers."[22] This was accomplished through the ongoing emphasis on Black women and girls' clubs to convince African Americans to remain in the rural South. In 1920, Mary J. McCain organized twenty-five clubs and 440 cooperators—apparently the largest enrollment of any county in the state. In addition, McCain established homemakers' clubs in eight Mississippi County communities with members who also enrolled in poultry club work.[23]

The extension service also aided agents' efforts through the use of USDA-produced documentaries. The thirty-two minute silent film *Helping Negroes to Become Better Farmers and Homemakers* (1921) was shown at movable-school gatherings to encourage rural Blacks to stay on the farm.[24] Movable schools, operated by extension service agents, were developed in the early twentieth century to provide agricultural knowledge to rural communities. While it is not known if movable-school agents showed this government film in Arkansas, it was impactful because it simultaneously reinforced negative stereotypes of African Americans and implicitly endorsed southern white supremacy.[25] It further positioned white agents and USDA supervisors as the real catalysts of change in Black farmers' lives, while subordinating African American agents as mere assistants. In fact, local and national Black leaders like Booker T. Washington had long initiated agricultural and rural improvement programs for African Americans.[26] Despite the film's condescending portrayals of African Americans, image did not necessarily correspond to reality. Black people never accepted their oppressed conditions. Although white landowners utilized a variety of economic, political, and violent means to keep African Americans on the farm during World War I, Black workers continued to resist by exercising their mobility.[27] They empowered themselves by questioning, contesting, and physically extracting themselves from the economic and political structures that held them captive.

African Americans who remained in the rural South consistently confronted extreme racism. Like their enslaved ancestors, they engaged in everyday acts of resistance, since they knew that outright confrontation was risky at best and deadly at worst. They astutely observed and skillfully maneuvered around local white power structures. Such activism often required quick decision-making. Instances of feigning sickness, noncompliance, and evasion did not make headlines, but such self-empowerment allowed rural Black Arkansans to impress their economic value, if not their political power, on white landowners.[28]

Home and farm agents' work exemplified African Americans' efforts to reshape the agricultural South's oppressive social landscape through their interactions with other agents, social workers, Jeanes Supervisors, and community leaders to consider ways to make Black farm life as productive as possible. This included cooperating across racial lines with white extension service agents. In 1921, an integrated group of agents met at the Pulaski County Courthouse for annual meeting of Negro farm and home demonstration agents where white home demonstration agent Connie Bonslagel discussed "co-operation between the races in the betterment of farm life."[29] She extolled the virtues of the agricultural extension service's work in rural Black communities. Commenting at a meeting in 1924, Bonslagel asserted, "negro women follow the advice of their college trained negro advisers as readily as they follow the advice of white demonstrators." Clearly not understanding the agency and autonomy that Black women exercised in their own communities and organizations, Bonslagel went on to heap patronizing praise upon them:

> It is a real picture to see a group of colored girls—dressed in all white—put on a demonstration. They even imitate the vocal mannerisms of their instructors when repeating recipes. Our Negro women make unusually good reports. They show interest and enthusiasm even in the face of great difficulties. Our efforts among Negro women and children are indeed worthwhile. And our workers—both white and colored—are the delighted at the response of the Negro women of Arkansas.[30]

African American leaders further heard from J. A. Presson, the white state supervisor of Negro rural schools and W. J. Jernigan, state director of boys and girls club work. The Black farm and home demonstration agents at the meeting included T. D. Speaks (Chicot County), S. H. Ellis (Columbia County), J. D. Rice and Alice Winston (Conway County), Louise Jones and Jennie Lou Woodard (Lee County), Mary J. McCain (Mississippi County),

B. H. Bennett (Little River County), William Harris and Dora Hollman (Phillips County), J. M. Harris (Pulaski County), and H. H. Mitchell and Lugenia Christmas (Saint Francis County).[31] Many of these agents also met in March 1922 with M. T. Payne, the University of Arkansas agricultural extension work director, where they voiced their support for gender divisions in farm and home demonstration work.[32] Black agents were compelled to attend meetings at which they were often subjected to patronizing lectures by white Arkansas extension service officials. It stands to reason, then, that they preferred to gather in predominantly Black spaces with their Black colleagues from other parts of the South to discuss the issues impacting their communities.[33]

In addition to the patronizing, racist attitudes they confronted, Black extension service agents were also chronically underpaid in comparison to their white colleagues. In 1919 in Ashley County, $1,600 was appropriated for a white home agent while only $600 was allowed for a Black home agent.[34] In 1925, the Pope County quorum court voted to retain Black home demonstration agent Lula Whickam for another year at a salary of $600, while her white counterpart was paid $1,300.[35] Virtually all of the Arkansas counties that employed African American extension agents in the 1920s paid them half the salary given to white agents. In counties without Black home demonstration agents, white agents received salaries of at least $900 to $1,000 per year.[36] In one especially egregious case in 1919, the white home demonstration agent for Chicot County was paid an annual salary of $2,000, while the county's Black home agent was paid $300.[37]

In some years, Black home demonstration agents were not hired at all. African Americans in Pulaski County did not have a home agent in 1920, even though agent Mary McCain was credited in the *Arkansas Gazette* for assisting with the "nine hundred and fifty cans of vegetables . . . put up by the negro club women of Pulaski County" in 1919.[38] Even so, the amount of money appropriated for extension service agents was usually paltry. In 1927, the Mississippi County quorum court only appropriated $3,500 for two white farm agents, a white home demonstration agent, and Black farm and home agents.[39]

Though their numbers were few and their pay dismal and unequal, Black home demonstration agents' presence was critical for Arkansas's Black agrarian communities, as they impressed upon women the importance of food preservation, particularly as the nation began sinking into an economic depression following World War I. In 1924, Black home demonstration clubs showcased clothing, poultry, and fruit and vegetable preserves—

reflecting an idealized, gender-driven division of labor on the farm—for which they won prizes at the Pulaski County State Fair.[40]

Agricultural fairs such as the one held in Pulaski County were a part of a nationwide movement established in the nineteenth century and enjoyed a "golden period" between 1850 and 1870. They continued to occur in rural communities well into the twentieth century.[41] Fairs provided spaces where large numbers of rural people gathered to be directly addressed by farm and home demonstration agents. Before the 1914 Smith-Lever Act, fairs exposed farmers to new ideas about scientific farming.[42] African Americans often attended extension agents' demonstrations of their own volition to enhance their skills by learning new scientific agricultural and home-management methods and to address the issue of depopulation in rural areas. Learning about new scientific home-management methods might have also allowed rural women, as Canadian historian Margaret Kechnie has argued, to "reduce the most debilitating aspects of farm life."[43] Home demonstration agents encouraged farm women to display their wares and skills in county fair competitions. At the 1923 fair, fourteen-year-old Bessie Jones won first prize in a bread-making contest sponsored by agent Dora B. Holman and held at the Pulaski County Courthouse. Jones also participated in the segregated fall state fair organized by Mary L. Ray.[44]

White community support was important for ensuring the success of state fairs. When the bread-making contest was held at the 1925 fair under agent Ella M. Parker's direction, it was sponsored by Little Rock's Union Trust Company, the Bracy and Ace Hardware Companies, the American Southern Trust Company, the Exchange Trust Company, and the Parkin Stationary Company, which all contributed prizes, money, and materials. Mary L. Ray donated fifty cents as well.[45]

At times, Black agents' responsibilities involved sharing reports about their successes in rural African American communities with those who did not or perhaps could not attend the fairs; for these reports, they used a relatively new media form in the 1920s, the radio. In 1926, Mary L. Ray and Pope County agent Jennie Lou Woodard shared Black home demonstration agents' work on KUOA radio in Fayetteville, Arkansas. Ray talked about "What Home Demonstration Work Is Doing for Our Negro Women," and Woodward discussed "The Value of Exhibits in Home Demonstration Work for Negroes."[46] Ray was clearly respected in the Black and white communities for her leadership skills. At the 1927 Pulaski County State Fair, she was lauded for training Black farm women whose canned goods were considered among the most successful in the exhibit hall. Also present were Arkansas

Jeanes Supervisors from eleven counties, whose pupils exhibited home life improvements through health posters, consumer items for the home, and rural arts and crafts.[47]

A Black presence at the county fair was about more than just displaying food and domestic arts and science products. For Black home demonstration agents like Mary L. Ray, a good showing at the fair was a means by which to combat racial stereotypes with a more nuanced representation of the "Negro citizen" by showing them at their best.[48] It bolstered rural women's sense of their own worth outside the domestic sphere by emphasizing the significance of their labor.[49] It further demonstrated that, although interpretations of Progressive-era domestic science on focused on white women, African American women also understood and utilized the knowledge to effect gender and racial progress in their communities.[50] These skills would prove especially useful during and after the Mississippi River flood of 1927.

The Mississippi River Flood of 1927 and Agrarian Activism in 1930s Arkansas

IN 1927, LULA TOLER, a Pine Bluff home demonstration agent turned relief worker, noted the suffering she encountered while working with the American Red Cross to assist African Americans whose homes and lives had been devastated by environmental crisis known as the Mississippi River flood of 1927 (also known as the Great Flood): "My first day's work with the sufferers were ones long to be remembered. The scene was most pitiful and shall ever haunt me while life lasts. The screams of the people and the lowing of cattle could be heard in the distance."[1] Toler resigned her post in 1927; she had served as the Jefferson County home demonstration agent since 1925, the year during which she also established the county's local council. Under her leadership, the council enjoyed many accomplishments, notably that club members were trained as "health leaders" and improved access to health care in their communities by assisting with community x-rays and providing polio vaccinations.[2]

Like many Black women, Toler had held different positions that had allowed her to serve Black communities elsewhere before coming to Arkansas. She had previously been a home demonstration agent in Meridian, Mississippi,[3] and a high school science teacher in Birmingham, Alabama.[4] She was well-versed in the struggles that African Americans faced in the rural South and the frequency with which Black extension service agents were denied adequate resources to assist them. The stress of extension service work caused her to seek other work, and she later became a noted ordained minister and the founder of Pine Bluff's first African American convalescent home.[5]

Rural Black families were devastated by Mississippi River flood. Surging flood waters covered four million acres in eastern Arkansas, destroyed $38 million in property, resulted in $12.5 million in crop loses, and cost 127 lives. Of Arkansas's seventy-five counties, thirty-six were impacted by the flood.[6] The flood further revealed the extreme poverty of residents of the Mississippi River Delta, most of whom were African American.[7] American Red Cross relief camps aided flood evacuees throughout the area, although only 19 percent of Black Arkansans availed themselves of Red Cross facilities.[8] African Americans nationwide expressed deep concerns about the American Red Cross's deference to the South's racial hierarchy, which resulted in unchecked white abuses and mistreatment and peonage of Black people.[9] Reports about brutality at the hands of armed National Guard officers within the relief camps, for instance, were widespread in the Black press.[10] Ironically, the flood's devastation also allowed many African Americans who had been trapped in debt peonage the freedom to migrate out of the South and away from abusive planters.[11] The Black press conceded that African American extension agents were perhaps best suited to participate in flood relief efforts to assist those who could not leave.[12] Black home demonstration agents and club members worked with the Red Cross to provide food and housing to destitute but proud African Americans as they struggled to survive the storm.[13]

In Saint Francis County, agent Lugenia Bell Christmas, who had been employed by the extension service since 1917, worked with the Red Cross to assist African Americans who had waded through floodwater for miles in search of food, clothing, medical care, and shelter for their families.[14] Christmas was not alone in her efforts, as local home demonstration club members distributed food to patients in an emergency hospital under the direction of Forrest City club leader Henrietta E. Ankrum.[15] Agents never missed an opportunity to impart important extension service lessons to flood refugees, whom they regarded as a captive audience. Lee County agent Annie L. Smith was in charge of securing sanitary "sweet milk" for Black infants from the Red Cross. Providing children with sanitary milk was important, since rural Arkansans, regardless of race, often ingested unsanitary and unsafe milk, which led to increased child mortality rates. At times, unsafe milk had been obtained from unhealthy cows. At others, milk-related illness was due to unclean utensils and equipment that had been used to handle milk such as buckets, vessels, and separators. Extension service agents warned against the dangers of milk-borne diseases such as typhoid fever, tuberculosis, scarlet fever, diphtheria, and septic sore throat.

They also stressed the importance of serving children fresh, cold milk in order to avoid outbreaks of dysentery and diarrhea.[16]

Annie Smith also attempted to combat food insecurity among Black flood victims by organizing home demonstration club members into four "canning club units" that were then responsible for holding demonstrations in their assigned section of the camp. Using canneries, cans, and sugar provided by the Red Cross, they produced several hundred quarts of canned berries.[17] This initiative was also aided by Jeanes Supervisors, who helped construct canneries in rural Black communities. Their efforts to combat food shortages lasted beyond the flood crisis. In the 1930s, Mississippi County Jeanes Supervisor Bessie Dupree Partee (later Ivy), worked with the Red Cross to provide schoolchildren with hot lunches as part of a countywide relief program. This was a cooperative venture involving the white county home demonstration agent and the county health unit and was an outreach program designed to assist all who suffered from food insecurity regardless of race. Yet white schools were consistently serviced before Black schools. Partee, who in 1937 was elected the Mississippi County Negro Teachers Association secretary and later earned an education degree from Arkansas AM&N College in 1948, was initially only authorized to "investigate conditions in the colored schools." Only later was she authorized "to serve the lunches in some of these schools also," thereby underscoring the inherently unfair treatment Black schools and children endured.

Very likely, the overwhelming responsibility and strain of helping flood victims and bearing witness to the devastating poverty and the extreme racism they endured proved too much for some Black home demonstration agents. African American flood victims were routinely denied food until they could prove they had worked to control the flood's damage. American Red Cross officials were largely uninterested in disrupting rural Jim Crow laws and customs and left the administration of its resources to local whites. Landowners often used Black food insecurity as leverage to ensure that they retained African American laborers.[18] They confiscated food distributed by the American Red Cross to sell in camp commissaries and charged Black victims between 100 and 500 percent of regular store prices. At least one Arkansas camp charged $0.60 for a twelve-pound sack of flour that cost $0.30 pre-flood, and $1.05 for shirts that sold elsewhere for $0.35.[19] These gross displays of racial injustice surely exhausted Black home demonstration agents who were laboring under overwhelming circumstances. As the 1927 flood ended, Annie L. Smith and Lula Toler resigned; as a result, white Lee County

home demonstration agent Flora Ferrill assumed responsibility for organizing canning clubs in what was euphemistically called "the bottoms"—the
separate and certainly unequal space designated for Black flood victims.[20]

In some cases, Black home demonstration agents found their white
colleagues willing to help African American flood victims. Mary L. Ray
was District Negro Home Demonstration Agent and Director of Negro
Work during the 1927 flood. Her husband, H. C., was a Special Advisor
for Colored Relief Work in Arkansas, a subsidiary of the Colored Advisory
Commission on the Mississippi Valley Flood, chaired by Tuskegee Institute
president Robert R. Moton.[21] Mary Ray noted this important professional,
if not quite equal, exercise in interracial cooperation while highlighting
Black women's accomplishments under difficult circumstances.[22] In a 1927
report, she credited Black women all over Arkansas with producing more
than 130,000 quarts of canned fruits, vegetables, and meats. But even as she
praised white agents' and officials' efforts, she validated their and perhaps
even her own beliefs about rural Blacks' inferiority when she asserted that
they "have always shown their interest and faith in the future of club work
and its effectiveness to advance a backward people."[23] It is likely the pressure
of Ray's responsibilities proved insurmountable. By 1928, she was replaced
by agent Jennie Lou Woodard after being granted a year's leave of absence
to attend to her health issues.[24]

Home demonstration agents were particularly concerned about the
poor dietary habits they encountered among rural African Americans.
Phillips County agent Carrie W. Moore used the flood crisis as an opportunity to teach impoverished Blacks better nutritional habits. More than
one thousand victims were sheltered at Eliza Miller County High School,
a Rosenwald School in West Helena, and at local churches. Moore noted
that when these people were given what she considered nutritious food,
they rejected it in favor of the high-fat and -calorie foods (grits, gravy, and
bacon for breakfast and cabbage with salt pork for dinner) to which they
were long accustomed. Moore helped flood victims, but she may have further sought to impart better dietary choices and domestic-science lessons
onto African Americans as a means of uplifting the race and refuting the
white stereotypes about Black inferiority, which circulated widely via early
twentieth-century eugenics arguments.[25] But she clearly did not take into
account flood victims' ability to resist attempted changes to their dietary
habits, particularly when they were under duress. Moore's resolve was not
defeated, and she later instituted nutritional programs in many of Arkansas's
Rosenwald Schools.[26]

Moore's activism was apropos, because Rosenwald Schools were spaces specifically created by and for Black Arkansans. Her role in the nutrition program was part of a statewide effort among home demonstration agents, regardless of race, to provide hot lunches to students and to, as a consequence, improve their academic performance. Such programs were particularly important, because impoverished people in rural areas consumed diets that were often tied to a "cash-crop economic system," and as a result often suffered from pellagra, a dietary deficiency. Combating poor nutrition, an initiative that had long been part of home demonstration agents' rural activism, became even more important during the 1927 flood.[27] Although Moore had to make concessions to the victims' dietary habits, she and the public health nurse cared for those who required medical assistance. This included women with newborn babies and those who suffered from tuberculosis, smallpox, and rheumatism.[28]

Agents helped flood victims find lost loved ones, provided clothing, organized soup kitchens, and conducted sanitation and hygiene demonstrations. In cooperation with farm agents, they led agricultural demonstrations and provided landless and displaced victims in Arkansas Red Cross emergency relief camps with much-needed psychological support as they rebuilt their homes and lives.[29] Living conditions for some rural Blacks improved dramatically after the flood.[30] Agent Lugenia Christmas noted that an increasing number of tenant homes had better light and multiple rooms. Many African Americans previously had lived in homes that lacked even such basic amenities as screens and windows. And because unsanitary living conditions were often linked to chronic illnesses in rural areas, more homes were equipped with outhouses.[31]

Improved living conditions after the flood allowed some rural Black women to resume raising chickens and planting gardens to supplement their meager incomes and diets. Lillie Bondon in Wheatley, Arkansas, operated a hatchery that she allowed her entire community to use. Others generated surplus income by producing and selling goods to help family members pursue an education. For example, by selling eight pounds of butter for $0.25 a pound, Lottie Bond of Madison, Arkansas, was able to pay her son's $15 a month boarding fee at the Fargo Agricultural School, an industrial school for African Americans located just outside of Brinkley in Monroe County.[32]

Home demonstration agents wanted to reach African Americans who lived in rural areas to ensure that they were trained in the most current farming and home management techniques, and to also perpetuate the philosophy of rural uplift. That is, they extolled the virtues of Booker T.

Washington's philosophy that Black self-sufficiency and determination would allow African Americans to move up from the bottom of America's racial, social, economic, and political hierarchy. To this end, in 1928, the AACES established the Movable Demonstration School for Negro Farm Folks.[33] Developed by George Washington Carver and Booker T. Washington, these portable agricultural schools were moved by farm and home demonstration agents from one community to another. Traveling to the most isolated areas, agents used movable schools to demonstrate the latest agriculture, home management, and public health innovations.[34] Christopher "C. C." Haraway and Jennie Lou Woodard served as Arkansas Movable School agents in the 1920s.[35] They traveled around the state in a one-and-a-half ton Ford truck and performed demonstrations in approximately twenty-eight to thirty counties in the first year of the Movable School's existence.[36] In 1929, the duo, along with H. C. Ray, journeyed to Washington (Hempstead County) where they regaled local Blacks with lectures and canning and farming demonstrations at Lincoln School.[37] African Americans from Walnut Grove and Mount Pleasant Baptist Schools in Keiser, Arkansas, also "motored" to Wilson in Mississippi County to meet with Haraway and Woodard.[38] Since movable-school agents were also tasked with improving race relations by reinforcing local racial hierarchies, Haraway and Woodard often were the guests of landowners who relied upon Black agents' demonstrations to help sharecroppers improve their home and health habits. In 1931, the movable school conducted demonstrations at Mason Rice Jr.'s and W. F. Anderson's farms in Ellison, Arkansas.[39] Of course, the primary objective of landowners was always profit—they wanted to ensure that they had the most productive laborers possible.[40]

Extension service agents also availed themselves of opportunities to improve upon the skills they imparted to rural people. In 1930, Mary and H. C. Ray, Jennie Lou Woodard, and C. C. Haraway all participated in Special Summer Schools for Negro Extension Agents held at historically Black colleges in Orangeburg, South Carolina; Prairie View, Texas; and Nashville, Tennessee. Supported by the USDA's Office of Cooperative Extension Work, southern state extension services, and the Julius Rosenwald Fund, the summer schools were established at a meeting held at the Georgia State Industrial College (known today as Savannah State University) in January 1930. With scholarships underwritten by the Julius Rosenwald Fund, Black extension service agents had the opportunity to secure additional training in agricultural economics.[41]

Throughout the 1930s, home demonstration agents and other Black leaders cooperatively harnessed the power within rural Black women's networks to increase food and health security, childcare, and domestic uplift activism in African American communities. They navigated through a mélange of individual and collective activist networks. As PTA members, home demonstration clubs, extension service agents, and Jeanes Supervisors, Black women employed community networks to carry out extension service and reform programs. They served on "consumer-nutrition committees" and were often members of or worked with home demonstration and 4-H clubs and county agricultural planning committees.[42] They also turned to local home demonstration clubs to help them combat high infant mortality rates and provided them with child development lessons through the creation of Better Babies Clubs.

Better Babies Club members visited homes and provided mothers with bulletins on child care, development, and education.[43] Because so many rural children were born into extreme poverty and often suffered from chronic malnutrition, extension agents who wanted to help mothers give their children a "healthy start in life" provided them with information on pre-natal and postnatal care.[44] Child care and development were particularly important in rural Black communities where parents were often the poorest of the poor. The lessons provided by home demonstration agents greatly influenced how Black women cared for their children. Unfortunately, Better Babies Clubs were segregated, and woefully few of them existed for African American women. Arkansas had 428 Better Babies Clubs in the late 1930s, nine of which were African American. Black mothers enthusiastically utilized their services. In 1939, Black children participated in 115 clinics (289 clinics were held for white children) and were examined by county health nurses and doctors. Three hundred eighteen Black mothers created a "baby's canning budget" and 1,450 reported that they followed approved child feeding methods provided by the AACES.[45]

As the economic crisis deepened in the 1930s, Arkansas's Black leaders gathered to assess the best strategies for survival in rural communities. In 1932, home demonstration agents gathered at the Arkansas Negro Farmer Conference at Fargo Agricultural School, where they outlined plans to assist Black farmers throughout Arkansas who had been devastated by the Great Depression.[46] Jefferson County home demonstration agent Cassa H. Lawlah and H. C. Ray were among those present at the meeting.[47] Arkansas Jeanes Supervisors surely attended because their own work was so closely connected to that of extension service agents. Monroe County Jeanes Supervisor Viola Gabashane quite likely attended. Gabashane, a Jeanes Supervisor from 1931 to 1933, was one of the first teachers at the Osceola Rosenwald School in Mississippi County.[48]

At times, extension service messages from home and farm agents were meted out to African Americans from rural church pulpits. Black extension agents understood that churches were by far the most important institutions in rural Black communities. They provided spiritual succor to those who had been physically, psychologically, and emotionally assaulted by the demands of agricultural life. They also provided space for much needed rural social interaction and community uplift activities. And in agrarian communities, Christian churches were spaces where rural moral values were reinforced. Christianity and churches were "entwined with the power of government, especially through state universities and cooperative extension."[49] Home demonstration agents collaborated with rural pastors, whose approbation garnered local support for extension service programs which in turn promoted healthy rural communities. In doing so, they were able to access the core of African American communities. Pastors, who were often revered community leaders, welcomed agents' uplift activism in their congregants' homes and lives.[50]

Furthermore, Black churches allowed African Americans to quietly challenge the strictures of the rural Jim Crow South and to maintain their dignity and sense of self-worth.[51] Most African Americans belonged to a congregation and participated in church programs. Agricultural laborers worked long hours, and lacked transportation or even adequate clothing, but they still managed to attend services because church was the preeminent nucleus of the Black community, the place where African Americans gathered to share their intelligence, develop leadership abilities, and assume positions of authority. These components of community building were specifically of their making, because they were denied them in most other aspects of their lives in rural Arkansas.[52]

Ministers and other local and national leaders used their influence to urge rural Blacks to support extension service programs and to promote rural uplift. What little wealth southern African Americans possessed, they often invested in their churches. They attended service for spiritual guidance, psychological release, and as a talisman against hard times, but they also expected their churches and pastors to serve the community and often attended institutes conducted by the Home Missions Council of the National Council of Churches of Christ in the U.S.A. These institutes were intended for rural people and were most often held in conjunction with vocational and agricultural schools and churches.

Moreover, churches were meeting places for 4-H and home demonstration clubs and other extension service activities.[53] In 1933, Reverend S. B. Branch, pastor of St. James Methodist Episcopal Church in Roland, Arkansas, gave a sermon on "better homes" after which home and movable-school demonstration agent Ella M. Parker presided over a showing of local homes.[54] When Lugenia Christmas met with female 4-H club members in Saint Francis County in 1934, it was to hear reports about their poultry-raising, gardening, "dairying," sewing, "home beautification," and the county "bread and dress" contest.[55] But there again, local Black women leaders were also attuned to the benefits of the farm and home practices they learned from the extension service during the lean Depression years. Between 1925 and 1935 in Lee County, for example, their interaction and cooperation with home demonstration agents doubled from 22 percent to 42 percent.[56] During 1938 in Osceola, Arkansas, the local home demonstration council and the county farmers' association met with home demonstration agent Mary M. Banks Wingfield, who talked about "home improvement." Also at this meeting, attendees discussed plans for the first annual Colored Farmers' Cured Meats show.[57] Banks Wingfield additionally worked with the 4-H club and in 1934 sponsored a day-long rally where girls were taught bed-making, dishwashing, and canning. Boys listened to lectures which such titles as "What the Farmer Ought to Know about Cotton," and "I Know My Livestock." Jeanes Supervisor Annie Currie talked about the importance of school work and the possibility of opening a school for illiterate adults.[58]

Food preservation of course was of critical importance during the Depression. In 1938, food canned and preserved by Black club women and girls was valued at $199,248.[59] And despite their meager resources, in 1939 rural Black women in Little Rock, with the assistance of district home demonstration agent Cassa Lawlah, participated in Better Homes Week, during which 10,084 families participated in clean-up campaigns in 286 communities.[60] Like many Black Arkansan home demonstration agents, Lawlah possessed many community connections. She was a member of a Black women's federated club, the Social and Art Club, established in Pine Bluff in 1911. The club became affiliated with the AACW in 1912. At one point she also served as president of the Social and Art Club.[61] In the late 1960s, Lawlah also served on the Arkansas Council on Human Relations.[62]

After President Franklin Delano Roosevelt's 1932 election, the Democratic-controlled Congress passed New Deal legislation revolutionizing American agriculture.[63] In 1933, the Agricultural Adjustment Act's passage created the Agricultural Adjustment Administration (AAA). The AAA paid farmers to limit their production to such basic commodities as cotton, corn, hogs, rice, tobacco, and dairy products. In Arkansas and throughout the South, this largely meant reducing cotton acreage and production in order to reduce surpluses until prices increased to 1909–14 levels. In 1933, for instance, one million farmers were paid $112 million to destroy 10.4 acres of cotton. These crop-reduction efforts occurred with the full cooperation of extension agents, farmers' committees, and the Farm Bureau.[64] Despite their employment with the extension service and the federal government and their critical roles in rural Black communities, however, Black home demonstration agents and African Americans in general were routinely denied access to information about New Deal programs, particularly the Agricultural Adjustment Administration; this denial dramatically impacted African American farmers.

Similarly, tenant farmers or sharecroppers were often denied the kinds of federal government subsidies given to large landowners. In Marked Tree, for instance, tenants received only one third of the payments due to them from their landlords.[65] Such parsimoniousness often spurred on African Americans' decision to leave rural environs for southern cities or northern and western locales, or to join organizations like the biracial Southern Tenant Farmers Union (STFU), established in 1934 in Tyronza, Arkansas. This integrated group of tenant farmers went on strike in 1935 and 1936, to demand direct payments from the AAA for the reduction of cotton production, and fought eviction by landowners who in 1934 had evicted forty families in violation of Section 7 of the Agricultural Adjustment Act that was supposed to protect tenants' rights.[66]

Rural Black women were among the most active members of the STFU. According to STFU founder Henry L. Mitchell, "women always had more courage than men and were usually able to get more done than men."[67] Describing southern landowners to an STFU official in 1936, Lula Parchman said, "[They] don't regard my rights at all." The landlord for whom she worked had planned to "consolidate his holdings, replaced his tenant farmers with wage laborers, and charge rent for the house she had occupied rent free under her sharecropping agreement." By the next year, Parchman had become a STFU member and well-known activist for the organization, recruiting sixty-four of her neighbors into the STFU.[68] Mississippi-born Gould resident Carrie Dilworth was secretary of her STFU local in the 1930s, an experience that informed her later civil rights and political activism in rural Arkansas. In the 1960s, Dilworth, who had lived in Lincoln County since 1919, housed Student Nonviolent Coordinating Committee workers who also helped her establish a Freedom School in a building she owned.[69] Like many rural Black women, Dilworth was also a home demonstration club member. In 1962, she was the segregated State Home Demonstration Council parliamentarian.[70]

Unfortunately, violence often accompanied African American rural laborers' challenges to economic, social, and political marginalization and the firm hold planters had over land and their agricultural labor force. This was particularly the case for Black women, who were fundamentally denied the protections of womanhood theoretically granted to white women. In 1936, Eliza Nolden, a sixty-year-old Black sharecropper from Earle, Arkansas, was severely beaten by white planters "with sticks the size of axe handles," for her activism.[71] Nolden, who had been born in Mississippi between 1878 and 1880, looked to the court system for justice.[72] Nolden, along with Willie Sue Blagden, a white Memphis social worker who was flogged for investigating the beating of a Black sharecropper, and a white minister who had also been assaulted, each filed separate $15,000 lawsuits against their attackers, to no avail. In the suit, Nolden alleged that she had been abducted by planters and members of the East Arkansas Planters collective John "Boss" Dulaney, H. S. Watson, Percy Magmus, and L. L. Barham in Earle's business district. The men took her to jail and then to Barham's cotton gin, where she was beaten and quite possibly sexually assaulted.[73] During the trial, the men all denied any knowledge of Nolden's beating. Percy Magmus described himself as "just a farmer," and L. L. Barham denied even knowing Nolden.[74] Nolden died from her injuries in May 1938 at John Gaston Hospital in Memphis, Tennessee.[75] The charges against the planters were dropped in November 1938.[76] Although it was never proven that Nolden's death resulted from her beating, STFU president J. R. Butler commented:

> There is no doubt in my mind that the death of Eliza Nolden was hastened by the brutal beating she received at the hands of this brutal planter mob. As yet we do not have conclusive proof that death was caused by this attack on the Negro woman, but we do know that up until the time she was assaulted she was in good health and that since the beating she has been confined to her bed almost continuously.[77]

Generally, the federal government was reluctant to intervene and curb racial and sexual violence and discrimination in AAA programs, preferring instead to defer to local authorities.[78] But in 1936, the federal government finally investigated violations of tenants' rights in eastern Arkansas and sent a special agent to appear before the Little Rock federal grand jury to present data of alleged violations of peonage laws. Additionally, Arkansas governor Junius Marion Futrell established an honorary Arkansas Tenancy Commission to consider solutions to sharecropper issues.[79]

Increasingly, the USDA and the AAA were also forced to address Black farmers' and agricultural extension service agents' discontent.[80] They did so by looking to prominent and connected African Americans like Jennie Moton, who in turn leveraged her contacts and relationships with rural southern Black communities that had been devastated and further impoverished by the economic downturn.

From 1936 until 1942, the AAA employed Jennie Booth Moton as a field agent to inform local Blacks about the programs' benefits and to galvanize their support. Moton, a prominent African American clubwoman and the wife of Tuskegee Institute president Robert Russa Moton, visited Black churches and clubs throughout the South, often with home demonstration agents, to extol the virtues of the AAA. In 1936, she went to Little Rock and Pine Bluff and talked to Black and white extension officers and agents about organizing a statewide meeting to inform rural women about farm conservation measures.[81] Because Jim Crow laws prohibited her from staying in local hotels, Moton often stayed with H. C. Ray and his second wife, Julia, when she was in Arkansas.[82]

Jennie Moton visited Arkansas again in 1937, where she addressed the Saint Francis County Farm Bureau, the home demonstration council, and Black club women. She toured farms with Osceola home demonstration agent Mary M. Banks Wingfield. She and district agent Cassa Lawlah further sojourned to Hickman and Wilson, Arkansas, to inspect a model farm and rural home.[83]

The primary focus of Moton's efforts were African American farm women, with whom she shared information about the AAA and whom she encouraged to participate in soil conservation efforts by planting gardens. In most cases, the AAA and other New Deal programs did not fully meet the needs of African Americans or the extension service agents who represented them; agents were often denied access to critical information.[84] Cassa Lawlah informed Moton, "Unfortunately, we have not participated in this program at all. . . . Nor have any of our staff of Negro Home Demonstration Agents been called in for any meetings or conferences pertaining to the Agricultural Programs and for this reason. . . . Our knowledge of the program is very limited."[85] Though Moton did not leave behind much that speaks to how AAA programs actually aided rural Black women, she did support and promote the work of home demonstration agents. In writing to Cassa Lawlah, she expressed how she endeavored to "put on the map home demonstration as never before. I know we can do it working together, with the officials and the farm families, and it is certainly a rare privilege we have, those of us who are employed, and are held responsible for the demonstrational teaching of family and home improvement."[86]

Moton's influence, then, was critical to advocating for Black home demonstration agents' increased numbers and presence in rural communities.[87] Her visits to Arkansas also included meetings with predominantly Black local and state organizations. In 1937, she met with Annie Gilliam, state president of the AACW, a group that was heavily invested in improving rural Black life. Moton also visited Marianna, Arkansas, in September 1941 and met with Anna M. P. Strong, principal of Robert R. Moton High School and president of the National Colored Parent Teacher Association and yet another African American woman whose activism helped ameliorate social, economic, and political ills in rural communities.

Anna Strong was born in Phillips County in 1884 to parents who were active in the Religious Society of Friends, also known as the Quakers.[88] Strong attended Southland College, a Quaker institution in Lexa, Arkansas, and later attended Tuskegee Institute and Columbia University on a one-year scholarship from the General Education Board, although she never earned a degree from either institution.[89]

From 1929 to 1930, Strong was the president of the Arkansas Colored Teachers Association and in the 1930s established the Key Schools Program. This program, which began with twenty schools in 1934 and grew to one hundred by 1940, allowed educators to attend a ten-week summer workshop at Arkansas AM&N College to continue their educational training.[90] They attended using scholarships provided by the General Education Board. Educators then returned to their institutions and worked cooperatively with homes, schools, and churches to address conditions in rural communities.[91] In 1932, Strong was appointed assistant supervisor of rural Black schools by the ADE, a position she held for eight years before resuming her position as principal of Moton High School.[92] Strong advocated for rural Black Arkansans' educational access on a national level as well. In 1934, she was named the rural education committee vice chairperson at the National Conference on Fundamentals in the Education of Negroes in Washington, DC.[93] Strong was further awarded an honorary doctorate in education in 1938 from Bishop College in Marshall, Texas. She was the only woman who had been so honored in the college's history.[94] In 1939, Strong, R. C. Childress, and the white supervisor of the Arkansas Division of Negro Education further highlighted the social, economic, civic, and health inequities in rural Black communities when they published *Problems of Negro Health in Arkansas: Preliminary Study Bulletin*, a health education course for Black parents and teachers, in corporation with Arkansas AM&N College (where Strong was a visiting professor of rural education), Philander Smith College, the Arkansas Tuberculosis Association, and the Arkansas State Board of Health.[95] Strong remained principal of Robert R. Moton High School in Marianna until she retired in 1957. She died on March 14, 1966.[96]

The severe privation African Americans faced following the Great Flood of 1927 and during the Depression years underscored the importance of Black women's activism in rural Arkansas communities. Extension service agents often found their hands tied when it came to assisting their constituents, because they were intentionally denied access to important resources.[97] Moton's travels continued to take her around the South until her death in 1942, but her interactions with Black women leaders such as Anna B. Strong and home demonstration agents helped bring increased national attention to the depth of the issues they were battling in rural communities. Similarly, their locally cultivated organizational network of home demonstration clubs, discussed in the next chapter, strengthened their resolve in attending to the needs of the most impoverished communities in rural Arkansas and developing agrarian women leaders.

— 5 —

The State Council of Home
Demonstration Clubs

BLACK HOME DEMONSTRATION agents' interactions with communities, particularly the leadership abilities they exhibited, often deeply influenced young women. They were community role models particularly for young women like Pine City's Cynthia Weems. In 1935, agent Cassa Lawlah, who at the time was unmarried, recognized Weems's leadership potential during their interactions in demonstration club meetings. Lawlah and other Black women in the Pine City community encouraged Weems to pursue a career with the AACES. Weems, who had always enjoyed canning and cooking and described them as "hobbies," asserted, "My aim in life is to finish school and be a county home demonstration agent like Miss C. L. Hamilton [Lawlah's maiden name] and from that to the state agent of Arkansas."[1]

For most rural women, training in food canning and preservation methods began at a very young age. It was not unusual to find young women in local canneries who had learned from older women in home demonstration club meetings or operating the establishment themselves. In 1935, a sixteen-year-old Weems supervised a canning kitchen.[2] Weems, who was originally from Holly Grove and currently a ninth grader at Arkansas AM&N's laboratory high school, was one of Pine City's youngest and most productive supervisors. In the previous year, her cannery produced more cans (5,196) than any other kitchen, Black or white, in Monroe County.

As the demand for home demonstration agents grew across Arkansas, so too did the need for a statewide organization of clubs to unite rural women and coordinate their activities. Home demonstration clubs served many purposes in rural communities. They created all-female spaces for rural women to ask questions and to discuss health, family, and child care concerns. The clubs also combined educational programs with the extension service's agenda. Agents disseminated information and educated rural women who were then expected to share their newfound knowledge. with others.[3] And because farming families often lived far from their neighbors, home demonstration clubs also provided opportunities for women to socialize.[4]

In 1929 white demonstration agents organized the Arkansas Council of Home Demonstration Clubs.[5] As was typical of the Jim Crow restrictions of the time and extension service policies, its membership excluded Black women. But because Black women served the most impoverished communities around the state and often had to do so with fewer resources, they craftily coordinated their efforts and formed state organization of their own. In 1936, Cassa Lawlah, and Connie J. Bonslagel, established the segregated State Council of Home Demonstration Clubs (SCHDC) at a farmers' conference at Arkansas AM&N College. Mary B. Doxy from Widener (Saint Francis County) was elected the council's first president.[6] Like the Arkansas Council, the SCHDC created a network of county clubs in rural Black communities around the state.

Some of the agents who were SCHDC members also had long tenures with the AACES.[7] Parliamentarian Fannie Mae Boone had been a public school educator in Luxora, Arkansas, before she was employed by the AACES in 1929. Born in Alpine, Georgia, in 1892 and trained at the Kansas Industrial and Educational Institute (also known as the "Western Tuskegee"), and later at Tuskegee, Boone was appointed the Lee County home demonstration agent in 1929.[8] She became the supervisor of Black home demonstration agents in Arkansas in 1942, a position she held until her retirement in 1958.[9] Boone was later honored in 1960 as one of three outstanding rural leaders by President Dwight D. Eisenhower at the Thirteenth Annual Regional 4-H Club Camp at Howard University in Washington, DC.[10] In her retirement, Boone became a girls' counselor at Arkansas AM&N, where she worked for ten years before moving to St. Louis, Missouri, to live with her daughter. She died in 1985 and is buried in the Luxora City Cemetery.[11]

Although the SCHDC had been founded in the 1930s, local Black home demonstration clubs in Arkansas had been around at least since World War I. As discussed in chapter 2, in 1917 Mary L. Ray formed the first club in in Forrest City, Arkansas. The Saint Francis County Home Demonstration Council was established in March 1921.[12] In Hot Spring County, membership in the local home demonstration clubs increased from 20 percent in 1925 to over 50 percent in 1935.[13] Two factors account for this growth during the Depression years. First, the impoverished conditions in which many rural Blacks found themselves made it imperative for them to learn new farming and home techniques. Second, malnutrition and chronic underemployment or unemployment and destitution was endemic among rural families regardless of race. As a consequence, most found themselves on relief rolls. Black women in particular often tended to be the sole source of support for their households. Already poor, they were particularly devastated by the economic downturn. Starting in 1932, approximately twelve hundred canneries or canning kitchens and sewing projects, created using state funds subsidized by the Civil Works Administration, put many of these women back to work in areas like North Little Rock where the first canning program was established.[14] By 1934, there were 1,379 canning kitchens in Arkansas. The state emergency relief commission hired 1,025 home demonstration club members to supervise the kitchens, thus skillfully harnessing women's control over household finances and food production.[15]

Professional educated women like the aforementioned Cassa Lawlah exposed rural Black women to new opportunities within and beyond their rural communities and allowed them to develop their leadership skills.[16] Indeed, when they engaged women in all-female settings, the impact was often transformative. Women realized that they possessed the power to carve out spaces for their agency and in doing so created empowering women-centered communities within the larger rural community. This often resulted in them learning about and accessing opportunities they might not have otherwise been aware of. This was particularly important for rural southern Black women, whose race overwhelmingly limited them to agricultural or domestic employment.

Many of the women like Cynthia Weems who worked in cannery kitchens were also members of 4-H or local home demonstration clubs. Their employment not only allowed them to help others who were in similar circumstances, but it also generated much-needed, if limited, cash income.[17] Such skills also readily lent themselves to the inculcation of the ethic of community improvement and self-sufficiency among rural Blacks.

Home demonstration agents and club members often sponsored 4-H clubs, the youth component of the extension service, in their communities. Although extension work in many areas of the country began after the passage of the 1914 Smith-Lever Act, 4-H work actually predated any federal legislation. Club work among rural girls and boys actually grew in part out of a desire to "to create future generations of rural leaders."[18] Like home demonstration clubs, 4-H clubs were created to teach girls and boys to embrace rural life with the additional objective of keeping young people from abandoning farming life.[19]

The 4-H, like the extension service, was housed under the auspices of the USDA. The organization's public face and the national conception of rural life was considered quintessentially American and therefore implicitly white. In reality 4-H membership was diverse, though clubs throughout the South were segregated.[20] This remained the case even after the USDA used the 4-H to deploy democratic language and citizenship programming in the late 1930s and during World War II.[21] Although they espoused the rhetoric of American citizenship during the wartime, Black 4-H members were not permitted full roles in its practice: they were excluded from such national events as the National 4-H Congress in Chicago and the National 4-H Camp in Washington, DC. In the South, white 4-Hers attended subsidized camps. No such options existed for African American 4-Hers.[22] The state 4-H Club Congress remained segregated into the 1960s.

Despite these racial disparities, Black women's home demonstration clubs supported 4-H youth activities, as did African American extension service agents. Limited financial resources did not impede them from celebrating Black youth's achievements in their own communities. In 1930, for instance, H. C. and Mary L. Ray held contests for 4-H club members at their annual rally in Osceola, Arkansas.[23] At the 1932 4-H rally in Forrest City, the couple spoke to the approximately eight hundred club members about "improved agriculture and home life."[24] Mary L. Ray continued to engage in this kind of public labor throughout her career until her untimely death in July 1934 from chronic interstitial nephritis and arteriosclerosis.[25]

By 1937, twenty-four 4-H clubs for African American youth had been established in Arkansas.[26] Black home demonstration agents also encouraged Black 4-Hers to display their accomplishments at local fairs. In 1949, "negro booths" were set up by 4-H clubs from Clear Lake, Promised Land, Grider Round Lake, Flat Lake, Joiner, Birdsong, Holt, and Rosa, all Black communities in Mississippi County. Booths were also manned by home economics students from Harrison Negro High School and the New Farmers of America.[27]

Like white women, Black women also supported 4-H club members' educational pursuits through their entrepreneurial ventures by supporting college scholarships through the SCHDC. Black women further showcased 4-Hers' accomplishments in local newspapers. In 1948, for instance, the SCHDC awarded a scholarship to Gracie Mae Tatum, a graduate of Lincoln High School from the Spring Hill community in Camden. She won the scholarship as a result of her club projects in 1947 and 1948.[28] Additionally, in 1950 Burdette 4-Her Loretha Blackburn was named "State Girl Leadership Champion" at the annual dinner for Arkansas Live-At-Home contest winners held at Shorter College in Little Rock.[29] For a final example, the Hempstead County 4-H club held its achievement banquet in November 1954 for which the theme was "Serving as a Loyal Citizen Through 4-H Club Work," perhaps a nod to the civil rights activism occurring nationally. The banquet was sponsored by the local white Retail Merchants' Association and the Meyers Bakery in Hope, Arkansas. Home demonstration agent Lena Eddington was the event's keynote speaker.[30]

Home demonstration agents were aware of the environments in which they operated. They were mindful of how important it was to respect rural African Americans and earn their trust. In short, local support for extension programs was critical. Rather than positioning themselves as representatives of the federal or state government sent to work on poor rural Blacks' behalf, agents instead cultivated working partnerships with them even as they sought to uplift them from their impoverished circumstances. This tactic held great import for home demonstration and farm agents and Black Arkansan leaders throughout the 1930s and beyond, as they approached African American communities cautiously and respectfully even while imparting the "politics of respectability" to encourage them to embrace middle-class notions of self-determination.[31]

Club involvement further helped Black women develop leadership skills that enabled them to conduct meetings when home demonstration agents were unavailable.[32] This did not challenge white authority, but it did allow Blacks to challenge assumptions about African American inferiority and pathology some of which had been internalized.[33] It further encouraged them to engage self-empowering and communal discourses beyond the observation of white landowners by employing what one scholar termed "hidden transcripts," or unnoticed strategies of resistance.[34] Black women, like marginalized people the world over, obliquely critiqued the power structures that regulated and restricted their lives. This was yet another tool of resistance that poor rural Blacks had long wielded in private spaces to assert their dignity and pride at a time when their psyches were constantly under siege.[35]

Although joining or becoming leaders in home demonstration clubs was an important way for Black women to empower themselves and their communities, there were also compelling reasons why many were not inclined to assume leadership positions. Black and white rural women often had no way of getting to home demonstration club meetings. The responsibility of farm life required women to work inside and outside the home, thereby leaving relatively little time to attend meetings, even if they could arrange transportation. Women who were mothers found it difficult to find someone to care for their children in their absence. In some cases, women were simply indifferent to the home and health practices available at home demonstration club meetings. In other cases, they were unaware of the services the extension service provided.[36] And some women simply distrusted the motives of outsiders and agents of the federal government.[37] On the whole, however, once they were convinced that extension service agents were interested in the most pressing issues in their communities and sought to work with them rather than marginalize them, rural women enthusiastically joined local home demonstration clubs and welcomed the information and training they provided. They additionally availed themselves of opportunities to increase their knowledge of and ability to lead and serve the rural Black communities in which they resided.[38]

These opportunities often included attending short courses. In 1938, twenty-five 4-H and home demonstration club members from Hempstead County sojourned to Arkansas AM&N College, to attend the annual Farmers' Conference and Short Course. Established in the late nineteenth century and a fixture on land-grant agricultural college campuses by 1914, short courses were made available to rural people around the country and were considered a form of extension agricultural work in and of themselves. Short courses did not grant degrees, but they provided rural people access to short-term agricultural education—most did not have the means or the time to attend a four-year institution. Short courses were practical, flexible, concentrated, and mobile courses that could best meet and instruct rural people right in their communities or at nearby institutions. They were also relatively inexpensive. By 1907, such courses were available in Virginia, New Jersey, and Arkansas.[39]

Most short courses instructed rural people in crop, soils, animal husbandry, dairying, and, for women, domestic science. Any reading materials for the short course were typically provided by the USDA and experiment station publications.[40] Short courses also targeted the young. 4-H girls participated in contests for food canning and salad-, bread-, and dress-making, while the boys were scored on their ability to judge mules, cows, poultry, and hogs.[41] Mary and H. C. Ray supervised such a short course at the Branch Normal College in 1921. The instructional style was practical and made extensive use of demonstrations. During a three-day course, African

Americans not only witnessed cattle- and hog-judging, canning, and mattress-making demonstrations, they also were addressed by educational specialists and state and local extension service leaders and other luminaries. C. P. Newton, who represented Arkansas governor Thomas McRae and Black agents from Tuskegee and Hampton Institutes, spoke at these gatherings.[42]

What was most evident from these actions is that rural Blacks of all ages availed themselves of opportunities to enhance the living standards and agricultural productivity of their communities. The SCHDC specifically utilized rural Black women's resources, talents, and limited influence as a chance to not only improve conditions in Black communities but to also showcase African Americans' agricultural skills. They further allowed women from different communities to network, share ideas, and experiences. These women's connections to one another were not limited to the SCHDC. As the next chapter reveals, Black women's statewide affiliation through the AACW allowed larger formations of solidarity and cooperative action, including among Black women based in urban spaces. Through these larger formations, they were able to confront a multitude of issues while challenging discrimination and realizing meaningful change among rural Arkansans.

— 6 —

The Arkansas Association
of Colored Women

AT THE 1920 National Association of Colored Women's (NACW) biennial convention at Tuskegee Institute, Black club women discussed what had happened to African Americans in Phillips County during and after the 1919 Elaine Massacre. Mary Jackson, a Young Women's Christian Association industrial secretary, relayed the details of her visit to the prison in Little Rock, where the men were held at one point. She asked the NACW to send a letter to African American attorney Scipio A. Jones to support him in his efforts to have them released.[1] Arkansas Association of Colored Women (AACW) members also addressed racial violence in the state and throughout the nation during and after World War I. When Black Arkansans established the Citizens Defense Fund to support the twelve men who had been imprisoned for their alleged role in the massacre, club women in Little Rock raised over $1,000 to support the organization.[2]

Also present at the meeting was AACW representative Henrietta Carolina along with three other Black women including Pine Bluff's Ladye B. O'Bryant, who later headed Arkansas's NAACP Anti-Lynching Crusaders chapter.[3] Carolina advocated a "very strong and heart appealing plea" for the "condemned men awaiting execution for rioting in Elaine, Ark."[4] Each state federation was then asked to appeal to Arkansas's governor to commute the men's sentences to life imprisonment.[5] Black women's rural reform activism was buttressed by their participation in the women's club movement in the late nineteenth and early twentieth centuries. Their national connections were a significant means through which they were able to simultaneously challenge racial violence and address issues in African American communities in the wake of World War I.

National women's organizations with local chapters often addressed issues in rural communities by underscoring the importance of home economics. Although home economics was considered a "white" occupation, Black women also obtained domestic-science education, because courses were offered at most African American institutions of higher learning.[6]

After the Civil War, the women's club movement spread throughout the nation, reflecting Progressive-era concerns about impoverished communities nationwide. These organizations were particularly important sites of empowerment for women, not least because women founded and led them. Furthermore, the issues they addressed were often considered a natural extension of their roles as wives and mothers.[7]

Such activism was even more important in African American communities, because they were generally not included in white progressives' plans for community uplift activism. Black women were typically not considered true wives or mothers, a notion that they vociferously contested through their organizational and community activities. Excluded from white women's clubs, in 1896 they founded the NACW to support local African American women's clubs around the country. The NACW did not seek to emulate white women's clubs. Rather, as middle-class, educated women, the members were best were positioned to dedicate their lives to activism in African American communities.[8] Although scholarship on the NACW has often focused on members' uplift activism in urban spaces, the organization also sought to alleviate poor conditions in rural communities through its network of Black women leaders.[9]

Members of the AACW, which was established in Little Rock in 1905, often cooperated with home demonstration agents, clubs, and Jeanes Supervisors—who were often AACW members themselves—to enact rural school, health, and sanitation improvements.[10] Like the national body, the AACW adopted the motto "Lifting as We Climb" and its members were middle-class, educated Black women from all over the state. The AACW held its first annual meeting in 1905 in Hot Springs, with Little Rock educator Mary Harris Speight serving as its first president until 1915.[11] At its second annual meeting in Little Rock in 1909, the AACW hosted thirty clubs from around the state. Black club women understood their work was intimately connected to the plight of African Americans in Arkansas and throughout the nation. AACW president Mary H. Speight, an 1880 Oberlin College graduate and an English teacher at Little Rock's Mifflin Wistar Gibbs High School, underscored this idea during her opening address, remarking that the "hope of any race depended on its women and that no nation ever rises above its women."[12]

For Black club women, racial uplift invariably meant caring for African

American homes and children. The AACW's primary objective during its first two decades was to establish industrial homes for young Black women who had been sent to adult prisons for criminal activity.[13] The major topic of discussion at the 1909 and subsequent AACW meetings was parenting and homemaking. One Hot Springs member stressed that the "happiness of both the child and its parents depends upon discipline, which in turn necessitates correction and occasional punishment." She further advised that "homes be made attractive for children and that they should be kept off the streets and out of alleys." The politics of respectability resonated strongly among Black club women and formed part of the mantra of NACW officials, who maintained close contact with the AACW.[14]

NACW officials often visited Arkansas. In 1911, president and cofounder Elizabeth C. Carter lectured to AACW members at North Little Rock's Mount Pleasant Baptist Church.[15] AACW members also supported the NACW's campaigns against the motion picture industry's racist portrayals of Black people. In 1917, twenty-three Black women's clubs presented a petition to Little Rock's mayor and the Board of Censors protesting the showing of the silent film *The Birth of a Nation*.[16] The controversial film, which premiered in 1915, perpetuated negative stereotypes of African Americans during Reconstruction and led to a nationwide revival of the Ku Klux Klan and increased anti-Black violence.[17]

Arkansas club women were also officers in the national organization. When the NACW met at Arkansas Baptist College in 1905, it elected Little Rock's Mary H. Speight secretary and Hot Springs resident Nettie P. Eden vice president.[18] Margaret Murray Washington, Booker T. Washington's third wife, also attended this meeting.[19] The Washingtons were also friends with Arkansas club woman and Fort Smith resident Mame Stewart Josenberger, who in 1915 accompanied the couple on a cruise from Boston, Massachusetts, to Halifax, Nova Scotia, and Charlottetown, Prince Edward Island, in Canada.[20] Josenberger, one of the AACW's most prominent members, was born Mame Stewart in either 1868 or 1872 in Owego, New York, to Frank and Mary Elizabeth Stewart, both of whom had been born in Virginia.[21] After attending the Owego Free Academy in upstate New York, Josenberger graduated in 1888 from Fisk University in Nashville, Tennessee, with a degree in education. Among her classmates was scholar and political activist W. E. B. Du Bois, with whom she often corresponded throughout the years, and Margaret Murray Washington.[22] After graduation, Stewart moved to Holly Springs, Mississippi, where she taught at the State Normal School for Negroes (known today as Rust College). In 1890, she relocated to Fort Smith to teach at Howard School, the second oldest school in the city, built in 1870 and named for Union General and Freedman Bureau commissioner Oliver Otis Howard.[23] In 1892, she married African American mortician and postman William Ernest Josenberger.[24] Mame gave birth to their only child, a daughter bearing her father's name, William Ernest Josenberger (later Stevens) in 1893. Like her mother, Stevens also attended Tuskegee Institute. Unfortunately, Stevens died in May 1919 in Denver, Colorado, of peritonitis, an inflammation of the membrane lining the abdominal wall and organs.[25]

Mame Josenberger's organizational affiliations were many. In 1903, she was elected the Grand Register of Deeds of Arkansas of the Grand Court Order of Calanthe, a fraternal benefit organization founded in Texas in 1897 to provide burial insurance for African Americans.[26] The Grand Court Order of Calanthe challenged racial stereotypes by promoting positive portrayals of African Americans. For instance, in 1915 the Supreme Court of Calanthe, a division of the larger order, passed a resolution "promoting cultivation of negro ideals, reading of Negro literature, possessing of Negro pictures, the patronizing of Negro business enterprises," and "support of all interests tending to upbuild the Negro race."[27]

Josenberger took over the family mortuary business after her husband died in 1909.[28] As an African American business owner, she was also a member of the National Negro Business League (NNBL) and organization founded in 1900 by Booker T. Washington "to promote the commercial and financial development of the Negro."[29] The NNBL had affiliates in Little Rock, Pine Bluff, and Helena that had been organized by prominent African American businesspeople.[30]

Josenberger thoroughly imbibed the NNBL's message of African American financial self-determination and continued to acquire property, in addition to running the family undertaking business. She owned Josenberger Hall, an entertainment venue on 619 1/2 Ninth Street in Fort Smith, and a hardware and retail store.[31] Josenberger Hall was a welcoming spot for African American entertainers and performers until the early 1960s. In the 1940s, for instance, Christine Chatman and Her Orchestra, King Kolax and His NBC Band, and Irvin C. Miller's Brown Skin Models all performed there for Fort Smith's Black residents.[32]

In 1913, Josenberger purchased property in Little Rock's Taborian Heights area.[33] Josenberger's business acumen, which included owning a burial insurance company, served her well. She was considered "one of the most capable and efficient business propositions" and regarded as the "wealthiest as well as one of the most successful colored persons" in Fort Smith, who owned a "palatial residence" on 703 North Eleventh Street and was considered "a true factor" in making African Americans a "better race."[34] Josenberger was allegedly worth $30,000 in 1919 (approximately $398,782.54 in 2019 dollars).[35] She was also a Fort Smith Negro Business League life member. After Booker T. Washington's death in 1915, Josenberger was among the NNBL members who gathered in Kansas City, Missouri, in 1916 to memorialize their fallen leader.[36]

In addition to running her businesses, Josenberger was affiliated with the NACW and the AACW. She attended the sixth biennial NACW session in Brooklyn, New York, in 1908.[37] When the NACW met at Wilberforce University in Ohio in 1914, Josenberger was there with her longtime friend, NACW president Margaret Murray Washington, when the organization endorsed women's suffrage.[38] She was on the Peace Committee following World War I, and served as the NACW auditor in the early 1920s and its first recording secretary in the 1930s.[39] Josenberger often interacted with such nationally known Black women club leaders and activists as Ida B. Wells-Barnett, Mary Church Terrell (the NACW's first president), and Nannie Burroughs (president of the National Trade and Professional School for Women and Girls in Washington, DC.)[40] Furthermore, Josenberger participated in the 1898 founding of Fort Smith's Phillis Wheatley Federated Club, serving as its president for fifty-six years. She also held the position of AACW president from 1929 to 1931.[41]

Club women like Josenberger utilized the NACW's resources and their connections to advocate for women's and Black people's suffrage in Arkansas. Josenberger was on the African American-owned and Atlanta-based Standard Life Insurance Company and the Frederick Douglass Memorial and Historical Association's board of directors.[42] She was also a lifetime member of the NAACP, yet another organization dedicated to Black voting rights.[43]

Josenberger and other elite Black women monitored global events through such organizations as the International Council of Women of the Darker Races of the World (ICWDR).[44] Established in 1922 in Richmond, Virginia, by Margaret Murray Washington, the ICWDR's objective was the "dissemination of knowledge of people of color so that the world could better appreciate their history and accomplishment." Although it only existed until 1940, the ICWDR's members included politically astute African American women activists from around the country who dedicated themselves to international relations and world peace in the years following

World War I. In 1923, Josenberger was elected treasurer and attended an ICWDR meeting in Washington, DC, at the National Training School with such nationally known Black women leaders as Mary McLeod Bethune (also one of the ICWDR's founding members) and Mary Church Terrell.[45]

Beginning in the 1920s, Josenberger remained involved with the NACW, the AACW, the ICWDR, the NNBL, and the NAACP, in addition to managing her businesses in Fort Smith. She died in September 1964 and is buried in Oak Cemetery in Fort Smith.[46]

AACW members like Josenberger, and Black club women nationwide, promoted respectability to as a means to uplift African Americans from their disadvantaged situations. That program always included the maintenance of proper homes. In 1930, for example, the main topic of discussion at the NACW's biennial convention in Hot Springs was "better homes and better environments for children."[47] The Better Homes Movement, a national housing improvement campaign, existed between 1922 and 1935 and was led by US president Herbert Hoover, editor and journalist Marie Meloney, and Harvard University professor James Ford.[48]

Mary L. Ray, the AACW Better Homes committee state chairperson, attended the 1930 meeting as a speaker on behalf of the Better Homes Movement in Arkansas, along with Julia Conroy, the Better Homes Movement assistant director, and Mary McLeod Bethune.[49] Ray not only utilized her relationships with national Black leaders to uplift rural communities, but she also reached across the racial divide. In June 1930, she participated in the fourth annual Christian Conference for Colored Women held at Philander Smith College in Little Rock. Sponsored by the Presbyterian Church's Woman's Synodical Auxiliary of Arkansas, the interracial and interdenominational conference included white women like Erle Chambers, from the Arkansas Tuberculosis Association, and Lillian McDermott, the state's first licensed social worker.[50] Both women were also members of the all-white Arkansas chapter of the Association of Southern Women for the Prevention of Lynching, which had been established in 1930 to end lynching and mob violence.[51] Other Black women who attended the interracial conference included home demonstration agents Inola Childress and Ella Parker.[52]

Better Homes committees had been established for white women in Arkansas in 1924, and in six Pulaski County communities for African Americans in 1929. This initiative was clearly as important to Black women as it was to white women—perhaps even more so, because it encompassed all of the work in which Black women leaders were engaged to address con-

ditions in rural communities and schools and to counteract negative stereotypes of African Americans. When the Ouachita County Colored Teacher's
Association met at a segregated high school in 1930, its members, under the
leadership of Jeanes Supervisor Cleo N. McDonald, created committees for
"Better Health Week," "Better Home Week," "Better English Week," and
"Negro Week" (the last, presumably, to celebrate Black history).[53] McDonald,
the county Better Homes Chairman for the Colored, emphasized reforming rural residential spaces, as doing so would at least hold psychological
benefits for African Americans. According to McDonald, "much good has
been accomplished in the Better Homes campaign throughout the county.
The clean-up campaign covered much territory and met with great success. Many homes were repaired and beautified."[54] McDonald's 1932 report
indicated that many segments of the community converged to improve the
quality of life among rural Blacks in Ouachita County:

> Homes have been cleaned, steps repaired and built, fences built,
> yards beautified, gardens planted, old rubbish and woodpiles
> moved and many other things have been done to make the home
> a better place to live in. They were requested by the Jeanes agent
> who is the county chairman for the colored. . . . In the Elliot
> and Kirkland communities, men and women led by Rev. William
> Elliott and wife, campaigned from house to house, leveling yards
> and helping to clean up and beautify in general. In some commu-
> nities, the teachers took an active part stressing home sanitation
> and also had the school premises beautified by cleaning, planting
> flowers, leveling grounds, and white washing trees.[55]

Cleo Nunn Anderson McDonald was born in Arkansas between 1892
and 1897. A Ouachita County Jeanes Supervisor since 1923, she had formerly taught at Tuskegee. Of the experience, she said, "[It] prepared me
to do the work in this county, for to do anything successfully, you must
prepare for the task." Like many Black women, McDonald had been a home
demonstration agent and before becoming a Jeanes Supervisor. When she
first arrived in Ouachita County, she conducted a survey to assess community needs and then began establishing boys' and girls' industrial and agricultural clubs. McDonald discovered very quickly that African American
schools were either nonexistent or in very poor condition. Knowing that
local school officials did not provide enough resources to ensure equal educational opportunities for Black children, McDonald pleaded with Julius
Rosenwald and the Arkansas state education supervisor to provide money to

improve school facilities. By 1930, McDonald secured $2,300 to add a shop building to the Camden Colored High School. In total, McDonald's efforts led to $16,450 being appropriated from the Rosenwald Fund to enhance or construct Black schools in Ouachita County.[56] Always mindful of the need to ingratiate herself to the local white community to ensure their continued support, McDonald said of her achievements, "I want to thank the good white people who supported me and my good colored people who cooperated with me these seven years to make this work a success, for without your support and cooperation, my work would have been a failure.[57]

The Better Homes Movement's goals were not only to improve conditions in the home but to also encourage homemakers to purchase consumer items. In Arkansas, local Better Homes committees created "ideal room settings in demonstration homes."[58] Extension agents encouraged rural women to embrace consumer culture by purchasing household items despite the financial limitations they faced as largely impoverished agricultural laborers.[59] The "ideal room setting" was cost-prohibitive for rural dwellers, regardless of race. Yet African American club women eagerly embraced the Better Homes campaign as a part of their rural uplift development initiatives, because they were tied to national concerns about Black domestic life as a reflection of racial progress.[60] That is, some Black leaders believed that material culture within homes enhanced racial pride and self-determination, which in turn helped to counter stereotypes about Black moral degeneracy.[61] Rural Black homemakers and leaders in Saint Francis County were elated when they were recognized in 1933 with a special merit award from the New York City–based national Better Homes in America program:

> This award was made primarily for the instructive educational tours conducted by your committee and for the extensive work in home improvement and the widespread participation in contests. St. Francis County, under your direction [Lugenia B. Christmas, local home demonstration agent], has developed a significant community campaign for home improvement and one well adapted to meet the needs of the present economic situation. I wish, therefore, to extend to you personally and to all of the members of your Committee and co-operating organizations, our sincere appreciation of all that has been done.[62]

Because of the dire needs in rural Black communities, the Better Homes Movement lasted among African American women beyond 1935. In 1939, home demonstration agent Cassa Lawlah noted that 10,084 farm families had participated in community clean-up campaigns during "Better Homes Week," which included building or repairing 1,437 toilets in the Watson, Bayou Mason, Halley, and Kelso communities.[63] African American Better Homes clubs also continued to receive national recognition for their work. In 1944, the state Black Better Homes committee was awarded a special merit award from the national Better Homes in America office.[64]

While AACW members strove to create better homes in Black communities, they consistently advocated for African American women and girls. Throughout the nation, women's clubs created a space for Black women's community activism. Because they were often excluded from leadership positions or marginalized in Black male-led organizations or denied membership in predominantly white female organizations, Black women's clubs allowed them to act freely and independently of racial and gender limitations.[65] The AACW's labors reflected the national body's creed. Mame Josenberger said of the state organization, "Arkansas never desires to lag, but to do her best to maintain her own organization, meet all the demands of the National Association of Colored Women, and ever 'Lift As We Climb.'"[66]

Of necessity, Black club women engaged in "race" work to address social, educational, and health issues in African American communities.[67] Chief among the AACW's concerns in the 1930s was the prevalence of tuberculosis among African Americans, youth education, and the creation of an "industrial school for race girls." Josenberger stated, "Our real objective is the erection of a Girl's Industrial Home where our wayward girls may have a chance to recover themselves and perhaps become good and useful citizens."[68]

The AACW was the voice of African American women statewide, yet the organization struggled mightily throughout the years to obtain facilities for delinquent Black girls and boys. In 1910, just five years after its establishment, the AACW wielded their limited political influence when they met with Arkansas governor George Donaghey to urge him to ask the state legislature for an appropriation. He supported the request but urged them to obtain four to five hundred acres "as a site suited to agricultural purposes" as a condition of them "doing something for themselves" and claimed that he would then ask the legislature for an appropriation to construct buildings. This was apparently the same deal offered to white Arkansans when they established an institution for white boys and girls. Donaghey refused to make any recommendations unless "the tract of land or its equivalent in money is provided by the negroes themselves, just as was done when the state established the school for white boys and girls." This task proved extremely difficult, because so few African Americans possessed the resources necessary to purchase land or property or any sort. Informed by racist stereotypes about Black criminality and dependence, Donaghey also believed the school was necessary because African Americans convicted of crimes were sent to the penitentiary regardless of their age. But it seems he was less concerned about the well-being of Black youth than about the cost to the state when he said, "This is not right for the Negro, nor is it best for the state. Such a condition means a bigger bill for the state to pay in the long run." He also believed a reform school for African Americans would "make the Negro more efficient and develop him into a productive citizen instead of a renegade, making him an asset instead of a liability to the state."[69] Black club women remained steadfast and in 1915 also reached out to then governor George Hays, who endorsed the organization's efforts, which were led in part by Little Rock's Annie T. Strickland, the AACW's superintendent of reform school work.[70]

Two years later, AACW club members Annie T. Strickland, Mary H. Speight, Lillian Murphy, and Jennie A. Johnson called on Arkansas's new governor, Charles Brough, and urged him to recommend that the state legislature appropriate funds to build an industrial school for Black boys. The AACW had purchased sixty acres of land in Jefferson County to use for the school, significantly less than the amount recommended by Governor Donaghey in 1910. Governor Brough promised Black club women that the state legislature would "consider the matter."[71] By 1918, the AACW had built a cottage on the land. They repeatedly offered it to the state as proof of their determination, in the hope of obtaining financial support; but their efforts were to no avail.[72] By 1923, at least, the Arkansas Negro Boys Industrial School was built just outside of Pine Bluff in Jefferson County.[73]

Unfortunately, an industrial school for African American girls did not materialize until much later. As early as 1915, white women had established a committee to build an industrial school for white girls. Erle Chambers, the Arkansas Tuberculosis Association executive secretary, served on this committee.[74] Many southern whites believed delinquent white girls needed to be reformed for their own good, to curb their "sexual self-determination" and, more importantly, to maintain the "South's foundational association between chastity and whiteness."[75] They held no such expectations for delinquent Black girls, who were considered sexually mature beyond their years and unworthy of reform. Yet AACW members had long confronted complex sexual politics, including stereotypes about Black women's sexuality, and the problem of juvenile delinquency among Black girls. For them, Black women were absolutely worth saving, and they consistently urged Arkansas state senators to vote for appropriations to build the school. When their efforts failed, they relied on club resources and the African American community. At their annual meeting in 1939, after a keynote address by African American Pine Bluff attorney W. Harold Flowers, AACW members voted to raise funds to care for a thirteen-year-old girl who had been sentenced to ten years in prison. The AACW procured the funds for the girl to be sent instead to the Fargo Agricultural School in Monroe County. County home demonstration agent Mildred C. Smith, likely an AACW member herself, lauded the school as a nurturing space for African American children:

> The Fargo Agricultural School is to Monroe County as the rural girls and boys as an oasis is to a traveler in the desert. . . . The rural youths that are not able to attend other schools have the opportunity of learning, not only the literary subjects of a first rate high school, but industrial work for girls, as cooking, sewing, canning, art work, mattress making; and for boys, as farming and shop work.[76]

Smith further believed that Floyd Brown, the school's founder, was "doing a much needed work of moulding the rural youth into a better citizenship, and more efficient service to humanity."[77]

The AACW's decision to support the young woman at Fargo was also assisted by Lillian Epps Brown, an AACW trustee and the wife of Fargo's founder. African Americans continued to petition Arkansas governors for appropriations to build an industrial school for Black girls. As late as 1943, Governor Homer Adkins recommended to the state legislature that monies be procured for this important cause.[78] It was not until 1949 that the Arkansas state legislature finally decided to appropriate $25,000 to convert the institution into the Fargo Negro Girls Training School.[79] It further provided $75,000 for its operation over the next two years.[80] Governor Sid McMath only appointed one African American, educator Anna M. P. Strong, to the school's board of control.[81] The Fargo Training School for Negro Girls closed in 1968, when it was integrated with the white school in Alexander, Arkansas.[82] For the time that it existed, the school was the long-sought realization of the AACW's dream to provide a safe environment for Arkansas's indigent young Black women.

World War II

WHILE THE AACW was consumed by their efforts to establish a home for wayward young Black women, home demonstration agents and Jeanes Supervisors utilized the democratic sentiment of the World War II years to help Black farming families meet the USDA's food production goals. When the fourteenth annual Negro Farmers Conference met at Fargo Agricultural School in February 1941, before the United States officially entered World War II, participants discussed the practical applications of the conference's theme, "More food and less credit, more work and less talk." Black women leaders commandeered space to make their voices heard and their activism visible in arenas typically dominated by men. During the meeting, which included presentations by H. C. Ray and Cassa Lawlah, farmers and their families witnessed the requisite farm and home demonstrations.

The conference discussion topics belied a not-so-hidden agenda designed not only to uplift rural Black residents but to also enlist them as agents of change on their farms and within their communities. While they considered such issues as "problems confronting us on the farm and how to solve them," others, such as "what women can do to help solve some of our farm problems," reflected an understanding of Black women's important roles in rural communities. Topics like "community pride," "how gossip hurts the neighbors in the community," and "learn to cooperate for the sake of the cause regardless of our personal differences" held that rural Blacks were collectively responsible for their community's growth.[1] And such themes as "grow more food and do less credit as possible [sic]," and "money that is borrowed to finance, let us not use if for other purposes" spoke to Black extension agents' mission to teach rural African Americans financial responsibility.[2]

Unfortunately, Blacks still suffered disproportionately from the economic privation of the depression years. In light of this, Black home demonstration agents focused on teaching farm women to augment the quality of their homes, families, and communities by doing more with less. As mentioned in the previous chapter, the Better Homes Movement remained important in rural Black communities long after it ended nationally. In 1940, local home demonstration agents in Pine Bluff sponsored a "Cotton Dress Revue" as part of a weeklong community-wide campaign that included a showcase of home improvement activities.[3] Home demonstration agents worked with club women to uplift those living in poor, rural communities. Pine Bluff resident Beatrice Kahn, the AACW president, and chairperson of its rural women committee and the city Better Homes campaign, endorsed their efforts.[4] Such activities were further undertaken by home demonstration and 4-H clubs in Desha County, where African American women conducted home tours in McGehee, Watson, Bayou Mason, Halley, and Kelso.[5]

During the war years, Black women leaders were primarily concerned with endeavors to enhance African Americans' access to employment opportunities and to create learning and recreational spaces for young people in the Arkansas Delta. Savannah Parr, the wife of a local mortician in in Poinsett County, founded the Boys and Girls Canning Club in Marked Tree and later led a community initiative to purchase seven acres of land, where she established a school with a fully equipped canning kitchen in 1939.[6]

African Americans increasingly sought spaces for young people's educational and recreational needs for a number of reasons: once the United States entered World War II, many parents were employed and thus away from home and unable to supervise their children, and, crucially, Black children were not permitted to utilize predominantly white facilities. The Blytheville Social Arts Club, organized in 1944 and affiliated with the AACW, along with members of the Royal Brotherhood club, purchased a building to provide a day-care and recreational center for young Black people. The center hosted segregated Boy Scout meetings and also charged working mothers a minimal fee to care for their children.[7] The Royal Brotherhood had been founded in 1935 by Black men employed by the Blytheville Compress Company, which stored and baled cotton.[8] The Brotherhood, like Little Rock's Mosaic Templars, had been organized to aid members and their families in times of crisis.[9] In 1945, the group sold $1 tickets for a chance to win a bale of cotton, the proceeds of which went to support the day-care center.[10] After World War II, the Royal Brotherhood and the Blytheville Social Arts Club cohosted an open house that included discussions on such topics as "Echoes from the Child's Welfare Dept." and "Echoes from the Negro Youth," once again reaffirming their commitment to providing opportunities for African American children whom they feared might otherwise engage in criminal activity.[11]

Mississippi County educator Alena Erby Wiley was one of the Blytheville Social Art Club's most active charter members. Wiley was born in Jackson, Arkansas, in 1909 or 1910 and educated in Carthage, Magnolia, Pine Bluff, and Fort Smith, Arkansas, where she had been persuaded by Mame Stewart Josenberger to become involved in the AACW's junior affiliate.[12] Wiley attended Arkansas AM&N College in 1931. A popular student, she was named the school's first college queen. Also an author, Wiley was noted in the college's yearbook for publishing, "Points on Barbering."[13] She left Arkansas AM&N and in 1934 graduated from Spelman College, in Atlanta, Georgia.[14] Wiley met and married Robert Wiley, a fellow educator, in 1937.[15] Wiley became a Jeanes Supervisor in 1942 and was treasurer of the Mississippi County Negro Teachers Association and assistant director of the Black school system in Blytheville.[16]

Wiley was an AACW member and, like most Jeanes Supervisors and Black home demonstration agents, possessed multi-organizational connections that allowed her to cooperatively utilize the extension service's resources to provide community clothing, canning, and handicraft demonstrations.[17] Members of AACW affiliates like the Semper Fidelis Club and the Friendly Twelve Club in Saint Francis County, guided by extension service agents, crocheted bedspreads and knitted woolen garments to help the less fortunate in their community. The Friendly Twelve Club additionally constructed a building that home demonstration agents and clubs used for their meetings and presentations.[18] The AACW and home demonstration agents and clubs and other Black organizations used such facilities to address rural Blacks' food security and preservation concerns during the war. In 1944, the Unity, Benevolent Industrial Club (UBI) in Madison, Arkansas, reached out to home demonstration agents and requested information on nutrition and food preservation demonstrations. UBI's president, Mrs. C. E. Allen, found the discussion on the seven basic food groups particularly important because it complemented the work in which its members were already engaged:

> The President and leaders in our club are putting forth a special effort to get this information to our people in this community and stress the necessity, as you did to us, of eating the right kinds of food in order to have healthy bodies. Each member has pledged herself to see to it that at least 5 people not belonging to our club

use your one-dish-dinner plan on the 2nd Sunday in May. . . .
If this plan works, 240 families will be reached.[19] ·

But food preservation was only one among several ways Black women
sought to increase living standards in rural communities. Reforming home
life remained a part of Jeanes Supervisors and home demonstration agents'
race work, because it allowed them to directly tackle the problems that
impacted Black families through demonstration clubs. In Lee County, for
instance, rural homemakers were encouraged to improve and sanitize their
homes by making bed mattresses stuffed with cotton as part of a USDA
program that had begun in 1932. Because store-bought mattresses were so
expensive, averaging about $15, many poor Blacks—and whites, for that
matter—often slept on bundles of rags or "ticks" (bags of made of cloth)
stuffed with straw, chicken feathers, or pine needles.[20] At a mere $4 per per-
son to create home demonstration agents saw mattress-making workshops
as a way to upgrade and modernize rural homes at minimal expense.[21] For
some African Americans, their first opportunity to sleep on a cotton mattress
was memorable. Forrest City resident Delores Twillie Woods recalled from
her childhood that "mama and them made those mattresses. And I know
that we had several mattresses, straw mattresses before then."[22] Mattresses
were more than items for the improved comforts of home. Indeed, new
mattresses may have served as a means to prevent diseases. At a time when
many rural people, particularly African Americans, died of contagious diseases such as tuberculosis, mattresses were promoted as a means to not only
create "better homes," but also to help families prevent an array of health
problems and to popularize home sanitation techniques.[23]

In keeping with the patriotic theme of the war years, club women also
constructed "Victory Garments" from flour sacks, in addition to their usual
home improvement efforts, which included demonstrating pride in resi-
dences and their country by embellishing their home furnishings, planting
shrubbery, and removing hedges.[24] Such tasks were particularly emphasized
in demonstration club meetings. Some agents, like Mary Stubblefield in
Woodruff County, reported that home furnishings often were of inferior
quality. Her goal for 1944 was to ensure that women made more "home-
made rugs, slip covers, and better color selection." Stubblefield's desires
did not fall upon deaf ears, and again, Black women leaders played a crucial role in getting their neighbors to embrace home demonstration agents'
programs. For example, A. C. Hollis was aided by other New Salem Home
Demonstration Club members in reupholstering her living room furniture

slip covers. There was further a patriotic imperative involved: Hollis's home-made slipcovers assisted the wartime conservation effort by allowing her to save money she would have otherwise spent on a new living room suite.[25] One agent noted that the money women saved was used to purchase war bonds.[26]

Black women certainly had fewer resources to adorn their homes and yards than their white counterparts, but they were no less receptive to the home and community development information they received from extension service agents. African Americans felt that internal and external home improvements were the most obvious ways they could demonstrate rural Black progress in the Jim Crow South. Well-stocked and -furnished homes represented home demonstration agents' and clubs' positive impact in rural communities. Cotton Plant resident Alberta Cade, a Shady Grove Home Demonstration Club member, replaced her old fence, planted flowers, and removed the hedges to beautify her yard.[27] And because sanitation was always an issue, particularly due to concerns about hookworms, Cade, like many rural dwellers, built outdoor toilets.[28]

These initiatives also extended to Black community institutions. In 1944, African Americans in the Nelson community (Saint Francis County) raised money to refurbish the local one-room school. Not only was the school where local Black children were educated, it was also where women held their home demonstration club meetings. Advised and assisted by movable-school and home demonstration agents, by September 1944 community members had reframed windows, added a small kitchen (quite likely to provide hot lunches for their children), and donated dishes, among other improvements. In Palestine, Arkansas, African Americans fenced in and planted grass, trees, and shrubs at the Weaver School to enhance its appearance.[29]

PTA members further worked with home demonstration agents and clubs to counteract food insecurity among school-age children. Twenty of the twenty-five rural schools in Saint Francis County provided children with hot lunches. In Caldwell, educator and home demonstration club president Eula Gilliam ensured that children consumed nutritious meals. In Forrest City, the local home demonstration agent teamed up with the PTA to gather resources to feed children at the all-Black Lincoln High School.[30]

At times, such work occurred in collaboration with white PTAs. In October 1943, Gilliam and Nelson teacher Laura Jones attended a home demonstration club call meeting at Lincoln High School, where they reportedly served children 150 hot lunches. Mrs. Earnest Bordon, the Saint

Francis County Hot Lunches Project chairperson and the white high school PTA president, also attended this meeting and voiced her support for the women's efforts on Black school children's behalf.[31]

African American PTA members were further concerned about ensuring that their children were properly inoculated. Supported by the Arkansas Congress of Colored Parents and Teachers (ACCPT), the PTA sponsored a "Summer Round-Up" to ensure that Black children began the schoolyear protected against diphtheria and smallpox.[32]

Rural Black women understood that they had to do the best they could with limited resources during World War II. This also pertained to clothing for themselves and their families. Learning to "make do" informed their participation in the war conservation effort. Clothes made out of leftover materials like flour sacks allowed rural women to inexpensively clothe their families and again, demonstrated their significant contributions to farm and household economies. Delores Twillie Woods remembered home demonstration agents teaching local women how to sew and make clothes using fifty-pound flour sacks. The women tried to make clothing out of similarly colored sacks. When they could not do so, they cultivated their own sense of fashion in their rural couture. According to Woods, "The country girl would be wearing them two-toned dresses we call them now, they wearing that stuff, but the people then knew how to make 'em just like they making them now."[33]

Woods's recollection demonstrates that rural women were not simply the passive recipients of home demonstration agents' teachings. Home demonstration agents may have wanted Black women to improve the quality of their clothing while refraining from creating items that historian Blain Roberts argued were seen as "loud, ostentatious, and unsophisticated" and which thereby "betrayed the race" by undermining improvement efforts among African Americans.[34] Instead, when the situation warranted, rural women depended upon their own skills to make the best use of limited, or in this case mismatched, resources in ways that suited their conception of a rural aesthetic. In doing so, they pushed back against home demonstration agents' conservative proscriptions.

Despite, or perhaps because of, their own ingenuity under difficult circumstances, Black women often acted in ways that demonstrated their respect for home demonstration agents and the skills they imparted. Yet rural Black women also revealed their confidence in their own abilities when they selectively incorporated the aspects of agents' instruction that best suited them. In Conway County, women from Oliver, New Hope, Morrilton,

Union Chapel, Keenwood, Spring Valley, Menifee, Plummerville, and Center enthusiastically exhibited their homemade products and participated in community contests, even though their agent only served their communities on a part-time basis.[35] Even infrequent visits from home demonstration agents were impactful in rural areas with scarce resources. In these feminized spaces, Black women were also able to better feed their families and develop their business acumen as a result of what they learned from extension agents and from fellow home demonstration club members.

In 1944, the aforementioned Alberta Cade took three hundred eggs to an electric hatchery from which she received 294 baby chicks. After placing the baby chicks in a brooder, she was able to feed her family from her supply, sell over one hundred fryers, and save enough pullets for laying hens for the next year. August home demonstration club member Katie Brunson also raised chickens and asserted that "poultry production . . . increased her income through the assistance of the Negro Agent and the Movable School Agent." Brunson was able to cull all of her chickens for market and save the best layers for future use.[36] She also maintained a garden in which she grew green and butter beans, squash, radish, corn, and greens that allowed her to feed her family year-round.[37]

Rural women often augmented their family income and kept the family solvent by selling goods at curb markets. In the Telico Community in Saint Francis County, Black women sold three hundred fryers for $0.75 each, fifty bushels of apples for $1.50 each, and twenty bushels of peaches for $3.00 each. Surplus garden produce had greater import beyond providing supplementary income, however. It allowed women to share the wealth with their community. In Forrest City, Mrs. Arthur Jacks gave Mrs. Frenchie Woods from the Nelson community beans in exchange for beets so that the latter woman would not fall behind in her canning.[38] Environmental historian Dianne Glave has noted that African American women's gardening habits and practices revealed their interpretations of agricultural extension service lessons "within a gendered and racial milieu" that lent itself to a "complex social potency." This sense of empowerment allowed African American women gardeners to dictate and control "how and where they gardened, and by implication, why they gardened."[39] The tenacity Black women exhibited in their farming and gardening practices further illustrates their determination to assert their independence as producers and business-minded women who were responsible for supporting their families and communities.

Agrarian women understood their critical roles and indeed their patriotic duty as farmers to shore up the nation's food security during the war.

At the Negro Farmers Conference in 1945, Cotton Plant resident Mrs. George Wilson proclaimed that she was a farmer and proud of it; she further asserted, "The Government is looking to farmers to lead the nation. If production stops, the world will go down." Mrs. Paul Kelly from Clarendon, Arkansas, discussed, "How I Help My Husband Solve Our Farm Problems," by growing a garden year-round and maintaining accurate records for the farm, thereby highlighting the importance of women and men's cooperative efforts in the overall function of farm life.[40]

Home demonstration agents also reinforced the extension services' lessons about food preservation to farm women. Underscoring the AACES's message "Food Is Strength—Make Arkansas Strong!," Pulaski County agent Mary P. Gaines wrote to the president and leaders of the Hill Lake Home Demonstration Club that she had met with farm families at night because they were working in the fields during that day. Although their club was new, Gaines expected its leaders to "call all of the families together as soon as possible to check on the progress they are making in the fall gardens."[41]

Messages about the importance of food preservation compelled Black home demonstration and extension agents, ministers, educators, and farmers to meet in Little Rock, Forrest City, and El Dorado during the war to discuss how the AAA's features could be used to implement the USDA's "Food for Freedom" program.[42] The program's plenary sessions stressed galvanizing rural Black communities' support for the war effort by increasing food production and preservation. Because they worked closely with farm women, home demonstration agents' input into federal food-security programs was especially important. Agents Lugenia B. Christmas and Marguerite P. Williams spoke at the Forrest City and El Dorado meetings.[43] Black female representation from the AAA was also critical. Field staff director Jennie B. Moton spoke to African Americans who attended the Little Rock meeting about the "Negro Farm Home."[44]

Agent Fannie Boone implicitly underscored the patriotic rhetoric of the gathering in Little Rock with a talk titled "Cooking for Freedom." She highlighted the more practical imperative of encouraging rural Blacks to cook nutritional meals and to preserve food because of the shortage of rationed goods during the war years. Additionally, movable-school agent Ella P. Neely demonstrated the latest cooking innovations for conference attendees.[45]

Wartime programs linked proper nutrition to patriotism.[46] The Union County Committee for Better Nutrition among Negroes, for instance, cosponsored a series of cooking schools with home demonstration clubs,

African American educators, the Black PTA, and Black women's federated clubs.[47] Improved food security encouraged increased patriotism in rural Black communities. African Americans in Union County pledged to support the "Food for Victory" campaign at the county courthouse and met with the county defense council executive vice chair, who talked about the importance of national civilian defense and the "patriotic spirit of American negro citizens" during the war years.[48]

The USDA even touted food security as a priority and a patriotic duty in Black newspapers. An *Arkansas State Press* article titled "Only Saboteurs Neglect Their Victory Gardens" stressed "food for freedom" goals and urged rural gardeners to "use every precaution to insure an adequate supply of vegetables for home use, because it helps the war effort."[49] Food security concerns also extended to showcasing African Americans' meat curing and canning skills as a way to publicly demonstrate African Americans' dedication to the war effort. Mississippi County farm agent William Barabin and home demonstration agent Mary M. Banks sponsored the seventh annual canned and cured meat exhibition in Osceola in cooperation with the segregated agricultural planning committee and the county farm bureau. Women exhibited and competed to win awards for ham, sausage, spare ribs, roast beef, beef stew, stewed chicken, roast chicken, and market-quality eggs. Men displayed hams, shoulders, middlings, bacon, and sausage. The event was covered by KLCN, the local radio station.[50]

At the conference for "Negro Farm and Home Demonstration Agents" held at the Pulaski County courthouse in January 1943, African American extension agents emphasized increased food production and home and farm practices, but also money-saving habits like "wise spending and thrift buying." And they encouraged rural Blacks to purchase war bonds and stamps. Fannie Mae Boone and H. C. Ray co-chaired the meeting and helped rural African Americans learn the benefits of extension service programs.[51]

Unfortunately, raising food for the war effort proved difficult if not impossible for many Black farm laborers. In 1943, J. E. Clayton, a STFU general executive council member, wrote the NAACP's Walter White to express his dismay that "sharecroppers are not allowed to raise any food for themselves much less raise any to help win the war."[52] Black extension agents were certainly aware of this issue, but their more immediate concern was the improved race relations and expanded civil rights for African Americans that they believed would surely emanate from the democratic rhetoric of the war years and African Americans' patriotism.

Home demonstration club meetings also lent themselves to rural Black

women's increased attention to political education and efficacy . They identified as Americans despite the impoverished state in which many of them
lived and the racism to which they were subjected daily. In a 1943–44 report,
Monroe County home demonstration agent Mildred Smith Davis recorded
that club members received "citizenship training" by singing patriotic songs
at meetings and by displaying the American flag on Flag Day. To support
the war effort, each home demonstration club appointed a "Victory Leader"
who was responsible for encouraging members to save paper, scrap rubber,
and iron, and to assist with Red Cross drives. Holly Grove and Clarendon
home demonstration club members enrolled in Red Cross first aid and
home nursing courses and attended civilian defense meetings.[53]

Local Black leaders also joined the Minutemen, a program designed to
help rural dwellers increase their food production and preservation by creating "Victory Gardens," sell war bonds, and collect scrap metal during the
war years. In Union County, the Minutemen were comprised of women and
men from fifty-two neighborhoods who met with extension service agents
who explained the "Food for Victory" program and shared other extension
service information. Black women appeared most frequently as leaders in
this program. They supervised community canning centers sponsored by
the federal government.[54] Minutemen's duties further included collecting
grease, conducting nutrition schools, repairing farm equipment, preventing
fires, and explaining how government rationing and price control programs
operated.[55]

But food security remained the most consistent and prevalent issue
for rural Black women and home demonstration agents during the war. In
Poinsett County, home demonstration agent Lena H. Eddington helped
Black families implement dietary plans and instructed them in food production and preservation techniques. She, like Fannie Mae Boone, also linked
good nutrition and health to national wartime goals when she asserted that
"health on the home front" would lead to "victory on the war front."[56]

Eddington, a graduate of Arkansas AM&N College and the University
of Minnesota, began her career as home demonstration agent in 1941. Like
many of her fellow African American leaders, she encouraged Black people
to remain on the land. Eddington supported the Live-At-Home program,
established in Arkansas in 1931. Funded by politicians, the extension service,
and state and local government agencies, the program emphasized the value
and benefits of agrarian life.[57] Indeed, one of the home demonstration clubs'
objectives throughout Arkansas and across racial lines was to instill in the
agrarian "individual responsibilities toward himself and his surroundings

in the Live-At-Home program."[58] Through the Live-At-Home program, agents promoted crop diversification and self-sufficiency among farming families in poverty stricken rural areas.[59] For Black Arkansans, it served additional purposes. Not only were they able to improve their standard of living by becoming self-supporting, but home demonstration agents also used the program to dissuade African American migration to the North and empowered them to secure concessions from local whites.[60] This was of great importance in areas like Saint Francis County, where the outmigration of Black families to cities created labor shortages in rural areas. The reasons for leaving Arkansas and the South were indeed compelling. Extreme rural underdevelopment left African Americans few options. In the face of racial segregation, economic privation, discriminatory agricultural programs, and poor access to health care and educational opportunities, many felt they had little choice but to employ the only strategy they had left to resist their marginalization.[61]

Between 1940 and 1960, 850,000 African Americans left Arkansas—many for employment in Midwestern cities such as Chicago, Detroit, and St. Louis—resulting in a 44 percent drop in the state's population.[62] The northward migration was considered a wartime emergency, and so public meetings and gatherings were held in cooperation with Black extension service agents to convince African Americans not to leave farms. At the annual Black farmers' visiting day at the University of Arkansas College of Agriculture's Fruit and Truck Branch Experiment Station in June 1941, Cassa Lawlah and Union County agent Marguerite P. Williams demonstrated the importance of establishing healthy food habits in rural areas to African Americans after they had toured the station's farm. Afterward, College of Agriculture dean Dr. Walter R. Horlacher underscored the importance of African Americans' patriotic duty to remain on the farm by urging them to participate in the Live-At-Home, AAA, and soil conservation programs to fulfill their "part and responsibility in national defense."[63] Live-At-Home supporters also included Jeanes Supervisors. During the same year, Nevada County Jeanes Supervisor Ila Upchurch accompanied a couple from the Upchurch Community to Memphis, Tennessee, to represent the county in a weeklong Live-At-Home program.[64]

Black women did not passively accept the rhetoric of the Live-At-Home program, however. They assessed program instruction to understand the ways they could benefit from the program and further their interest in home and community improvement to complement their own goals. Using local programs to augment one's economic opportunities and achieve "better living" was the most effective way for Blacks to challenge and protest conditions in rural environments. The Live-At-Home program clearly helped farmer's wife Alwilda B. Jackson in Lexa, Arkansas, survive the Depression and develop her business and budgeting skills when she turned to raising and selling chickens at a curb market to supplement her family's income.[65] Live-At-Home activities were facilitated by the Memphis *Commercial Appeal* and its chamber of commerce agricultural committee, which began sponsoring a Live-At-Home competition in Tennessee, Arkansas, and Mississippi in 1937. In 1941 and 1944, two farm families from Crittenden County won the prize, which included a $250 award. County home demonstration agents Corrie J. Jarrett and Clara M. Howard were awarded trophies for selecting the winners. This was quite likely done as an incentive to continue encouraging rural Blacks to remain in the tristate area.[66]

African American agents were also rewarded for procuring farm families to participate in the program, which continued to hold sway among rural Black Arkansans even after the war's end.[67] In 1947, C. H. and Georgia Highley, owners of a four-hundred-acre farm near Wycamp in Phillips County, and tenant farmers Elmo and Doll Walton, who rented 246 acres on "Mrs. Mary Martin's farm" three miles west of Ratio (also in Phillips County), won the Arkansas Live-At-Home contest. Agent Gertrude LeMay had provided them with valuable extension services to improve their farms and homes. The couples received their awards at a Live-At-Home celebration at Arkansas Baptist College.[68]

Living at home also meant addressing Black agrarians' poor health. Movable-school agent Ella P. Neely traveled throughout Arkansas to Rosenwald schools and local Black churches, teaching farm women how to make a "one dish meal from the basic seven food groups," salad, and "tooth powder."[69] Neely, an Ogden native, was the Little River County home demonstration agent from 1925 to 1935 and was later appointed the "Negro district agent." She had attended East Texas Academy, in Tyler, and Tuskegee Institute and had taught public school for five years before joining the extension service.[70]

Concerns about African Americans' health also meant addressing the spread of venereal disease in rural Black communities. Back in 1939, Anna M. P. Strong, Fred McCuiston, and R. C. Childress created a health education course supported by such African American organizations as ACCPT and ACTA that specifically addressed this issue. Black leaders recognized that venereal disease was among a range of illnesses that disproportionately impacted impoverished African American communities.[71]

Black leaders like Anna Strong joined forces with women from around the country to discuss the pervasiveness of venereal disease during the war years. In 1944, Strong represented the National Congress of Colored Parents and Teachers on the National Women's Advisory Committee on Social Protection (NWACSP) executive committee. The NWACSP was founded after the Social Protection Division (SPD) of the Federal Security Agency held a conference in 1943 to discuss the "woman's role in social protection."[72] The SPD believed that "respectable" women and their organizations were the best conduit through which to marshal public opinion to suppress prostitution and control venereal disease.[73] These issues were particularly concerning for Strong and other Black women activists in Arkansas who feared that poor, rural, and uneducated women and girls might be lured into sex trafficking to earn an income.

The NWACSP consisted of thirty-three women's organizations.[74] In 1943, in conjunction with the Office of Community War Service and the Federal Security Agency, the NWACSP published *Meet Your Enemy, Venereal Disease*, a booklet that discussed ways to combat venereal disease and was distributed throughout communities nationwide. Strong helped draft the resolution to support a social protection program, curb prostitution, and prevent "sexual promiscuity" during the war years.[75]

National social protection initiatives clearly impacted local activism in Arkansas both during and after World War II. When the Black PTA in Arkansas held its annual meeting at Little Rock's Dunbar High School in 1943, its state president, Ila Upchurch, had SPD representatives Alice Clemmet and Melba Feltz address the conference theme, "For These We Fight: Child, Church, Home, School, Community."[76] By 1949, Mississippi County Blacks could go to Blytheville's Richard B. Harrison High School year-round to be immunized and to take the Wasserman blood test to detect syphilis.[77]

As World War II ended, Black women leaders turned their attention to planning for the future. Like other Americans around the country, they were concerned about the direction the nation would take as it demobilized. Like white landowners, they were also concerned about the record numbers of African Americans who had left the South during the war, never to return. Some good did come out of this exodus: Black extension service agents were often able to leverage this shortage of labor not only to improve programming for rural Blacks, whom white landowners desperately wanted to remain in the South, but also, increasingly, to achieve greater closer parity of salaries between themselves and white agents.[78]

In the postwar years, as before, African American home demonstration agents most often found themselves performing dual roles in rural Black communities. They had to tread lightly, as the longevity of their programs was largely dependent upon cooperation with white landowners and officials. Agents taught farm women home management techniques. But many of them also advocated Booker T. Washington's rural uplift philosophy. Home improvement, which was to include better health access for African Americans, was tantamount to racial uplift, and Black women promoted their work as such.[79] But home demonstration agents were mindful of the changing racial environment in which they worked, as the next decade presented new challenges that increasingly complicated their labors in agrarian spaces.[80]

Rural spaces and the people who dwelled therein were not without champions. The tumultuous postwar years were a primary opportunity for agrarian Blacks, most often led by women, to utilize their connections through such organizations as the Arkansas Farm Bureau Federation's Negro Division to challenge the forces that marginalized rural African American communities and overlooked their substantial contributions to the state's agricultural production.

— 8 —

The Arkansas Farm Bureau Federation Negro Division and the Spirit of Cotton Pageant

BORN IN 1909 in Plainview (Yell County), Leoda Berry-Gammon earned a home economics degree from Arkansas AM&N College and later a master's degree in special education from the University of Central Arkansas. She began working for the AACES after graduating from college and served as the Jefferson County home demonstration agent from the 1930s until she resigned in 1941.[1] In 1938, Black home demonstration clubs under Berry-Gammon's direction won an honorable mention in a national Better Homes campaign and, with 332 Black farm homes, led the state in entries to the Live-At-Home contest sponsored by the Memphis-based *Commercial Appeal*.[2]

Like other home demonstration agents and Jeanes Supervisors, Berry-Gammon was dedicated to achieving equitable educational access for African Americans. When the ACCPT held its fourteenth annual convention at Little Rock's Dunbar High School in 1942, she met Black women like Anna M. P. Strong, the National Congress of Colored Parents and Teachers president, and Jeanes Supervisor Ila Upchurch. It was also at this meeting that Berry-Gammon was elected recording secretary of the ACCPT.[3]

Even after her time as a home demonstration agent, Berry-Gammon remained active in club activities. She was elected the fifth president of the Crittenden County Home Demonstration Council, organized in 1943, to serve for the 1954–55 term.[4] Later in her career, Berry-Gammon was a Memphis Dairy Council nutritionist and an educator in Memphis (Tennessee) and Flint (Michigan) and an NAACP and Democratic Party member. Berry-Gammon was also the wife of prominent Crittenden County planter and Arkansas Farm Bureau Federation Negro Division president

John Henry Gammon Jr. She died in 2003.[5] This chapter focuses on her and other rural Black women's activism through this organization as they carved out spaces to assert their identities as wives, mothers, and farmers.[6]

The American Farm Bureau Federation (AFBF) has received relatively little scholarly attention as an organization, and its segregated Black chapters even less so. Throughout rural America, county farm bureaus were established to support local agricultural communities and extension service agents. At least as early as 1918, state and local leaders contemplated consolidating county farm bureaus to create a national organization. In 1920, the AFBF was formed, thereby solidifying an alliance between county agents and farm people and ensuring a collaboration that lobbied on both groups' behalf. In time, it was clear that this alliance posed a conflict of interests, because extension service agents were supported by tax dollars and the AFBF was a separate and private economic entity. In 1921, this issue was resolved with a memorandum of understanding establishing extension agents as public employees who "worked with and for all farmers," although their efforts could be supported by farm bureau funds and other resources. Despite this seemingly innocuous separation however, farm bureaus and extension service agents were inextricably linked, as both were concerned about shrinking rural populations and the impact of agricultural mechanization.[7]

The Arkansas Farm Bureau, a similar consortium of county farm bureaus, was founded in 1935. By the early 1950s, it had become the Arkansas Farm Bureau Federation (ARFBF). State farm bureaus did not necessarily represent all farmers equally. African American farmers were most often underrepresented because state federations had the autonomy to set their own rules about admitting Black members. Alabama allowed Black members, for instance, but Louisiana did not. And in cases where African Americans were admitted, local circumstances dictated whether or not they had access to all the responsibilities and privileges of membership.[8] Soon after 1935, however, the ARFBF developed plans establish a "negro division," although Black county farm bureaus largely operated independently of one another and often focused on increasing their own memberships. When the "colored unit of the Mississippi County Farm Bureau" met in Osceola in 1936, for instance, it launched a membership drive to increase its ranks to two hundred members by 1938.[9] A segregated ARFBF affiliate known as the "negro division" was not established until 1948 at Arkansas AM&N College. The organization, originally named the Arkansas Negro Farmers Association, was led by Crittenden County farmer-planter John Henry Gammon Jr.[10]

While it appears that men were the Negro Division's most visible members a close reading of the sources reveals Black women's involvement as well. In 1955, Black women like Crittenden County home demonstration agent Levada Parker Mason attended the Negro Division's annual meeting.[11] In 1958, agents Marguerite P. Williams and Jennie B. Wright were on the "Women's Committee" and addressed the convention with a talk titled "A Woman's Voice Is Heard," and asserted their importance in the ARFBF Negro Division's work. Additionally, home demonstration agents such as Saint Francis County's Carreather Banks, Phillips County's Gertrude LeMay, and Cross County's Sylvania May were members of the division's segregated fair committee.[12]

Because of their deep connections to rural communities and their numerous and often overlapping organizational memberships, Black women were particularly important to the ARFBF's Negro Division when it came to recruiting members. Indeed, in 1959, Monroe County's S. Kelly received an award for the "largest number of memberships by individuals."[13]

Like their male counterparts, women farm bureau members paid close attention to state legislation that impacted income production on family farms. The passage of the 1959 Arkansas Egg Marketing Act or "Egg Law" directly affected many rural women, regardless of race. Passed by the state's general assembly at the ARFBF's insistence, the law regulated the sale of eggs and the registration of business hours dedicated to "buying, selling, trading, or trafficking in eggs." The law further established standards for grading, classification, and marking of eggs, along with a penalty for failure to comply with the act.[14] Most rural women sold eggs as "pin money" for their families. This money was often a significant contribution to the family income during lean economic times. Egg production had long been understood as a female pursuit in rural areas, but the passage of the Egg Law heralded the mass production and marketing of egg sales. As egg production became increasingly perceived as a male enterprise, women who often used eggs to barter with other women as part of a localized economy were displaced. This dramatically impacted rural Black women, who overwhelmingly lacked the means to participate in the mass egg-production market.

Farm bureau women further participated in ARFBF conventions and Rural Life Conferences. The Rural Life Conference began in 1946, when Simon Alexander Haley, father of *Roots* author Alex Haley and AM&N College's director of agriculture, decided to organize a gathering to increase Pine Bluff's Black farm community's exposure to and awareness of the most recent agricultural programs and innovations. The first Rural Life

Conference was held in 1950 and had only fifteen attendees. Dr. Sellers J. Parker, the first dean of what became AM&N's Division of Agriculture and Technology, significantly expanded the conference after attending a similar event at Tuskegee Institute also in 1950. After Parker met with ARFBF Negro Division president John Gammon, the two decided to combine the organizations to found the Rural Life Conference and Farm Bureau Leaders.[15] By 1955, under Parker's direction, the meeting was firmly established as an annual college event, which he then went on to chair for thirty years.[16]

Black women attended the annual Rural Life Conference as extension agents, home demonstration and 4-H club leaders, and farmers. For instance, Marianna farmers Willa Howard and Gladys McFadden were listed among the planning committee members for the 1956 meeting.[17] When the sixth annual Rural Life Conference met in 1958 with the theme "Improving Family Living Through Better Farm and Home Management," ARFBF representatives, home economics instructors, students, and church and community leaders were present. This included home demonstration agents Fannie Mae Boone, Marguerite P. Williams, LaVerne Feaster, and Carreather F. Banks.[18] Willa Howard led a session on "ginners, cooperatives, and heavy machinery operators" thus demonstrating that rural Black women were not necessarily limited to discussions about home management.[19] When the ARFBF Negro Division met at its annual meeting, also in 1958, Black home demonstration agents from Lafayette and Columbia Counties presented on "How to Present Yourself as a Leader," thereby underscoring the importance of African American women's leadership roles in rural communities.[20]

Local ARFBF-sponsored educational experiences always included women. In 1963, Black farmers attended a meeting that focused on machinery schools, instructions on cotton-gin operations, and leadership development. Black women were expected to perform in traditional gender roles even as they oversaw leadership sessions. For example, the Heth home demonstration club in Saint Francis County served lunch at the meeting while the men discussed the "fine points of cooperative management and the efficiency of operations." In contrast, Lee County's Willie Mae Collier and Desha County's Hazel Baker presided over leadership meetings held in Forrest City and Cullendale.[21]

By the mid- to late 1960s, women had assumed leadership positions in local segregated ARFBF chapters. In 1964, Jefferson County's Mable Hubbard and Lee County's Willie Mae Collier co-chaired the women's auxiliary. Women were also leaders in the organization's main body. During this same year, Desha County's Hazel Baker was elected the Negro Division vice president.[22] Again, rural Black women's ability to recruit farm bureau members by utilizing their multifarious organizational and community connections remained as important as their homemaking skills. At the Negro Division's annual meeting in 1964, Crittenden County agent Lula Farley received an award for being the "Best Woman Solicitor," and Gertrude T. Henderson from Chicot County was awarded "Woman of the Year in Home Economics."[23]

Incidentally, the ARFBF formed its own auxiliary, the Associated Women of the Arkansas Farm Bureau (AWARFB) at its 1947 annual convention. It promoted school lunch programs, rural libraries, and churches—all initiatives that were well within the purview of rural Black women's activism. All women holding farm bureau memberships could become AWARFB members. There is no evidence that Black women chose to do so, as they wielded considerable influence within the negro division until the ARFBF integrated in 1966.[24]

African Americans also employed Black women's bodies as a commodity to celebrate and sell southern agriculture. Blain Roberts has noted how rural white women's bodies were commoditized through beauty pageants as a reaction to economic, political, and social change in southern communities. These pageants firmly centered white women as the ideal of rural southern beauty and the epitome of womanhood. Black women were not viewed similarly and consequently were not represented in these contests. Nor were Black people recognized as the critical labor force in southern agriculture. Yet they, too, intentionally adopted a gendered understanding of agrarianism by using rural Black women's bodies in agricultural beauty contests as sites of consumption to project respectability politics and to highlight Black people's critical roles in southern cotton production.[25] Black women's bodies were, furthermore, the means by which to demonstrate racial progress and Black potential.[26]

In 1935, Black Memphis dentist Ranson Q. Venson and his wife Ethyl Horton Venson founded the Cotton Makers Jubilee after taking their nephew to a parade sponsored by the all-white Cotton Carnival, which had been established in 1931. The young man noted the marginalization of Black people in the mid-South's agricultural narrative.[27] For the Vensons, creating the Cotton Makers Jubilee offered a counter-narrative to what Anna Thompson Hajdik called a "nostalgic reimagining of the nation's rural past."[28] Like the Cotton Carnival, the Jubilee highlighted cotton production, but it also celebrated African Americans' agricultural contributions and celebrated Black women's beauty and femininity by presenting them as "queens" in African American communities.[29]

Black Arkansans attended and participated in the festival as well. In 1948, Mississippi County Jeanes Supervisor Bessie P. Ivy accompanied seventy-five students from Harrison Elementary School to Memphis for the twelfth annual Cotton Makers Jubilee. The free trip was the students' reward for perfect school attendance.[30] Arkansas women were well-represented in the Cotton Makers Jubilee, which emphasized "beauty, talent, and person-ality."[31] Preliminary contests were typically held in rural communities and extension service agents were often the most ardent recruiters. In 1940, for instance, Mississippi County farm agent W. S. Barabin announced that preliminary contests were going to be held in Blytheville and Osceola for the "Sepia Venus of the Mid-South," who would be awarded a trip to Chicago.[32]

From 1948 to 1956, the Cotton Makers Jubilee added the Spirit of Cotton Pageant as the Black analogue to the white-only Maid of Cotton Contest. Contestants were chosen for both their beauty and their tailoring skills. Daisy Lee Gaston Bates, who in 1952 became the Arkansas State Conference NAACP president, served as local chairperson of the pageant from 1950 to 1954. While Bates is typically known for leading and advising the Little Rock Nine during the 1957 Central High School integration cri-sis, she was also a rural activist. Born in 1914 and raised in Huttig (Union County), she married insurance salesman and newspaperman Lucius C. Bates in 1941. The couple settled in Little Rock, where they established the newspaper the *Arkansas State Press*. In 1968, Bates moved to Mitchellville (Desha County) where she became a community organizer for the local Office of Economic Opportunity's Self-Help Project. As a result of her activism, the rural Delta community gained a new water system in 1970, a sewer system in 1971, and paved roads, a community center, and a swim-ming pool in 1972, and a Head Start program. Bates, who died in 1999, lived in Mitchellville until 1974.[33]

Most Spirit of Cotton contestants came from middle-class families. Betty Johnson, a graduate of Dunbar High School (Little Rock) who had also attended Howard University and Philander Smith College, was selected to compete in the pageant in Memphis, which she subsequently won in 1950. Johnson's mother owned Johnson Business College, where Betty was enrolled in a secretarial course.[34] After her national tour, Johnson returned to Little Rock where she and Ethyl Venson met with the local chapter of the National Council of Negro Women and where Johnson modeled her cotton gowns. Johnson, referred to as the "Spirit," was further welcomed to the city by Little Rock and North Little Rock mayors Sam Wassell and Ross Lawhon.[35] It was also important for the winner to meet USDA officials to impress upon them the importance of African Americans' role in cotton production. In 1951, Spirit of Cotton winner Ernestine Jones, then a student at Arkansas AM&N College, embarked upon a national tour to represent the Memphis Cotton Makers Jubilee, which included a stop in Washington, DC, where she met African American USDA information specialist Sherman Brisco.[36]

Winners often became celebrities among African Americans nationwide. Ernestine Jones was lauded by Black fashion designer Nelle Noall as the "ambassador of cotton fashion," praising Jones for her "extensive wardrobe . . . every garment, from a velveteen flight coat to a pair of glazed chintz shorts, was made of cotton." She was especially impressed by the fact that Jones had "made nearly every one of the garments during free time from her studies."[37] Arkansas Baptist College student Minnie Pearl Henry placed second in the 1952 Spirit of Cotton contest. A source of pride for African Americans, Henry was sponsored by the Chicago Arkansas Baptist College alumni club and had been prepared for the contest by a local dentist and a Pine Bluff hair stylist.[38] The eventual winner, Texas native Barbara O'Cele Thompson, was accompanied by Daisy Bates on her nationwide tour of fifteen cities, which included being entertained by members of Chicago's Arkansas Club, and a slew of radio interviews, fashion shows, and photo shoots.[39]

The ARFBF's Negro Division supported the "Spirit of Cotton" as well. Leoda and John Gammon's daughter Ida Mae Gammon presented a $100 check from the ARFBF to Maxine Perryman—a student at Mississippi Vocational College (now Mississippi Valley State University) near Itta Bena—as the winner of the 1956 Spirit of Cotton Makers Jubilee.[40] As Blain Roberts has astutely noted, Black bodies, like white bodies, were utilized to promote southern agriculture. Black women were the wives and daughters of farmers and sharecroppers. Furthermore, their lives were not only impacted by agricultural calendars but also by racialized interpretations of "healthy and well-dressed bodies" which were key to promoting rural uplift among African Americans.[41] Black Arkansas women and communities continued to participate in the Jubilee and the Spirit of Cotton contest throughout the decades. The Cotton Makers Jubilee and the Cotton Carnival ran parallel to each other for nearly fifty years until they became part of Carnival Memphis in 1985.[42]

Rural Black women employed a number of strategies to impress the importance of African American laborers upon white landowners. More significantly, organizations as the ARFBF's Negro Division and events such as the Spirit of Cotton contest enabled Black women to continue to address African Americans concerns in agrarian communities. Their presence and leadership vividly demonstrated that rural Black people, and women in particular, sought recognition and, more importantly, a return on their roles as agricultural producers. Their efficacy as ARFBF Negro Division members and organizers provided much support and guidance in rural Black communities as they reckoned with the changes occurring in Arkansas agriculture from the mid-1950s to the late 1960s.

Rural Activism in 1950s Arkansas

IN THE 1950S, Black home demonstration agents and club members were impacted by the undercurrents of the burgeoning modern civil rights movement as they utilized extension service resources to improve conditions in rural Black communities. At a February 1950 meeting in Woodruff County, club members discussed strategies for "Better Rural Living," a campaign that encompassed Black agents' labor but that also underscored their understanding of the legal changes afoot, such as the challenge to segregated education. But they also renewed their focus on African Americans' needs in rural Arkansas, especially access to food security and health care.[1] Within this atmosphere, leadership development remained important. During that same month, in Camden the Lafayette County Home Demonstration Club met with agent Ernestine Wilson to discuss training local women to for prepare diets for the sick.[2] In March 1950, Faulkner County assistant demonstration agent Maude B. Davis showed Black women how to store home cured meats and preserve eggs so that they could increase their food supply.[3]

Local leadership was paramount. Lee County home demonstration agent Verna Gillard Mixon stressed to farm women the importance of attending meetings in a letter addressed to "food preservation leaders," wherein she asserted, "You are the Canning Leaders in your community. We are depending on you to come up and get this information to carry back to your community. Everyone can't come, only the leaders are invited. You are a leader. Please come."[4] Women also were often recognized for their club and community leadership and reminded that their labors were, in fact, patriotic during the Cold War years. In May 1950, for instance, Cross County agent Sylvania R. Mays and council president Frances McFerrin awarded certificates to its members with the following words of tribute:

> We pay homage to you for your . . . years of service as an extension club member. Your neighbors have welcomed your help. Your

family is proud of the service you have given to the community. The county is a better place to live in because of you. Homemaking is a serious job, and offers a real opportunity for you to serve your country. We commend you for the fine job you are doing.[5]

Home demonstration club leaders were not just concerned about food insecurity and poor health care among rural Blacks, however. They were likely aware of the changes resulting from the Supreme Court's 1944 decision in the *Smith v. Allwright* case, which overturned the white primary elections from which African Americans had been excluded since the early twentieth century. Rural women attended political training meetings, recognizing that access to voting rights was critical to fomenting change in their communities. After African Americans regained their right to vote in 1950 in Little River County, Black club women gathered with home demonstration agent Geneva R. Zachery at the Ashdown County Training School, also a Rosenwald school, to discuss "how to interpret the ballot." According to Zachery, these discussions helped Black women better understand "how to cast [their] vote, and stimulated interest in going to the polls to vote." Each member was then "urged to take her part in the community affairs, and to accept her right to vote as a responsibility."[6] This renewed sense of political engagement intensified throughout rural Black communities. In 1951, encouraged by agent Carreather Banks to vote in city elections, Saint Francis County club women learned about the importance of paying their poll taxes.[7]

Black women residing in Arkansas's rural communities found it profoundly important to fine-tune their leadership skills. In 1954, club officers convened at First Baptist Church in Union County for the "Home Demonstration Club Officer Meeting." As part of the program, they participated in a discussion, led by agent Marguerite P. Williams, titled "What Determines Good Leadership?" and which outlined club officers' duties. Using this information, they later performed a skit conducted by Williams and titled "What Kind of Leader Are You? Autocratic? Laissez-faire? Democratic?"[8]

Marguerite Williams further led by example in her efforts to train rural Black women leaders. In 1954, she led the negro Girl Scout movement in El Dorado, the segregated PTA, and helped to establish an African American YWCA. And because Williams was cognizant of political changes happening nationwide, she assisted Black women as they planned a countywide citizenship program.[9]

Home demonstration agents also helped Black women embrace home improvements through technological conveniences. Women in Lafayette County attended a wiring demonstration in 1953 and learned to wire their own homes.[10] In 1955, members of the Lucky Twenty home demonstration club in Lake Village (Chicot County) learned to make cypress knee lamps, an item that could be made inexpensively and provided rural homes with better lighting.[11]

Installing telephones and electrical service were important technological advancements in rural communities. Lafayette County assistant home demonstration agent Ruby L. Curry noted in her 1953–54 report that five women were the "first colored in Bradley to get telephones." Club women in Dermott learned how to use a "dial telephone" in 1956 at extension service demonstrations. Telephones were an important development in rural Arkansas that resulted from the passage of the 1949 Hill-Poage Act. Overseen by the Rural Electrification Administration (REA), a New Deal program begun in 1935, the act was designed to increase the quantity and quality of telephones in rural areas.[12]

As they were increasingly woven into the fabric of rural life, telephones allowed people to communicate more efficiently—though extension service agents did encounter some resistance to their efforts to implement a technology of urban communities. Because of the increased availability of telephones in rural homes, farmers were better able to conduct business, and residents aided each other during emergencies. Telephones further enhanced access to news and improved communication between neighbors and family members who had migrated out of the area.[13] Many rural Arkansans still did not have access to telephones until well into the 1960s. In November 1964, the Southwest General Telephone Company presented a proposal to the Arkansas Public Service Commission for a comprehensive statewide rural expansion program between 1965 and 1967. When it was implemented in places like Marvell (Phillips County), the program provided telephone service without requiring people to pay the higher costs associated with constructing lines. Because the new lines were placed underground, residents enjoyed improved and more reliable service.[14]

Some Black families did well enough that they could afford to invest in new technologies. In 1956, the Newsome family of Proctor (Crittenden County) owned a fifty-three-acre farm from which they sold $500 of okra, $475 of soybeans, $90 of broccoli, and, most importantly, $2,000 of cotton. The skills Mrs. Newsome gained from home demonstration agents and as the local home demonstration club president also contributed to her

family's success. Black agents carefully guided farm-owners as the latter learned how to diversify their crops and increase livestock to augment their income. As a result, the agents believed rural Black Arkansans were well on the way to "lifting themselves to better living by their own bootstraps."[15] Such efforts continued to underscore agents' longstanding goal to encourage Blacks to become self-sufficient producers.

The REA also enabled rural people to improve the quality of their lives through electrical technology. Newsome was not only able to produce and preserve large quantities of food for her family, she also learned how to reupholster furniture and convert kerosene lamps to electric—and subsequently taught those skills to other Black women.[16] The REA loaned money to cooperatives with a twenty-five-year amortization period. Extension agents and agricultural professionals had long understood electricity and

Assistant Home Demonstration Agents for Negro Work, 1950. *Image courtesy of UACESR, Special Collections, University of Arkansas Libraries, Fayetteville.*

technology as a means to "solve" and "modernize" the problems of rural life and to save families farms by "urbanizing" and bringing them "city conveniences."[17] Families who needed money for wiring and appliances could apply for individual loans. The REA did not begin loaning money to Arkansas rural electric cooperatives until 1937 resulting in the construction of in the state's first rural electric cooperative utility pole.[18]

While power companies like Arkansas Power and Light were, according to Jeannie Whayne, not enthusiastic about using federal funds to subsidize competitors for the rural market, increased electricity transformed agrarian life.[19] Electricity had been available in Arkansas cities and towns by the time the REA was enacted. But an embrace of a "utopian view of rural electrification" and "technological determinism," as one historian has described the views, came late to many communities.[20] The fantasies of technological determinism, imagined as a way to make rural dwellers more like their urban counterparts, rarely matched the cultural and economic realities of Black agrarians' lives.[21] Many still lived without electricity, much as their predecessors had, until well into the twentieth century largely because they were too impoverished to subscribe to a cooperative. As late as the 1950s and 1960s, home demonstration agents like Levada P. Mason introduced farm women to indoor plumbing, electric light fixtures, and an array of consumer items powered by electricity that were designed to promote family comfort and eradicate the drudgery of rural life.[22]

Home demonstration agents' presence in poor rural Black communities was important because the agents themselves had often been born into similar circumstances. Levada Mason was born in 1927 to sharecroppers in Albany (Nevada County) in southwest Arkansas.[23] She had labored in the cotton fields as a child. But her parents encouraged her to obtain an education, which began at Sweet Home Elementary, a one-room Rosenwald school.[24] Mason completed her public school education at the Nevada County Training School in Rosston and later earned a BA at Philander Smith College and a BS in home economics at Arkansas AM&N. She subsequently obtained a master's degree in home economics at the University of Central Arkansas and did additional graduate work at Prairie View A&M College in Texas, Tuskegee Institute, and the University of Arkansas. Mason worked as an educator in Hempstead County and became a home demonstration agent in Crittenden County. After leaving the extension service, she was an elementary school educator in West Memphis, Arkansas.[25]

While electricity slowly made its way into rural Black communities during the 1950s, some counties saw an increase in the number of African American home demonstration clubs. Club names often reflected the particular geographic location of the club within its county. Woodruff County, which already had at least seven clubs, witnessed the formation of three other organizations: the Harris Chapel Club, the Revel Club, and the Howell Club.

To be clear, not all home demonstration club members were farming or rural women. In Arkansas, rurality did not necessarily exist in opposition to urbanization.[26] During 1953–54, Lafayette County had eleven clubs. Of the total of 423 members, 292 were farm women, 106 were rural non-farm women, and 25 were listed as "urban ladies." And among their concerns, like most Black women's organizations, was the creation and maintenance of recreational spaces for young people. The Lewisville Negro Home Demonstration Club, for instance, celebrated the opening of a community park in 1954. After refurbishing donated land, club members held a dedication program which they began by singing "Lift Every Voice and Sing," often considered the "Black National Anthem." Lafayette County home demonstration agent Ruby L. Curry attended, along with Black agricultural agent T. R. Betton and a cross section of community dignitaries.[27] And the number of clubs continued to grow throughout the decade as was the case in Chicot County in southeast Arkansas, which was home to ten home demonstration clubs by 1958.[28]

Club women also learned about the world and culture beyond Arkansas, particularly as so many African Americans migrated out of the state. Pulaski County Home Demonstration Council members purchased material and a kit to construct a United Nations flag. The flag was then displayed at the county courthouse to celebrate United Nations Day.[29] In Lee County, not only did Black women produce a flag later featured in a high school homecoming parade, they also signed a petition supporting the United Nations Universal Declaration of Human Rights after it was adopted by the UN General Assembly in 1948.[30] Between 1952 and 1953, they attended study courses on religions in foreign countries and participated in an "All Nations" pageant at the 1952 SCHDC annual meeting, where they depicted local Arkansan social customs. Twenty-three of the twenty-eight counties with Black home demonstration clubs participated.[31]

Agrarian Black women understood well that the world was changing around them and increasingly, in the 1950s and 1960s, SCHDC meetings included themes with such implicit political messages as "The Home Maker, a World Citizen," "Working Together for World Understanding," "The Homemakers' Responsibilities in Changing Times," or "Symbols of the Sixties—Alert Homemakers."[32] Black extension service agents and home demonstration club members subtly merged the extension service's agenda with their interpretation of the changes occurring in Arkansas. In December 1960, they discussed their concerns at their annual conference at the segregated National Baptist Hotel in Hot Springs. The conference, for which the theme was "Agricultural Extension in a Decade of Change," also featured a talk titled "Our Job in a Decade of Change" by home demonstration agent Marguerite P. Williams.[33]

Ameliorating impoverished conditions in rural communities remained an important focus throughout the 1960s. As part of their duties, Black women agents attended in-service training conferences where their efforts toward this end were reinforced. In 1962, AACW president Marguerite P. Williams and farm agent T. R. Betton underscored this critical work in a joint talk and discussion titled "Your Responsibility in Economic Development and Social Improvement."[34] To celebrate the extension service's fiftieth anniversary in 1964, the state council presented a program at Arkansas Baptist College titled "The Homemaker: A World Citizen," which spoke volumes about rural Black women's understanding of and attention to the changes occurring both nationally and internationally.[35]

African American home demonstration agents and club members acknowledged the historical transformations in Black life as the civil rights movement gained momentum. Yet they still faced rampant discrimination and risked the loss of important funding and white community support if they became overtly involved in political activism. Still, directly confronting discrimination was not unusual. In 1956, Poinsett County home demonstration club members protested when the extension service decided to eliminate the county's Black home demonstration agent position. This was particularly alarming for African Americans, because the white home demonstration agent position was retained. Arkansas extension service associate director C. A. Vines argued that this was due to the decrease in Poinsett County's rural Black population.[36]

Vines argued that it was necessary to spend funds "where it will serve the most people" and observed that in 1954 Poinsett County had 332 non-white farm operators for a total non-white population of 1,604. In his estimation, it was unreasonable to pay an agent to serve such a small population when Lincoln County's population was three times larger and in greater need of their services. He further assured Poinsett County Blacks that "white agents are aware of your situation and have been asked to help in any way they can." As rural Blacks understood well the very real and tense nature of race relations in the 1950s South, Vine's promise was likely not very reassuring.[37]

Elveria Heard, a resident of the Cherry Beam community in Tyronza and the county home demonstration council president, sent Vines, the University of Arkansas president John Tyler Caldwell, Arkansas governor Orval E. Faubus, and P. V. Kepner, the USDA deputy administrator in Washington, DC, a petition signed by seventy-five African American Poinsett County residents who were determined to retain a Black home demonstration agent because of "past achievements that have been accomplished through extension work in the county, state, tristate and national activities," because they considered it a "great loss to the Negro Homemakers and Negro 4-H boys and girls of this county."[38]

A farmer's wife with only one year of high school education, Heard had been born in rural Monroe County, Mississippi, in 1911.[39] Between

1935 and 1940, Heard, her husband, Sidney, and their children moved to Arkansas in search of improved economic opportunities and to escape racial violence and political marginalization. They probably continued to move, as opportunities for agricultural labor continued to decline due to Arkansas's large-scale landowning farmers' increased dependence on mechanization. In 1940, the family was living in Wappanocca in Crittenden County. By the 1950s, they were in Poinsett County.

Couching her response in carefully chosen but politically loaded terms, Heard asserted, "In view of the past achievements that have been accomplished through Extension Work in the County, State, Tri-State and National activities, we feel that this will deprive these citizens of equal opportunities with other citizens of the State. We petition that you find a way to maintain the Home Demonstration and 4-H work in this county for all citizens."[40] Heard understood the benefits of 4-H clubs for African American children in particular. Her daughter Sedonia had been a member of the Houston High School 4-H club in Tyronza, where she was also class president, secretary of the home economics club, and was named Miss Houston High in 1950. After high school, Sedonia attended Arkansas Baptist College in Little Rock, where she majored in business education. Her education was quite likely funded in part by the monies raised by Black women's home demonstration club activities on the 4-H's behalf.[41]

Unfortunately, the USDA made it abundantly clear that it had neither the responsibility nor the right to determine the organization or staffing of state extension offices.[42] It is unclear whether Poinsett County Blacks were able to retain a home demonstration agent or what their assertiveness might have cost them. But it is noteworthy that Blacks in rural Arkansas communities relied heavily upon Black home demonstration agents' services and that their activism mattered even when they fell short of their goals. They had few qualms about organizing, petitioning, and challenging those in authority who threatened their access to beneficial resources.

African Americans were often adamant about retaining agents in their counties because they provided them with survival techniques. Health access was a pervasive concern among the rural poor. Agrarian Blacks however, were not "mere silent partners in the quest for health reform."[43] They understood that improved health was directly connected to rural development and often actively sought and embraced opportunities to address and alleviate issues in their communities.[44] In 1960, local Blacks in Amy organized a meeting to address the serious issues devastating their communities. Home demonstration agent Clothilde M. Shivers and the Ouachita

County Rural Development Advisory Committee worked with Amy residents to eradicate food shortages, low incomes, and inferior medical care. Shivers, the county agent since 1952, taught rural Black women how to conserve food and cook nutritious meals to feed their families. Extension agents helped Black families grow gardens and encouraged them to sell their surplus produce at market to augment their family income.[45] Shivers also regularly taught a "better housekeeping methods" course at the community center near the Ivory Heights housing development and, along with the local housing authority, sponsored a "Housekeeper of the Month" contest.[46] Furthermore, Amy residents participated in a quality of life program with a clean-up campaign, during which they removed two of the primary sources responsible for the transmission of disease and illness in their community: standing water and trash.[47] Even by the 1960s, few African Americans could afford the necessary inoculations to avoid communicable diseases like tuberculosis. Shivers and the Ouachita County Rural Development Advisory Committee additionally employed a public-health nurse to hold immunization clinics for African Americans.[48]

African American women leaders also advocated for health reform in rural Black communities by supporting the National Negro Health Movement. Established in 1915 by Booker T. Washington and such national Black organizations and institutions as the National Business League and Howard University, and based at Tuskegee Institute, the movement addressed African Americans' unequal access to health care, disproportionately high mortality rates, and living conditions. It brought Black community health problems to the attention of the federal government.[49] The National Negro Health Movement was supported by the Jeanes Foundation, the National Tuberculosis Association, local interracial commissions, the USDA extension service, the American Red Cross, and the National Medical Association.[50]

The movement later became known as National Negro Health Week (NNHW) and beginning in the 1930 was taken over by the United States Public Health Service.[51] During NNHW, usually held in April, Black extension service agents, educators, and community leaders encouraged African Americans to participate in clean-up campaigns, health education programs, and medical examinations.[52] When the Arkansas Colored Teachers Association launched their state's activities for NNHW in 1923, the organization invited ministers, doctors, and nurses to lecture on health concerns in African American communities. ACTA further designated a community clean-up day, for which it noted, "That the civic pride of the colored race is being stirred is satisfying."[53] In Mississippi County in 1930 Jeanes Supervisor Annie Currie organized 150 African Americans from Osceola, Grider, and Blytheville who were examined by Black doctors at clinics sponsored by the county health unit.[54]

White participation was a critical part of NNHW. Ouachita County Jeanes Supervisor Cleo McDonald lauded interracial health reform activism when she declared that the "colored teachers and pastors of Ouachita County are very grateful to the county health unit and the white physicians for their wholehearted support and cooperation." In doing so, she also subtly employed rhetoric that politicized and prioritized African Americans' health needs without infuriating whites. Asserting the primacy of Black health was in and of itself a political act that in turn allowed McDonald to stealthily advocate for Black civil and political rights.[55] McDonald further demonstrated how Black women wielded local influence over African American public health issues by advocating intergroup cooperation with the Arkansas Tuberculosis Association, the Metropolitan Life Insurance Company, the federal bureau of health, the ADE, and the National Colored Businessmen's League, all of which provided much needed health information to communities countywide.

Often, rural uplift events were held simultaneously. Ouachita County's seventh annual celebration of NNHW was held at Cotton Belt Rosenwald School in Bearden and sponsored by the Better Homes Movement.[56] McDonald continued to promote Black health access as a part of New Deal programs in the 1930s. In 1935, she taught a Federal Emergency Relief Administration home economics course to African American homemakers' clubs that focused on sanitation, hygiene, nutrition, and family budgeting. The experience clearly helped rural Black women, some of whom commented, "We wish we had known this before."[57]

Agents further combated the myriad health issues that plagued rural Black communities by demonstrating treatments for mastitis and by discussing the importance of mental and dental health care.[58] Although the records do not speak specifically to these issues, rural health care almost certainly included discussions about birth control and the prevalence of venereal disease.

Throughout the twentieth century, rural Black women were concerned with the issue of limiting the size of their families. Home demonstration clubs and agents were particularly important sources for the dissemination such information among rural residents. Farm agent H. C. Ray also supported birth control efforts within Black communities and underscored the critical role of rural club women's activism in his response to the newsletter: "We have more than 13,000 rural women working in home demonstration clubs. . . . It is in this connection that I feel our organization might work hand in hand with you in bringing about some very definite and desirable results in your phase of community improvement work. We will be glad to distribute any literature."[59] Jeanes Supervisors' responsibilities also included helping rural Black women with birth control concerns. According to records from the Planned Parenthood Federation of America's Division of Negro Service established in 1940, Jeanes Supervisors from Ashley, Bradley, Mississippi, and Nevada Counties all requested birth control information in 1942.[60]

Although NNHW ended in 1950, Black leaders continued to emphasize the importance of its themes and teachings. The 1953 SCHDC annual meeting, for instance, featured a "hearing-vision" consultant from the Arkansas Department of Health who gave a talk on "Eyes for Tomorrow." This was followed by a presentation by home demonstration agent Carreather Banks on "Proper Lighting for Reading."[61] In 1954, the Burnt Hill Home Demonstration Club in Union County displayed an exhibit titled "Who's Ruining Your Health" and outlined causes of poor health such as open wells and holes in the walls and screens that led to insect infestations. It also explained how electric pumps with sealed tanks and pasteurized milk were important to improved health in rural communities. The Union County Home Demonstration Council's exhibit "Mental Health Is Everybody's Business" outlined reasons for mental illness in rural communities.[62] Club women in the Lafayette County cities of Lewisville, Stamps, Buckner, and Bradley led the "Mothers' March for Polio" and contributed to the American Red Cross, the American Cancer Society, and the Christmas Seals drive.[63]

In the 1950s, rural Black women leaders' objectives were many. They continued to combat food insecurity and poor health access among African Americans, in addition to advocating for technological advancements to ease the burden of rural life. But they also utilized the postwar years to advance and support civil rights, even if subtly. In the years that followed civil rights became a pressing issue, particularly as African Americans increasingly moved from rural to urban areas. In the 1950s and beyond, Black women leaders like Ethel B. Dawson—the focus of the next chapter—consciously crafted a rural reform agenda that included political efficacy. Still, the underlying message Dawson imparted to agrarian Blacks, utilizing biblical text, continued to stress the importance of individual and community self-determination.

— 10 —

Ethel B. Dawson and the National Council of Churches of Christ Home Missions Division

IN 1949, ETHEL B. DAWSON penned letters to the *Arkansas State Press* to encourage Pine Bluff's Black community to own their role in improving their conditions and accessing their right to full citizenship. She called upon Black leaders to "talk about these unfavorable conditions," stating that they "required action on the part of everyone." Dawson's adamancy on this issue was informed by Christian principles and US law. She fervently believed that the "fundamental principles of our law books are based on the Bible," and that if the "spirit of the Book can get into men, it will make them just, impartial, and honest toward their fellowmen." She further asserted that "Christian citizens" in Pine Bluff had a responsibility to become involved in civic activism:

> Mothers, fathers, ministers, church, and public school teachers, and other professional groups and lay leaders should combine their efforts, make plans, and cooperate in programs designed to develop law abiding Christian citizens. They should attend and sit in on court hearings, beginning with the justice of the peace court on up to the highest courts, and listen to the practical Christian men hear testimony and administer justice. . . . We vote and help elect these men for the different offices. Let's attend courts and learn the facts including the source of many problems, then we will know how to attack and improve conditions.[1]

In the post–World War II years, some Black women activists increasingly engaged in rural religious activism in Arkansas as part of their battle against African Americans' economic and political marginalization; they did so through the National Council of Churches of Christ in the United States of America (NCC). Between 1946 and 1956, Lincoln County native Ethel B. Dawson was the NCC's Division of Home Missions religious extension director in Pine Bluff. Established in 1950, the NCC supported rural development and the USDA's programs to augment agrarian life by engaging Christians and church leaders. Concerned about increasing rural poverty, the NCC believed that rural people required not only economic assistance, but also moral direction. This emphasis on infusing the social gospel into Protestant churches was informed by concerns about the deleterious moral effect of rural communities' increasing shift to industrial agriculture.[2] As sociologist and director of the Committee for Cooperative Field Research of the Home Missions Council Harlan Paul Douglass noted, "every important denomination has an official social service agency either incorporated with its existing home missionary machinery or additional to and allied with it."[3] Historian Kevin Lowe has posited that concerns about moral deterioration in rural America resulted in a movement of those who "championed agrarianism—a vision of rural society based on family farms and small, face to face communities—in the face of agribusiness."[4] This version of Christian agrarianism became most pronounced in rural communities and churches through the Home Missions Council of North America.[5]

This Christian cooperative movement, began as two separate entities: the Home Missions Council and the Council of Women for Home Missions, both of which were founded in 1908. In 1940, they merged to become the interdenominational Home Missions Council of North America (HMCNA) to "promote fellowship, conference, and co-operation among Christian organizations doing missionary work in the United States and its dependences."[6] In 1950, the HMCNA was subsumed under the purview of the NCC. HMCNA activities were thereafter administered by the NCC's Division of Home Missions.[7] It was through this organization that Ethel Dawson combined religious doctrine with rural community uplift.

Born Ethel Beatrice Ross in 1907, she was raised on a farm in Lincoln County.[8] She knew well the difficulties of rural life and recalled of her childhood, "We went into the woods and cleared our land."[9] Ross also understood through firsthand experience the racial injustice that rural Blacks often faced when dealing with Arkansas's inhumane criminal justice system. Her father had been sent to the Cummins prison farm without a trial for six months when she was two years old.[10] Ross recalled, "We would see marks around his waist . . . we children would ask what were the marks and why were they there." Her father responded, "When I was in the county farm, those are the chain marks around my waist where they had me chained." Those marks remained on his body until he died.[11] This left a deep impression on Ross about the cruelty of the Arkansas prison system. Postbellum southern racial ideology defined African Americans as criminals. Throughout the South, perceived Black criminality resulted in the development of penal laws designed to control African Americans and exploit their labor.[12]

Ross attended elementary and high school at Arkansas AM&N College. After graduation, she taught in Jefferson and Garland Counties. In 1933, Ethel married Oscar G. Dawson, a tractor driver who had been born in Louisiana in 1904.[13] In 1940, she graduated from AM&N with a degree in home economics.[14] Almost immediately after college, Dawson began her career as a home demonstration agent in Gould in Lincoln County from 1941 to 1944 and later from 1944 to 1946, as a home economics instructor at Pine Bluff's Merrill High School.[15] She also pursued graduate work at New York's Columbia University, the University of Chicago, Northwestern University, and the University of Arkansas.[16]

Dawson became increasingly engaged in rural civil rights activism after starting a job with the NCC in 1946 to work in its sharecropper program in Lincoln County.[17] Although white landowners were not particularly interested in their laborers' exercising their right to vote, for Dawson, political efficacy was a key part of African Americans' ability to empower themselves and their communities to challenge the conditions that held them in perpetual bondage. She remembered, "We were always encouraging people to pay their poll taxes and vote."[18] In 1947, as the Arkansas director of religious extension service for the NCC Home Missions Division, she addressed the poor treatment rural Blacks endured at the National Conference of Church Leaders at Tuskegee Institute, noting, "Nearly every phase of the Negro's life in the deep South is overshadowed by discrimination and injustice."[19]

Dawson believed women were a critical part of agrarian racial activism in rural Arkansas. She was particularly skillful at harnessing Christian women's energies to aid her in her work and helped them to understand the importance of their involvement in rural religious, economic, and political advocacy. In 1947, she was one of the instructors at the Institute of Rural and Town Women, which met in Jackson, Tennessee, and was sponsored by the Home Missions Council under the auspices of the Phillips Theology School.[20] Dawson was also connected to Christian women through her membership in the United Council of Church Women (UCCW), an interracial and interdenominational organization founded in 1941. The UCCW brought together three women's religious organizations, the

National Council of Church Women, the Council of Women for Home Missions, and the Committee on Women's Work of the Foreign Missions Conference.[21]

In the years following World War II, the UCCW, like other female-led religious organizations such as the National Council of Jewish Women and the Young Women's Christian Association, focused its attention on fighting racial injustice in the United States. Indeed, religion had long been an arena for southern women to organize and discuss common concerns.[22] The UCCW was integrated at the national level.[23] Informed by this inclusive activist mandate, in 1948 Dawson attended the UCCW's fourth biennial meeting in Milwaukee, Wisconsin, where representatives from around the country unanimously endorsed a resolution to end segregation in the armed forces and other government establishments by declaring them "contrary to Christian principles and inimical to the democratic way of life."[24]

Because the moral and economic conditions in rural communities were so distressed, Christian leaders throughout Arkansas met frequently to discuss strategies and solutions for social and economic problems through local churches at the mid-winter institute held at the Phillips Theology School at Tennessee's Lane College.[25] The institute was designed to explore the "largest methods and techniques which are to be utilized in the effective administration of rural and town churches."[26] Dawson was one of its instructors. In 1948, she attended the Rural Regional Conference, for which the theme was "Meeting the Challenge of Rural America," held in Little Rock at Arkansas Baptist College. The conference was sponsored by the "Sunday School Publishing Board," the American Baptist Theological Seminary, and Arkansas Baptist College. This gathering was essentially a form of religious professional development that brought together "interested rural pastors, laymen, laywomen, and rural specialists to study the life conditions in rural America in relation to the Christian church" and to "formulate plans for more effective programs in State Baptist conventions, Baptist schools and colleges which serve rural areas."[27] Dawson also returned home to Lincoln County, where she gave a "demonstration on Biblical facts" at Gould High School as part of a panel on how "Negroes may obtain land and homes independently."[28]

Dawson was particularly concerned about the high mortality rate among mothers and children in Black communities caused by a lack of adequate health care. Like many women activists, she supported such campaigns as the March of Dimes as a way to galvanize community resources and to also increase awareness about rural health initiatives. In 1949, she worked with Jefferson County Jeanes Supervisor Mary Foster Cheatham to raise $1,764, collected largely from cash-strapped rural Black communities, to aid the March of Dimes efforts.[29]

By 1950, Dawson had become the NCC Division of Home Missions state director and, not coincidentally, the Pine Bluff NAACP assistant secretary.[30] Through the Division of Home Missions, she again employed a progressive and inclusive understanding of Christianity in ways that allowed her to work within rural Black communities to promote their political and economic efficacy. Dawson astutely combined Christian and political rhetoric as she labored in rural Arkansas. In particular, she understood the importance of building bridges and encouraging dialogue between progressive Black and white organizations so they could act cooperatively as "Christian citizens" and assume leadership roles as they addressed community issues and concerns. Part of this included inviting people to read and learn about conditions in Pine Bluff's Black communities. In 1950, Dawson encouraged locals to read Ralph A. Felton's *These My Brethren: A Study of 570 Negro Churches and 1,542 Negro Homes in the Rural South*, which described the limited educational opportunities and impoverished environments many African Americans endured throughout the rural South.[31]

Dawson was particularly outspoken about the disrespectful behavior Black women endured. In 1951, she and other Black leaders lambasted the *Pine Bluff Commercial* newspaper in an article in the Black-owned and -operated *Arkansas State Press* for referring to Black women by their first names while addressing white women as "Ms." or "Mrs."[32] Obtaining respect was an ongoing battle for Black women. Pine Bluff home demonstration agent Cassa Lawlah, whom Dawson likely knew, confronted Little Rock newspapers in 1952 for maligning Black women and their marital status.[33]

Dawson addressed these and other issues as a member of the Arkansas Division of the Southern Regional Council (SRC) when it met in Little Rock, Arkansas, in 1952.[34] The SRC, which evolved from the Commission on Interracial Cooperation founded in 1919, had been formed in Atlanta, Georgia, in 1944 to address southern racial injustice.[35] In 1954, when the Arkansas Division was reorganized as the Arkansas Council on Human Relations (ACHR), Dawson was elected secretary and served on the board of directors until the 1957–58 term with such individuals as Daisy Bates and ARFBF negro division president John Gammon Jr.[36] In this capacity, she called attention to the injustices and economic competition African American agricultural laborers faced when white farmers resorted to using Hispanic laborers, who were also known as "braceros." Between 1947 and

1964 approximately 300,000 immigrants from Mexico work in Arkansas Delta cotton fields. According to one source, the concentration of braceros peaked at 39,000 in 1959.[37] Because of labor shortages, the Mexican government was able to fight for and obtain a minimum $0.50 wage for braceros.[38] The fact that this was almost double what African American agricultural laborers earned incensed Dawson, who understood that economic exploitation had long allowed white landowners to retain control over Black workers by keeping them underemployed, indebted, and hence tied to the land. During the June 1955 ACHR board of directors' meeting, she voiced concerns about the "importation of Mexico farm labor at 50 cents, while native Negro labor received 25 cents and little employment."[39]

As the Division of Home Missions Religious Extension Director, Dawson, like other Black women leaders, combated rural food insecurity and poor educational access. She utilized predominantly Black spaces and institutions, namely churches, not only to impart important lessons about Christian civic responsibility, but to also provide basic educational and nutritional skills. She worked closely with historically Black schools and colleges and the extension service to encourage ecumenical cooperation between dominations and with colleges. Dawson also saw firsthand the changes that mechanization had wrought on agriculture in Jefferson County. By 1940, some 350 tractors and trucks had accelerated production and "tractored out," or replaced, agricultural laborers.[40] Dawson understood then that it was critical to help rural Blacks explore options to improve the quality of their lives, if they chose to remain on the farm, or to consider other opportunities, as mechanization and changes in the sharecropping system increasingly resulted in lower wages or complete displacement.[41]

Indeed, Dawson facilitated opportunities for rural Blacks to consider other vocations by inviting them to attend the 1951 Rural Life Conference at Arkansas AM&N. As always, she utilized Christian doctrine to justify her rural activism. She deployed Timothy 5:8, which says, "But if anyone does not provide for his own, and especially for those of his household, he has denied the faith and is worse than an unbeliever," to encourage African Americans to attend the conference. She knew that Black agricultural laborers had been mistreated by plantation owners. In fact, she wrote to the NCC's Department of Town and Country Church executive director, "Sharecroppers say that when they ask for contracts, itemized statements of accounts, or other legal papers, the landlords get angry and will begin cursing and abusing them." She wondered if "there isn't something that the federal government can do to help farm laborers and sharecroppers? For example, insure that these people [receive] better wages and a greater share in the profits from their crops."[42] Yet Dawson also believed that agricultural laborers were ultimately responsible for their own fate: "Why stay in one place and work for less—when you go to the store to buy anything, you have to pay the same price as the one who works for higher wages. You and your family are just as important and deserve the best if you want it."[43]

In 1952, Dawson attended the district congress of the twelfth Episcopal district at Little Rock's Shorter College, where she participated in the "Rural Life Institute," the theme of which was "Better Living, better health, better homes, better schools, better farms, and better community with the church as the center." The institute also included other Black women educational and health leaders, such as former Pine Bluff Jeanes Supervisor Maeleen Arrant, who now worked for the ADE, and state department health specialist Mamie O. Hale. All of these women labored in rural Black communities where their services were desperately needed.[44] Among their concerns was increasing unemployment among rural Blacks, as cotton acreage was reduced and large landowners switched to using farm machinery that only required three to four men to operate. Landowners encouraged them to find employment elsewhere, and many chose to relocate to Arkansas cities or to leave the state altogether to find jobs.[45] But some rural laborers chose to remain on the land where they had long worked, and where they lived in what were essentially shacks with little opportunity to own their own homes. In 1954, Dawson organized a "Housing Conference," the theme of which was "A Home—Every Man's Dream! How to Plan, Finance, and Build," at Arkansas AM&N, in cooperation with the Federal Housing Administration (FHA). Many rural Blacks were not familiar with the home construction options available to them through the federal government. Dawson arranged to have FHA specialists, including two "race relations" officers and a "minority group housing advisor," attend the conference in Pine Bluff to educate African Americans about home loans and mortgages. She urged local Blacks to "please come and help us to help you and others."[46]

While she addressed housing issues for rural Blacks, Dawson once again challenged the lack of bathroom facilities for African Americans who patronized Pine Bluff businesses. In November 1954, in a letter to the *Pine Bluff Commercial* titled "Rest Rooms Asked for the Colored," Dawson noted that she had asked that letters regarding this issue be published in the newspapers in 1952. While her request was accommodated, she asserted, "Within the last few months many colored people are experiencing difficulty with some salespersons regarding the use of rest rooms." Dawson was careful to note that African Americans were spending their dollars outside of Pine Bluff rather than face discrimination within the city. "Many colored people are spending hundreds of dollars in Little Rock because of the kind and respectful treatment they receive while shopping in those stores." As president of the Jefferson County Council of Church Women (organized in 1952) and co-chairperson of the Jefferson County Voters Association, Dawson asserted, "We earnestly hope that the city officials will arrange for the construction of public restrooms in our city. Large numbers of people come to Pine Bluff from rural areas to trade and search for jobs. We are all human beings and have need for these conveniences to prevent public embarrassment and to maintain health."[47] Dawson used the power of the dollar to appeal to white leaders not only to address the way Blacks were treated in stores in downtown Pine Bluff but also to encourage stores to employ Blacks as salespersons. Just a few days later, she took her concern before the Pine Bluff city council, where she once again emphasized that some African Americans had chosen to spend their hard-earned dollars in Little Rock rather than endure discriminatory treatment in local stores.[48]

To further address rural Blacks' myriad concerns, Dawson served on the state planning committee for the Town and Country Church Development Program, which was designed to instruct rural pastors through intensive training sessions.[49] Dawson planned an interdenominational and interracial seminar, which was held at the University of Arkansas in Fayetteville in 1955. That same year, Dawson attended the national convocation of the "Church in Town and Country," and then hosted the "Town and Country Church Rural Life Improvement Institute," at First Baptist Church in Gould. Sponsored by the Arkansas Town and Country advisory committee, Division of Home Missions, NCC, the institute, for which the theme was "Christianity at Work in All Areas of Life," brought together laypersons and agricultural specialists from Arkansas AM&N, all of whom were invested in helping rural Blacks achieve a better standard of living.[50] The program included sessions titled "Swine and Cows for Food and Marketing," "Farm Management for Improved Living Conditions," "The Objectives of the Employment (Social) Security Program," and "How Public School Teachers Can Apply Religious Principles in Their Work."[51]

Dawson taught rural Blacks many of the same skills that home demonstration agents and Jeanes Supervisors did. But she also addressed concerns about the over policing of Black communities and imparted important political education to Arkansans across racial lines as part of her duties. In August 1955, she attended a Civic Service Commission meeting with African

Americans to discuss police brutality, helped organize the Pine Bluff Council on Human Relations, and participated in the Arkansas Democratic Voters Association in Little Rock. Dawson also hosted community seminars in which she taught about "the Bible and Human Rights" or showed such films as *The Christian Citizen*.[52] She again called on women to help impart these lessons. In November 1955, Dawson urged the Jefferson County Council of Church Women and the Lincoln County Civic Association to share this information in their communities.[53] Members of the council may have also been members of the Progressive Women's Voters Association (PWVA), which Dawson helped to establish in 1953.

Women's collaboration across organizations strengthened Dawson's activist platform, as she believed that "good citizens and Christian women have a responsibility for civil and political action." She further asserted that what "good citizens and Christian women can do" informed the PWVA's objectives to:

> study government, political issues, civic and social problems and equality of opportunities. Equality of opportunities mean that we want a comfortable standard of living, as good an education that can be absorbed, a home in a decent residential community, a chance to enjoy the good life. When we insist that this chance, in terms of decent jobs, higher education, housing, and other needs of modern society, should be available to all regardless of skin color, birthplace, or religion, we are speaking up for equality of opportunity. We further aim to help educate all citizens to use their ballots wisely in the interest of good government.[54]

Dawson urged PWVA members to vote because, she believed, "good citizens and Christian women can change the world."[55]

Though Dawson left the NCC in 1956, her rural civil rights activism only increased in the 1960s. When the Student Nonviolent Coordinating Committee (SNCC) first arrived in Arkansas in 1962, and in Pine Bluff shortly thereafter, Dawson noted that discussions with local restaurants about allowing African Americans to eat in their establishments were already underway. She recalled that she and a committee of women had gone to the chamber of commerce, city council meetings, and Simmons National Bank to discuss African Americans' discriminatory treatment. She also recalled, "We could go to Woolworth's and other places to trade, but we couldn't eat at the lunch counters. The rest rooms were segregated, the water fountains were segregated. We went to Walgreens, to J. C. Penney." "We asked them

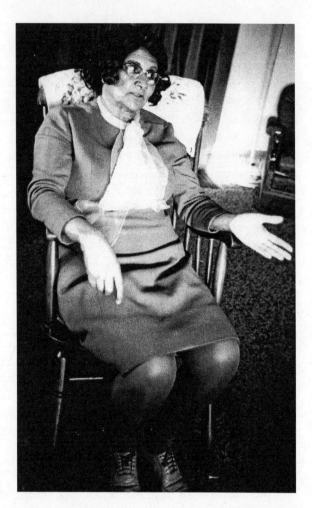

Mrs. O. G. Dawson
(Ethel B.), Pine
Bluff, 1976. *Image
courtesy of the Arts
& Sciences Center for
Southeast Arkansas.*

why we couldn't open up these places without these students coming in
here, because we've been living here all our lives. Why wait until we're under
pressure? They talked nicely, but they did nothing." When local businesses
failed to comply, SNCC members started sitting in at the Woolworth's
lunch counter. Dawson later met with SNCC members to ascertain how
they could assist them while simultaneously continuing to encourage white
businessmen to make their facilities accessible to African Americans without
external influence. Dawson and others supported SNCC members' activism
by raising funds from local churches and by providing them with food and
clothing during sit-ins and posting their bail when they were arrested.[56]

Dawson continued to work for educational and political opportunities for African Americans. In 1965, she unsuccessfully sought a seat on the Pine Bluff school board.[57] She additionally helped campaign for other African Americans who ran for political office. In 1965, Dawson campaigned for Florence Clay, a Black woman from Helena, when she ran to be a US representative for Arkansas's first congressional district. She subsequently lost to the incumbent, E. C. Gathings, who remained in office from 1939 to 1969.[58]

In her later years, Dawson continued to work with the Jefferson County Voters Association and the League of Women Voters by encouraging rural people to register to vote. She also remained an active NAACP member. Dawson recognized that, despite the passage of critical civil rights legislation, deeply entrenched local racism demanded that she and others keep impressing the importance of voting upon African Americans and continue to strive to get Blacks hired at the Jefferson County Court House.[59] The trajectory of her activism was buttressed by her concerns about improving lives for rural African Americans not only in Jefferson County, but throughout the state. Her humble beginnings on a farm in Lincoln County in the early twentieth century gave her a particularly fine-tuned understanding of the difficulties African Americans endured in rural communities. Utilizing her connections to the NCC, the AACES, and local and state organizations, Dawson helped to reshape the parameters of rural Arkansas in ways that created more opportunities and access for African Americans. She continued to do so until her death in 1984. These cross-organizational collaborations additionally informed the ongoing labors of Black home demonstration agents who created a national entity to address the problems they all faced in southern agrarian communities.

– 11 –

The National Negro Home Demonstration Agents' Association

MARGUERITE P. WILLIAMS'S work in the El Dorado Black community was intense. Williams was the second vice president of the National Negro Home Demonstration Agents' Association, but she also was deeply involved in many local African American organizations, like most professional and educated Black women in the state.[1] Williams was not only an AACW member, she was corresponding secretary and the president of El Dorado's Fairview Social and Art Club.[2] In 1967, she became an extension specialist and traveled throughout the state, training people to judge home economics exhibits at county fairs. Williams remained in this position until she retired in 1975, and her work provides evidence of the ongoing needs in rural African American communities well into the 1970s. The dire conditions in which they remained plagued Black home demonstration agents, as did the discrimination they faced from the extension service. These concerns were reflected in the founding of an organization to serve as an information clearinghouse for Black home demonstration agents throughout the South.[3]

Although African Americans worked for the AACES, they were not welcome in the all-white state council of home demonstration agents. Nor were they permitted to become members of the all-white National Home Demonstration Agents' Association (NHDAA), established in 1933.[4] Unfortunately, Black home demonstration agents lacked the resources to form a national organization until much later. In 1957, twenty-four years after the NHDAA was founded, Black women met in Jackson, Mississippi, and organized the National Negro Home Demonstration Agents' Association (NNHDAA).[5]

Arkansas Black home demonstration agents assumed prominent leadership positions in the NNHDAA. Women from El Dorado, Forrest City, Texarkana, and Lake Village were among its founders and first elected officials. Marguerite P. Williams, its second vice president, was born in Pine Bluff in 1910 and had worked for the Arkansas Extension Service since 1935. In 1946, Williams became vice president of the Union County Negro Extension Agents' Association.[6] During that same year, Williams also worked with local women who were part of a five-year home beautification program which resulted in a "model colored farming community" when their homes were moved to make way for the construction of an ammonia plant. The women met with Williams to create a home improvement plan for their community that embraced the agricultural extension service's ethic of rural self-sufficiency. The plan, which was submitted to the USDA by AACES, consisted of "a well-rounded food production program," which included year-round gardens, poultry flocks, milk cows, and home orchards." Williams was in charge of Black home demonstration work in Union County from 1936 to 1958.[7]

In 1958, the NNHDAA held its first annual meeting at Arkansas AM&N College. Twenty-five of the fifty-six home demonstration agents attending the gathering were from Arkansas.[8] Because they were subject to the control of white officials who ran the extension service, Black agents in the South had to be very careful about advancing any political positions or engaging individuals or organizations that challenged white supremacy. This was particularly true in Arkansas, where a tense racial atmosphere prevailed after the desegregation of Little Rock's Central High School in 1957. Black women implicitly tied their concerns to the overarching theme of farm and home improvement by encouraging agents to "readjust their teaching methods to changing conditions as a means of more effectively helping farm people achieve a higher standard of living."[9] Indeed, the theme of the meeting, "Readjusting for Better Living," encompassed their understanding of the changes occurring throughout Arkansas and the nation.[10] When the NNHDAA held its second meeting in Jackson, Mississippi, in October 1959, Ouachita County agent Clothilde Shivers was elected its third vice president; Saint Francis County's Carreather Feaster Banks was elected reporter; and Iola Rhone from Texarkana was re-elected as the organization's parliamentarian.[11]

Integrating the extension service was among Black home demonstration agents' primary concerns during the late 1950s and 1960s. The Title VI section of the 1964 Civil Rights Act prohibited discrimination based on race, color, religion, or national origin and denied federal funds to organizations that failed to integrate. Home demonstration clubs throughout Arkansas grappled with how they would comply with the act.[12]

Accordingly, in 1965 US secretary of agriculture Orville Freeman encouraged the USDA to enact polices to end discrimination: "The right of all of our citizens to participate with equal opportunity in both the administration and benefits of all programs of this department is not only legally required but morally right."[13] While it was not a federal agency, the NNHDAA complied with the directive and held its last annual conference in Hot Springs in 1965. It was subsequently absorbed into the NHDAA.[14] Although this was a seemingly progressive move, it is entirely plausible that many Black home demonstration agents feared that their leadership, skills, and voices might not be respected and honored and that the larger organization might not fully address the needs of rural African Americans.[15]

Because the extension service received federal dollars, the impact of the Civil Rights Act also gained traction among home demonstration agents in Arkansas. In 1965, in compliance with Title VI's requirement to eradicate discrimination, the Arkansas Council of Home Demonstration Clubs merged with the SCHDC. Throughout the state, Black and white county councils increasingly combined to form a single organization to serve the needs of all rural citizens. In 1966, the newly integrated state body became the Arkansas Extension Homemakers Council (AEHC) in order to align itself with the National Extension Homemakers Council (NEHC), which had changed its name from the National Home Demonstration Council in 1963.[16]

Despite the victories of the civil rights movement and the end of legal segregation in home demonstration clubs at the state and local levels, most rural Blacks in Arkansas were still poor and politically marginalized throughout the 1960s. Black extension service agents and the people they served still received less financial support and training than their white counterparts. Salaries remained unequal as well. In 1965, the Union County quorum court allocated $3,250 for Black county farm and home agents, in contrast to the $8,550 set aside for their white colleagues.[17] Even as late as 1966, the white home agent in Hope was paid $1,500 compared to the Black agent's salary of $1,100.[18]

The extent to which Black agents were fully integrated into the Arkansas extension service is questionable. The 1964 Civil Rights Act may have legally eliminated discrimination, but "equally" generally came at an agonizingly slow pace for African American agents. "Negro" agents became "associates," an insulting designation that conveyed their subordination to white agents, despite the fact that many of the Black agents had been employed by the extension service for decades.[19] Some were demoted, and others quite likely thought the end of segregation weakened the effectiveness of their services in predominantly African American communities, as some Black agents lost influence when white officials slowed the pace of compliance with federal law. African American agents were frequently absorbed into the extension service without supervisory duties, which negatively impacted the networks they had cultivated in rural communities. They also faced whites' resentment when they were promoted.[20]

The experiences of home demonstration agent LaVerne Williams Feaster exemplified these concerns. Born in 1926, Feaster grew up on Big Dixie Plantation in Cotton Plant in Woodruff County.[21] Educated at the private, Presbyterian-operated Arkadelphia Cotton Plant Academy, a coeducational boarding school founded in the 1880s, Feaster took home economics courses and graduated from the institution in 1945.[22] She attended Swift Presbyterian Junior College in Rogersville, Tennessee, a predominantly Black institution that existed from 1883 until 1955 and provided high school and normal school (teacher education) training.[23] Feaster graduated in 1949 from Tennessee State University in Nashville and later earned a master's degree in education at the University of Arkansas. She spent thirteen years teaching in high schools in Augusta and Dermott. In 1961, Feaster became an "Assistant Home Demonstration Agent for Negro Work" in Clark County. Some questioned her employment in the county. Feaster said that her supervisor, Marguerite P. Williams, was asked, "Who is this LaVerne Feaster who has been hired for the job in Arkadelphia? I understand she has been a teacher . . . that [Clark County] is one of the best counties in the state. She should be starting in a less desirable county." Williams's response to Feaster was "Don't worry, they are just frustrated."[24]

As a harbinger of the changes already underway, in 1963 the designation *for Negro Work* was dropped from Feaster's title, but she remembered well the difficulties associated with the integration of the extension service. According to her, "integration meant blacks' extension becoming a part of the 'white' extension program."[25] The Black extension office in Clark County closed in 1966, when Feaster, the Black assistant county agent, and the secretary moved to the county courthouse with white agents, an experience that Feaster described as "a shock for all of us, including the clients."[26]

To add insult to injury, white agents questioned the qualifications of Black agents who had been promoted. According to Feaster, some whites felt that Black agents had only been promoted to fulfill affirmative action quotas.[27] When asked about desegregation within the extension service, former Saint Francis County agent Carreather Banks Perry simply said, "It was hell!"[28]

Other Black home demonstration agents who had long careers with the extension service seemed to have a more positive experience. Born in 1922 in Wabbaseka (Jefferson County) to parents who had been born in Georgia, Lillie Mae Banks Doss received a degree in home economics from Philander Smith College and did some graduate work at Prairie View State College, Cornell University, Colorado State University, and the University of Arkansas. She was an educator before she became an assistant home demonstration agent in Nevada County in 1945. In 1966, she became the Union County associate extension home economist and the Pulaski County extension home economics agent. Like most female extension service agents, Doss was a member of multiple organizations including the El Dorado-based Sunshine Charity Club, which was affiliated with both the AACW and NACW.[29] Long recognized for her service to the community, particularly in providing clothing and combatting food and nutrition insecurity among low-income families, in 1975 Doss received the NEHC distinguished service award at the AEHC annual meeting at Henderson State University in Arkadelphia.[30] She continued to labor on behalf of the impoverished in Arkansas until her death in 1997.[31]

Changes occurred slowly, but some Black agents eventually found themselves positioned well enough in the extension service to serve all Arkansans. But rural Black homemakers required a bit more convincing. In Cross County in 1965, for instance, the Black home demonstration council continued to hold "Arkansas Home Demonstration Club Week" programs at Bethel African Methodist Episcopal Church.[32] LaVerne Feaster recalled that it "took many one on one contacts to convince [Black] families that they, too, were welcome at extension programs announced by people they did not know and held in places that had been off limits to them."[33] After being appointed the first Black state agent for 4-H programs in 1971, Feaster was again promoted to district home economist for Arkansas's northeast district. She held this position until she retired in 1981.[34] LaVerne Williams Feaster died in May 2013.[35]

Although the AACES was officially integrated by the 1970s, only about 1.8 percent of homemaker or home demonstration clubs and 20 out of 1,128 4-H clubs were integrated in actual practice. Indeed, because of deeply entrenched racism and local resistance to integration, African American women were not particularly enthusiastic about venturing into

unwelcoming, formerly all-white spaces. When LaVerne Feaster asked
Black farm women why they did not attend an extension program in Clark
County, one of them answered, "I got that letter about a meeting at the
First Methodist Church's Fellowship Hall." Despite the letter and a radio
announcement saying that the meeting was "open to all regardless of race,
color or national origin," the woman understood all too well the dangers of
entering a space that had formerly been off limits to her. She concluded, "I
knew that it did not mean me."[36]

Black women continued to struggle to gain access to and navigate
Arkansas home demonstration clubs and extension service activities in the
years following integration and the NNHDAA's dissolution. But the number of Black women members decreased precipitously, quite likely because
they were unwelcome in newly organized clubs. Furthermore, Black women
may have seen less use for home demonstration clubs as Arkansas agriculture became increasingly mechanized and opportunities for agricultural
employment eroded. But they were spaces in which Black women exercised
autonomy and developed leadership skills that allowed them to uplift their
families and their rural communities. This was certainly the case for Phillips
County farmer Annie Zachary Pike, whose connections to the AACES
provide the final example of how rural Black women used the resources
available to them to implement change African American communities,
and the focus of this book's final chapter.

— 12 —

Annie Zachary Pike:
Arkansas Homemaker, Farmer,
and Politician

IN 1967, AFTER REPUBLICAN Winthrop Rockefeller was elected governor of Arkansas, he appointed farmer Annie Zachary Pike—more commonly known as "Ms. Annie"—to serve on the state welfare board. The first African American to be appointed to any state board in the twentieth century, Ms. Annie recalled all of the media attention surrounding her and said that she was a "country lady, who was used to chickens and hogs and being out in the fields with the tenants, who had suddenly become a celebrity."[1] In the tumultuous years of the 1960s, southern governors lived in fear of the civil unrest that had occurred in other parts of the country and consequently took what they deemed necessary precautions to prevent similar events' occurring locally. Governor Rockefeller was also clearly concerned about the reaction when he appointed Ms. Annie to the Arkansas welfare board. When she arrived at the state capitol for her first meeting, the building was lined with state troopers and local officials. Ms. Annie remembered:

> They were just afraid that something was going to break out, that here comes this black woman in here. I didn't have a body guard. I thought, I'm going to walk up those steps and I'm going into this building alone and I'm going to show them, and if I ever need to show them, it's now. I took a cab to the building and I walked in with my head in the air.[2]

Annie Ruth Davidson was born in 1931 to farmers Cedel and Carrie Davidson in Big Creek, in the predominantly African American Phillips County, which lies in the southeastern part of the state known as the Arkansas Delta. Ms. Annie's father was born in Clay County, Mississippi, in 1892; her mother Carrie Washington Davidson was born in 1894 in Arkansas. Cedel Davidson was quite likely among the 200,000 African Americans who migrated to Arkansas from throughout the South during the late nineteenth and early twentieth centuries, searching for "cheap land, high wages, and state authorities' suppression of Ku Klux Klan violence during Reconstruction."[3]

A largely agricultural region, Phillips County had been established by the Arkansas territorial legislature in May 1820, before Arkansas gained statehood in 1836, and is located near the Saint Francis River, which empties into the Mississippi River.[4] Well into the twentieth century, African American residents of Phillips County, most of whom were agrarian laborers, lived with the memory of the 1919 Elaine massacre, which came to a head after Black farmers dared to organize to protest white landowners' unjust treatment and poverty wages. Hundreds of African Americans were murdered as a result of this act of Black economic assertiveness. Twelve Black men were convicted for "inciting a riot," although the courts later overturned their convictions.[5] Ms. Annie's parents would have certainly heard about the atrocity as memories of it reverberated in Black communities throughout Arkansas.

Ms. Annie vividly remembered the challenges and rewards of living and working on a farm.[6] She recalled that her mother, who was also a homemaker, produced everything the family needed to survive. Her father was known as one of the best blade sharpeners in Phillips County; according to Ms. Annie, people came from miles around just to have their blades sharpened by Cedel Davidson. Her father expected Annie and her siblings to be intimately involved in the business of farm life. Both of her parents stressed the importance of self-sufficiency and more importantly, education, particularly because African Americans were routinely denied equal educational access in rural Arkansas and throughout the South.[7]

Ms. Annie's formal education began at Trenton Elementary School. She went on to attend the Consolidated White River Academy (CWRA), a coeducational boarding school in Brinkley (Monroe County) founded in 1893 by local Black Baptists who wanted their children to attend a school that provided a Christian education.[8] While at CWRA, Ms. Annie was elected class secretary and president, played baseball and basketball, and was a glee club member. Her parents paid her tuition to attend the school, but CWRA students also helped cover their expenses by singing at venues around Arkansas. Ms. Annie graduated from CWRA in 1948, before the institution closed in 1950 due to a lack of funds.[9] Ms. Annie later earned a nursing degree from the Homer G. Phillips Hospital School of Nursing in St. Louis, Missouri. The hospital was founded in 1937 and named for a prominent African American lawyer. Phillips Hospital served over 70,000 local Blacks and provided medical training for doctors, nurses, and technicians of color until it closed in 1979.[10]

In 1952, Ms. Annie married Grover Cleveland Zachary, an African American plantation owner who had been born in Marvell in 1886. "Mr. Cleve," as he was known, owned and farmed 1,254 acres with twenty-seven tenants.[11] Mr. Cleve's continued farming was a major coup in 1950s Arkansas, as the number of Delta farms declined over 88 percent between 1945 and 1992. The rate of decline was even higher for African Americans, who were increasingly pushed out of farming by large and prominent landowners and could not rely upon the Farmers Home Administration to bail them out when they were overextended. The Zacharys managed to retain their land, but as farming became increasingly diversified and mechanized in the 1950s and 1960s, they rented out their land for commercial farming. (Ms. Annie continues to rent the land today, with assistance from a Jonesboro-based farm bureau agent.)[12] In 1959, the Zacharys' successful farming led to their being crowned the champions of the Arkansas "Plant to Prosper" competition in the landowner division.[13]

Unfortunately, Mr. Cleve suffered a stroke in 1962 and was partially paralyzed as a result. Ms. Annie assumed control over their farming operation. Like many rural women who ran farms when their husbands became ill or died, Ms. Annie did not think of herself as a feminist or a women's rights advocate when she became a farmer, which was a term traditionally used to define male rural landowners. She simply had done what was necessary to save the family farm. Furthermore, while dominant gender ideals may have informed farm life and work, the reality was quite different. Women's labor was an important component of the economic function of farm life and one from which women obtained significant power.[14]

Ms. Annie, who likely would have vehemently rejected being called a "farm wife," recalled well the challenges, stereotypes, and struggles she encountered as a farmer due to her gender, age, and race:

> When I first started, no one had ever heard of women's lib. I've been liberated all the time. . . . This responsibility came to me by no choice of my own. It fell on my shoulders and I have to take responsibility of a farm and when I took it, we had twenty-seven tenants, my son was ten years old, my husband was a lot older than

I, and right there I have a disadvantage; nobody believed in me
because I was so young and most of the tenants were old enough
to be my parents and some my grandparents. See, this was an old
established farm, and so we had families that had reared families. It
was a unique situation, and I had come in as an outsider.[15]

Ms. Annie, then, was the manager of a diversified farm and a nurse, in
addition to raising a small child. It was a challenging period, about which
she commented, "I shouldn't want to do over again."[16] Her role as a farm
wife and homemaker had been complicated by her family's dynamics and
economic needs. Ms. Annie's situation was typical of a "strange paradox," as
historian William Chafe has called it, that was most evident among women
in the post–World War II years. Gender roles were in flux when she became
the farm manager, yet Ms. Annie was still considered the "caretaker of home
and nurturer," and Mr. Cleve was still considered the breadwinning head
of the family.[17]

Like many farm women, Ms. Annie couched her experiences in terms
that demonstrated a clear sense of her own agency and autonomy. Nancy
Gray Osterud has maintained that "women who feel little control over
events recalled that things 'happened' to them, while women who had a
sense of agency referred to events as things they chose."[18] While Ms. Annie
may have begun her journey as a farmer to whom things happened, she
soon cultivated the resources and skills she needed to assert her authority
and agency as a farm manager.

Because she was a female farmer, and a relatively young one at that, Ms.
Annie worked diligently to get tractor drivers to respect her by assuming
an active role in the production work of the farm as it increasingly mechanized. Indeed, it is noteworthy that the Zacharys even owned tractors, since
southern Black farmers often lacked the resources to own land, let alone to
purchase mechanical devices. Key to Ms. Annie's success as a farm manager
was her willingness to adopt new technology and learn innovative techniques in order to maintain the farm's economic viability.[19] In order to learn
the skills necessary to operate the farm, Ms. Annie also relied on Phillips
County's Black agricultural extension service agents. They helped her test
soil samples from the farm for fertility. Soil science's roots lay in European
agricultural chemistry and became a major concern for American farmers
and agriculturalists in the mid-nineteenth century. The USDA Bureau of
Soils used soil typology to help farmers like Ms. Annie to improve and
determine the best use for their land. She used her close relationship with

the AACES to learn about fertilizers from USDA publications, also known as circulars, which she believed helped her to "become a good manager and to prove [herself] as a woman."[20] Ms. Annie also convinced Mr. Cleve, who obstinately clung to what she described as "old style farming," to embrace her newfound agricultural knowledge.

Under the guidance of Black Phillips County home demonstration agent Gertrude Banks LeMay, whom Ms. Annie described as her "guiding light," she developed the confidence and the agricultural knowledge she needed to convince the tractor drivers, in a process that took six months, to respect her skill and intelligence and to listen to her plans for the farm. Her gamble paid off and the Zachary farm thrived as a result.[21]

Because the Zacharys engaged in diversified farming and grew soybeans, oat, wheat, milo, and, chiefly, cotton on their farm, Ms. Annie not only had to learn about crop production, she also had to manage the farm's business, which meant negotiating and navigating with white cotton gin owners and bankers.[22]

Despite voluminous scholarship about Black migration to northern, western, and southern urban spaces throughout the twentieth century, relatively little has been written about the many, if not most, African Americans who remained in the rural Jim Crow South and in some cases actually thrived. According to rural women's historian Melissa Walker, key to all of this was a keen understanding of how "conditions of rural life gave unique shape to race relations in the countryside."[23] While racism and Jim Crow certainly existed, racial boundaries were far more fluid in rural spaces and customs were highly localized. This certainly was the case in rural Phillips County, where the population was and remains predominantly African American. Ms. Annie, however, recalled the difficulties she encountered when she went to local cotton sheds and challenged bankers who often cheated African Americans with little fear of legal recourse:

> They had never had a black woman to ask for their cotton. I started getting out asking for cotton samples and checking up on bales. I started going to the bank confronting the bankers and checking on mistakes and such things, and they were looking at me like, "Well, who are you and what do you want?"[24]

Undaunted, Ms. Annie believed in her own sense of agency and understood that she was quite likely protected by her status as the wife of an independent landowner. But she also knew it was potentially dangerous to be an assertive Black woman in an environment that demanded racial

Annie R.
Zachary, inter-
viewed and pho-
tographed by Ra
Hellman, 1976.
*Image courtesy
of the Arts &
Sciences Center
for Southeast
Arkansas.*

and gender subordination. Ms. Annie then drew upon the lessons she had
learned from her family about maintaining her dignity in her dealings with
southern whites. She was indeed "very proud that my parents taught me
patience and perseverance." Yet Ms. Annie was forthright about the racism
and sexism she encountered as a farmer:

> I definitely known that prejudice exists, because the road that I've
> traveled has been dark and lonely, and a lot of it, I feel, is because
> I'm a woman and sometimes people feel that you don't know
> things and that you're unprotected . . . that you're a lame duck.
> When I felt, though, that I was going to be cheated, I just had to
> stand up and say no.[25]

Along with the tenacity that made Ms. Annie a successful farmer was
her long history of community activism in Phillips County. She was "always
interested in a better way of life for my people."[26] Like many Black farm

women, Ms. Annie was member of the segregated the SCHDC. In 1963, she was elected vice president of the organization at its twenty-seventh annual meeting in Little Rock (she later served two terms as president).[27] In 1965, Ms. Annie was selected home demonstration clubwoman of the year.[28]

Ms. Annie led the local homemaker's club and the segregated Phillips County 4-H club. 4-H clubs developed, in part, out of a desire to provide "practical education in agriculture, manual arts, and homemaking and to create future generations of rural leaders."[29] At the 1963 Phillips County Fair, Ms. Annie co-chaired the "Colored Committees," the women's division, the 4-H exhibits, and was vice president of the Phillips County 4-H Council.[30] In 1965, she was honored by the 4-H for outstanding service to the organization.[31] She was also an active Arkansas Farm Bureau Federation member.

Ms. Annie was naturally inclined to become involved in anything, she said, that would "uplift or make a better way to learn the essentials of living" for rural Blacks.[32] From 1964 to 1965, she was a member of the Phillips County Development Council and its Family Living Committee. She and other Black women also worked with the white Phillips County Home Demonstration Council as they discussed compliance with the 1964 Civil Rights Act and planned to integrate their activities in 1966.[33]

Before the council's last meeting, Ms. Annie, Lula Farley, and Ietta Horton learned at the SCHDC annual meeting in Pine Bluff that they were to become the first African Americans delegates to attend the predominantly white National Home Demonstration Council's annual meeting.[34] The national organization was renamed the National Extension Homemakers Council at its twenty-seventh annual convention in Little Rock, for which Governor Orval Faubus was the keynote speaker; this was also the first time the meeting had ever been held in Arkansas.[35] Ms. Annie recalled that Little Rock was so crowded that it was difficult to find parking. And because the restaurants were still segregated, at lunchtime Black women had to go to Ninth Street, the main thoroughfare in Little Rock's African American community, in order to find a meal.[36] In 1964, SCHDC officers including song leader Ietta Horton, president Lula Mae Farley, vice president Annie Zachary, secretary Juanita Shelby, and treasurer Lula Johnson, and ASHDC officers met with white state home demonstration agent Hazel Jordon, who informed them that they had to integrate their organizations.[37] But according to one Black home demonstration agent, ". . . Arkansas was moving slowly. Mixing homemakers together in masses . . . was just too bold a move in 1965."[38]

When the AEHC held its first "integrated" meeting in 1966, the only

Black woman on the program was Ietta Horton, who was responsible for "Group Singing" and was the "Recreation" committee chairperson.[39] No Black women were elected officers, but Ms. Annie was selected the "Family Life, Education and Youth Committee" chairperson, an occupation she said was reserved for Black women. When she attended her first AEHC meeting in 1968, where she also led the group in singing the national anthem, she was not provided with any information about the committee.[40] Although Ms. Annie offered a class on "Building a Family Life Ed[ucation] Program," her experience at the meeting angered her, as Black women were blatantly marginalized.[41]

Ms. Annie was also a rural political activist at a time when most agrarian Blacks were deeply impoverished, barely educated, and lacked political access. In 1960, Phillips County, the largest in the Arkansas Delta, possessed an African American population of 25,308 (57.5 percent) and 18,222 whites (42.2 percent). However, less than one-fourth of registered voters were African American. Additionally, 65 percent of the Black population had less than a sixth-grade education, compared to 14 percent for whites. Three percent of African Americans had a high school diploma compared to 28 percent of whites. And African Americans earned an annual median income of $616; 1,923 Black households earned less than $1,000 in 1960 and only 147 earned more than $5,000. Annie and Cleve Zachary certainly fit comfortably into this latter category.[42]

In the 1960s, Ms. Annie became deeply involved in Republican Party politics. Throughout the South, whites fled the Democratic Party and its liberal civil rights platform for the increasingly conservative Republican Party. In Arkansas however, African Americans and progressive Democrats increasingly coalesced around changes promoted by New York millionaire and Republican Winthrop Rockefeller. When Ms. Annie recounted her experience with the Arkansas Republican Party, she made it abundantly clear that she was a "Rockefeller Republican," meaning she considered Rockefeller's reform politics more progressive and inclusive than the Democratic Party. Ms. Annie believed that, at least in the South at that time, the Democratic Party of the early 1960s still excluded African Americans, making it more similar to the contemporary version of the Republican Party which, in her estimation, bears little resemblance to the "Party of Lincoln."[43]

Born in New York in 1912, Rockefeller was a grandson of Standard Oil Company founder John D. Rockefeller. "Win," as he was more commonly known, moved to Arkansas in 1953 and established Winrock Enterprises and Farms on a 927-acre tract on Petit Jean Mountain, just outside Morrilton in

Conway County. Ms. Annie recalled that when Rockefeller, a racial moderate and National Urban League trustee who had long taken an interest in
the problems of African American communities, was considering running
for governor of Arkansas, he was appalled by the state's one-party political
system. He sent scouts to Phillips County to locate people who had "some
grit" to help him establish a two-party system in the state that would be
more responsive to the demands of the electorate. In 1964 Rockefeller ran
against Democratic incumbent Orval Faubus, whose political grasp on the
state seemed unassailable when he received 56 percent of Arkansas's white
voted. At the time, Ms. Annie was not terribly interested in politics; she
recalled, "All we knew was to pay poll taxes and you could vote, or someone
would vote for you." It was after someone contacted her and showed her the
advantages of a two-party state that Ms. Annie, with Mr. Cleve's support,
became the Phillips County Republican Party coordinator and collected
signatures for a petition to change the fate of politics in Arkansas. This
required her to travel door to door, which she often did with Mr. Cleve
in tow, to inform African Americans of Rockefeller's progressive plans to
improve Arkansas, a state which ranked only second to Mississippi in poverty levels, and to integrate Blacks into the state's politics in ways that had
not been achieved since Reconstruction.[44]

Ms. Annie emphasized Rockefeller's commitment to reform the state's
cruel penitentiary system and to investigate the revenue system. Although
Arkansas's convict lease system had been abolished in 1913, convicts at the
Tucker and Cummins prison farms in Jefferson and Lincoln Counties continued, during the 1960s, to produce their own food and sell the surplus, an
arrangement from which the state profited. Prison officials utilized armed
prisoners as guards. They maintained order in the prison with corporal
punishment, often employing the "Tucker telephone," a battery-powered
electrocution device used to torture prisoners.[45] Rockefeller's prison reform
would dramatically impact the lives of African Americans, who were subject
to disproportionately high rates of incarceration. After talking with Black
residents of Phillips County and leaving them to wrestle with the implications of this monumental political change, Ms. Annie would return to their
homes and collect their signatures for her petition.[46]

Ms. Annie supported Winthrop Rockefeller when he ran for governor in 1966, and African American women's organizations also endorsed
his campaign. The AACW, of which Ms. Annie was a member (she was
named "Queen of Women's Federated Clubs" in 1969), threw their weight
behind him, as they saw him as the candidate with the most progressive

and inclusive civil rights platform. When the AACW executive board met in October 1966, at the segregated Phyllis Wheatley YWCA in Little Rock, they stated their reasons for supporting Rockefeller:

> We the Arkansas Association of Colored Women's Clubs, Inc. appreciate your interest and broad vision in the cause of equality of education, economics, industry, and all facets of human progress and development, and your desire to be governor to serve all of the people in the areas of state activities. We as an organization committed ourselves to publicly endorse your candidacy for governor of the state of Arkansas, and we pledge to cast our votes for you and to use our influence to get other to do the same.[47]

Promising an "Era of Excellence," Rockefeller in 1967 was elected Arkansas' first Republican governor since Reconstruction in 1872. He won by a count of 306,324 to 257,203 votes (54.4 percent to 45.6 percent).[48] Eighty percent of Black Arkansans voted for Rockefeller.[49] Ms. Annie was rewarded for her loyalty by being appointed to the Arkansas Welfare Board. She replaced Max Coger of Danville. According to a newspaper report, Ms. Annie was "very elated over the appointment."[50] In 1968, the year he won reelection, Rockefeller was also the only Southern governor to memorialize Reverend Dr. Martin Luther King Jr. when he sang "We Shall Overcome" while holding hands with African American leaders on the capitol steps three days after King's assassination.[51] Rockefeller appointed an unprecedented number of Black Arkansans to state boards. The following year his reelection, he named Council on Community Affairs leader Ozell Sutton to serve on the Arkansas Human Resources Council and appointed William "Sonny" Walker as the South's only African American state head of the Office of Economic Opportunity (OEO), an agency of the War on Poverty. Ms. Annie also served on the OEO.[52] Rockefeller died of pancreatic cancer in 1973. He was sixty years old.[53]

Before Ms. Annie was appointed to the welfare board, it had consisted of nine "dyed in the wool" Democrats who had used their position to secure jobs and appointments for their families and friends. They were unaccustomed to interacting with a powerful Black woman. Ms. Annie used her position on the welfare board to address food insecurity and inadequate housing among Arkansas's poor. The impact of her activism was felt even in Marvell. Ms. Annie said she was never directly threatened while she served on the board and did not have to change her home phone number. In fact, when she returned home from her first meeting she was met by a pile of

letters and phone calls from local businessmen, most of whom she did not
know, to express how proud they were of her, because it was the first time
Marvell, despite its renown for cotton production, had even been "put on
the map."[54] Suddenly, Ms. Annie found herself attending seemingly endless
meetings with people who wanted to meet "the black lady who challenged
the system, who cared enough about the poor, the needy, and the indigent
to go to bat for them."[55]

In the years she spent on the Arkansas Welfare Board, Ms. Annie made
very important connections to powerful people, even as she aggressively
advocated for the poor and the marginalized. Never one to be silent in the
face of wrongdoing, she also fiercely challenged her colleagues' political
malfeasance. As she recalled, she "brought up some very hard issues . . . that
caused people to lose their jobs."[56] In 1967, Ms. Annie charged former
welfare commissioner A. J. Moss with receiving $3,000 from the Arkansas
Association of Public Welfare Workers while he served on the state welfare
board. Moss denied the charges and claimed it was an attempt to discredit
him, because he had been appointed by former Democratic governor Orval
Faubus.[57] But Ms. Annie urged the then current welfare commissioner,
Len Blaylock, to investigate. She observed that Moss's son-in-law, John H.
Keech, had also been on the Welfare Department's payroll from September
1966 to April 1967, but had "never performed any duties for the department
and was enrolled at the University of Iowa," adding that he had "never been
authorized to take an educational leave from the educational leave committee." Ms. Annie asked the attorney general's office to recover any monies
that had been paid to Keech and additionally called for a "full-scale investigation of the Arkansas Merit System" and asked Commissioner Blaylock to
place its director in a "position he is qualified for." Fine-tuning her political
acumen and dedicated to the welfare board's goal to help Arkansans in
need, Ms. Annie asked Commissioner Blaylock to take action to remove
"the political cancer that has existed in the Welfare Department."[58] Blaylock
agreed, and cited Ms. Annie and three other members of the welfare board
as those who were trying to "do right"; he called for the other five members
to resign, because their sole objective was to "perpetuate the Faubus political machine."[59]

Ms. Annie fought to maintain the welfare board's integrity among
Arkansans. In 1972, when the board was accused of giving welfare recipients $40 to purchase textbooks, she demanded an investigation into the
charges. If they were true, she remarked, it was "an insult to all the members of the social services board" and she would seek a special meeting

with the state welfare commissioner. According to Len Blaylock, it was likely that the checks were timed to coincide with Democratic governor Dale Bumpers's reelection efforts. Such political subterfuge infuriated Ms. Annie, who claimed that if the allegations were true it was "bad timing to take advantage of welfare recipients." As it turned out, checks were not sent to every welfare recipient, only those who were "in dire need with children in school."[60] Because of Ms. Annie's dedication to "doing right," Arkansas governors Dale Bumpers, David Pryor, Frank White, and Bill Clinton reappointed her to subsequent terms on the welfare board until the 1980s.[61]

Ms. Annie's prominence within the Arkansas Republican Party led to other local and national appointments. In 1970, she was appointed to the Arkansas Economic Development Advisory Council by Governor Rockefeller, and asked to serve on the USDA Citizens Advisory Committee on Civil Rights by secretary of agriculture Clifford Hardin and the Arkansas Farmers Home Administration Advisory Committee.[62] Her service for the advisory committee was particularly important, because it was the primary USDA lending agency for economically depressed farmers. The US Commission on Civil Rights, an agency created by the 1957 Civil Rights Act, investigated discrimination in farm policies. The report *Equal Opportunity in Farm Programs: An Appraisal of Services Rendered by Agencies of the United States Department of Agriculture* revealed that Black farmers had no input on policy or representation on county agricultural committees and were routinely refused loans and benefits.[63]

African American farmers in particular bore the brunt of the FHA's discriminatory policies and by the 1960s were rapidly losing their land as a result. Across the United States, the number of farms owned by African Americans fell from 74,132 to 45,428 during this period, and Black tenants declined from 132,011 to 16,113. This was particularly true as tenants and sharecroppers, according to scholar Pete Daniel, "became superfluous, as tractors, combines, mechanical cotton harvesters, and herbicides reduced the demand for intensive hand labor." Daniel has argued that "in some cases, it seemed that the more promising a black farmer was the less chance he had of getting an FHA loan." While USDA leaders claimed compliance with equal-opportunity laws, they routinely denied benefits not only to African Americans, but also to Native Americans, Hispanics, and women.[64] But poor and Black farmers in Phillips County had a representative and staunch ally in Ms. Annie, who was deeply concerned about the twenty-seven Arkansas farmers who had received rejection letters from the FHA in 1970 and had few qualms about utilizing her relationship with Governor Rockefeller to file a claim to review the applications and discriminatory practices.[65] When she accepted her appointment to the USDA Citizens Advisory Committee, she wrote to Secretary of Agriculture Hardin, underscoring the USDA's role in civil rights activism:

> For many years now, I have followed with interest the programs and functions of the U.S. Department of Agriculture and fully realize the broad scope of activities you are involved in. Certainly, as we attempt to strengthen the effectiveness of such programs, it is essential that the civil and human rights of citizens be preserved and protected.[66]

Informed by her experiences with her husband, then in his nineties, Ms. Annie was concerned about Black sharecroppers, including those employed on Zachary land, reaching retirement age and losing their jobs as agriculture became increasingly mechanized. In 1968, she was appointed to the White House Conference on Aging.[67] Selected by the president of the United States, the Secretary of Health, Education, and Welfare, and Governor Rockefeller, Ms. Annie attended the 1971 White House Conference on Aging and became a member of the Technical Committee on Nutrition, which allowed her to address concerns about malnutrition and food insecurity among the elderly, a particularly rampant problem among African Americans in rural Arkansas and other southern states.[68] By 1972, approximately 334,603 Arkansans, regardless of race, were over age sixty. Ms. Annie found herself among the Arkansans who partook in the process of asking Congress to amend the 1965 Old Age Act. President Richard Nixon supported this initiative and appointed Dr. Arthur Flemming, a former Health, Education, and Welfare secretary, "Chairman on Aging," an appointment that came with cabinet-level status. Ms. Annie further appealed to Arkansans to make the policies established at the conference come to fruition in the state. "Many long hours of hard work had been involved in preparation of the conference and that many committees worked overtime in policy making towards a better life for older Americans."[69]

Back in Arkansas, Ms. Annie remained concerned about poor rural Blacks' unequal access to job opportunities and the natural environment. Accordingly, she served on the Phillips County Office of Equal Opportunity (OEO) board, was secretary of the Marvell OEO, and was a member of the Arkansas Wildlife Federation, a group of landowners dedicated to preserving the state's wildlife, in particular the Cache River restoration project. She was additionally on the Arkansas Council on Human Relations, which in 1974 merged with the Little Rock chapter of the Urban League.[70]

Always concerned about impoverished agrarian communities, Ms. Annie was vice president of Marvell's Rural Water Commission. In 1975, the commission met with the Delta Utilities Service Company, which operated under the auspices of the National Water Demonstration Project in Marianna, to demonstrate how small, poor, rural communities could overcome design, funding, construction, operating, and maintenance problems in water and sewage systems with grant money and loans. It was these resources that in 1970 allowed Ms. Annie and Mr. Cleve to develop and sell forty-seven acres of their land to the federal government to build the Zachary Subdivision, which allowed poor and working-class African Americans, particularly those who might otherwise have been displaced from tenant farming by mechanization, to own homes. This was an important cause for Ms. Annie, because she had become friends with many of the people employed on the Zachary farm and they all had raised their children together.[71] Governor Rockefeller was among the attendees at the opening ceremony for the Zachary Subdivision.[72]

Passionate about African Americans' increased political involvement, Ms. Annie was a delegate at the 1972 National Black Political Convention held in Gary, Indiana. A diverse group that included Black elected officials, civil rights activists, Black integrationists, Black nationalists, and those affiliated with the Black Power movement, the convention met for three days to galvanize African American political power for the 1972 election.[73]

Ms. Annie also attended the 1972 Republican National Convention in Miami, Florida, as co-chairperson of the platform subcommittee along with the African American Missouri Republican Party vice chairperson, Joan G. Crawford, and Governor Rockefeller.[74] At the convention, Ms. Annie served on the Committee on Resolutions (where she demanded increased attention to sickle cell anemia) and as co-chairman of the Subcommittee on Human Concerns. She also was part of the Arkansas Republican Party delegation, along with two other Black women, Marianna farm wife Willa Howard and Little Rock educator Mildred Tennyson, both of whom were alternates.[75] The Arkansas Republican Party delegation was touted as the "State GOP Delegation 'Most Representative' in History," as a result of new state party rules requiring proportional representation by minorities, women, and youth among its delegates. The Arkansas Republican Party executive committee specified that the delegates had to include nine men and nine women, fifteen whites and three African Americans, fifteen people who were thirty and older, and three who were between ages eighteen and thirty. The same criteria applied to alternates.[76]

All of the Arkansas delegation stayed at the Golden Strand Ocean Villa Resort. This was notable: Ms. Annie recalled that Governor Rockefeller and his wife Jeanette, with whom she became close friends, were adamant that she and Tennyson not be segregated away from the rest of the delegation.[77] While in Miami, Ms. Annie met with the National Federation of Republican Women, founded in 1938, which included first lady Pat Nixon, her daughters, and Judy Agnew, the wife of vice president Spiro Agnew. While there, they discussed the difficulties women faced when running for political office. Many of the women had earned their place among the Republican elite in their states through their connections to husbands or fathers.[78] Ms. Annie stood out from them for having earned her stripes through her own work. She said she had become a Republican simply because "they asked me," and that she had been involved in politics for eight years. In terms of Black Arkansans' political involvement, according to Ms. Annie, "most Blacks consider themselves members of the other party, so it took some persuasion as well as education to get my people to see the need for a two-party system and that they needed to look at both sides of the coin."[79] She praised the Arkansas Republican Party for getting more African Americans involved in politics and for motivating her to "go further and seek ways to make America a better place to live. It was a statewide effort, not an individual one, but as a result, we elected the first Republican governor in the state in 100 years."[80]

Ms. Annie further offered the following perspective about being a southern Black woman in the Republican Party, "I have definitely been a guinea pig in this race. But to make progress, someone has to make great sacrifices. I feel that it is time for women to realize this, come forward, and get involved in the affairs of our country." Ms. Annie additionally said that she wanted to sound the alarm for American women to "wake up, get up, and go to work. . . . Then you can say and feel that as result of your efforts, what seemed an impossible dream can be made a reality."[81] When the Arkansas Republican Party convened in Little Rock, Ms. Annie, who was solidly behind Richard Nixon's candidacy for president and was named temporary convention chairperson, said the GOP was "the party that gives a damn" and that the "GOP opened a new door in Arkansas politics."[82]

In 1972, Ms. Annie became the first African American to file and successfully run for an elected position in twentieth century Arkansas when she vied for a state senate seat.[83] Representing District 34, which included predominantly African American Lee and Phillips Counties, Ms. Annie ran unopposed in the primary. In the general election, she sought to unseat incumbent Democrat Joe Lee Anderson of Helena. She lost by 1,259 votes, having obtained 6711 votes from Phillips and Lee County to Anderson's 7,970.[84] For Ms. Annie, fewer votes did not represent a loss; she had demonstrated that both Black and white Arkansans would vote for a qualified candidate: "The tally sheet shows that I lost, but I know that I didn't. I won practically in every box in the county, and the support that I got from both races was just tremendous. At the polls I didn't win, but deep down in my heart I still feel that I was a winner because this was the first time that a black person had attempted to go on a ballot."[85] That same year, Anderson was indicted on three counts of filing false income tax returns when he underestimated his taxable income for 1965, 1966, and 1967.[86] He resigned from the Arkansas state senate in 1973.[87]

Ms. Annie's affiliation with the Republican Party continued into the mid-1970s. In 1973, she was elected vice president of the Arkansas Minority Republican Organization, whose goal was to bring more African Americans into the Republican Party.[88] She also continued to represent the interests of African Americans who resided in Arkansas's fourth congressional district on the Republican State Committee.[89] Ms. Annie's presence and influence in the Arkansas Republican Party during the 1970s inspired other Black women who assumed positions in local Republican women's clubs and committees and ran for elected offices around the state.[90] She especially impacted younger rural Black women. In 1971, for instance, Marlyn Kelley from Poplar Grove, an unincorporated community in Phillips County, competed as a contestant in the first Miss Black Arkansas Pageant as Miss Black Young Republican. Her platform was "the importance of youth becoming more involved in politics."[91]

Ms. Annie maintained her astonishing level of activism, in addition to running the family farm, after Mr. Cleve died and she remarried.[92] Tireless in her local and national service, in 1977, she was appointed to serve on the Arkansas Social Services board and the board of directors of the National Conference of Christians and Jews. Tracing its origins to 1924, the conference remained a relatively small organization until World War II. It defined itself a "tri-faith enterprise" of Protestants, Catholics, and Jews whose goodwill efforts emphasized social justice and brotherhood.[93] Ms. Annie was also appointed to a term on the Arkansas Tobacco Control Board by Governor Mike Huckabee from 1999 to 2001. Ms. Annie understood the complexities

Image of the author
and Annie Zachary
Pike, July 14, 2016.
*Author's personal
collection.*

of her public service as an extension of her responsibilities as a housewife and
as a second-time widow, "I try to be a homemaker, but there are so many
things I have do to, being a widow now and trying to serve my community."[94]

Education was one of Ms. Annie's longtime passions. She had enjoyed
the benefit of a boarding school education, had pursued a nursing degree,
and wanted rural people to know they could access educational opportunities. In 1979, she negotiated formal legislation for Arkansas to celebrate
the first National Teacher's Day. Ms. Annie was a longtime member of the
PTA and the all-Black Arkansas Teachers Association before it merged with
the Arkansas Education Association (AEA) in 1969. The Marvell Education
Association and the AEA recognized her in 1983 and 1985 for her many years
of volunteer service. She also received their Human Relations award.[95] In
2002, Phillips County Road 125, which ran through Zachary farmland, was
renamed Annie Zachary Pike Road, in honor of Ms. Annie and her two
late husbands.[96] Arkansas lieutenant governor Winthrop "Paul" Rockefeller,

"In Honor of Annie
Zachary Pike" road
sign, Road 125,
Phillips County,
Arkansas, July 14,
2016. *Photo courtesy
of the author.*

whom Ms. Annie has known since he was a youngster and who was the
only child of Winthrop Rockefeller and his first wife Barbara, was invited
to attend the road dedication.[97] In an August 2002 letter to Pleasant Grove
Missionary Baptist Church, Rockefeller noted that Ms. Annie, who was
being honored for her exemplary service, had been a Rockefeller family
friend for over forty years and that "every Arkansan . . . owes a tremendous
debt to her and those she has influenced in her lifetime."[98]

Ms. Annie still resides on the Zachary farm. Well into her eighties, Ms.
Annie recently has slowed down a bit. In 2013, she retired as the Mattie Mae
Woodrich Teachers' Day committee chair after thirty years and received a
citation for her service from the Arkansas House of Representatives. She
also retired from the Phillips County Teachers' Day Committee in 2015. Ms.
Annie remains involved in community activism and has long been an active
member of Pleasant Grove Baptist Church in Marvell. She still rents out her
land for cash crops. The Zachary Subdivision still exists as well, although it
is currently in disrepair.

Annie Davidson Zachary Pike's remarkable story is a rare chronicle of the life of a Black woman farmer whose local, state, and national activism influenced monumental change, not only in rural Arkansas but throughout the nation. Her story lays bare the multifarious ways we can better understand how Black women engaged social, political, and economic issues in the rural South by revisiting and rereading long extant sources that have typically been marginalized if not completely ignored. It forces us to reckon with the complexities of agrarian women's identities and the ways they have complemented each other rather than merely existing and acting in isolation. Ms. Annie has been simultaneously a rural Black woman, a homemaker, a farmer, and a politician. Operating within and beyond each of these roles, she is a force to be reckoned with by anyone who has encountered her.

Conclusion

THROUGHOUT THE TWENTIETH CENTURY, and despite blatant discrimination, African American women and their allies remained focused on improving Black farms, homes, and communities and continuously employed the philosophies of self-help and community uplift as integral parts of their activism and as a crucial means of race survival. Home demonstration agents understood the social and racial complexities of the environment in which they operated and the realities of the lives of the poor Blacks they encountered. Working under the auspices of the AACES and utilizing the network of Black women created by the SCHDC, they often subverted those circumstances to exact the most change possible for rural Blacks.

But Black demonstration agents never acted alone. The AACW included members from a statewide spectrum of experiences and backgrounds. They gathered at local club meetings and at annual conventions to teach and learn from one another and to conceptualize the best means to implement important changes in their own communities. At some moments, as in the case of the AACW member and farmer Annie Zachary Pike, they used their limited political access to secure state governmental attention to address the issues plaguing African American communities, such as the harsh conditions Black people endured in Arkansas's prison system. As their collective voices and activism resonated throughout rural Black communities around the state, women deployed their interpretation of what has been described as the "strategies of female cooperation, collaboration, and female empowerment and used these to build upon existing notions of mutuality and rural traditions that valued shared work."[1]

This collaborative work included Jeanes Supervising Industrial Teachers. They were subjected to the authority of local white school and governmental officials who framed their understanding of and requirements for Jeanes Supervisors' work and activism in terms that helped them retain a compliant and disempowered agricultural labor force. Yet Jeanes Supervisors operated stealthily within and often beyond power structures as they assessed the needs of the environments in which they lived and work. As they did so, they made decisions informed by their everyday interactions with rural Blacks to determine the educational, health, and societal resources necessary to help them elevate living standards within their communities. Black women also emphasized the importance of African Americans in Arkansas's agricultural past and future through organizations like the ARFBF's Negro Division. Ethel Dawson, furthermore, did so by utilizing biblical rhetoric to empower agrarian Blacks as Arkansas agriculture increasingly became mechanized.

Whether they were home demonstration agents, Jeanes Supervisors, members of the Arkansas Association of Colored Women or the Arkansas Farm Bureau Federation's Negro Division, or individual or collectivized farmers and agricultural laborers, Black women organized on their own terms around the issues that most dramatically impacted their communities. They responded to shifting local, national, and international historical contexts that continually informed the contours of their activism. As they did so however, they made it abundantly clear that they were all, in various ways, dedicated to ensuring that African Americans were able to elevate themselves to better living by their own bootstraps as they engaged in uplift activism in rural Arkansas.

NOTES

INTRODUCTION

1. Jones-Branch, *Crossing the Line*, 18–19, 62.
2. Grim, "From the Yazoo Mississippi Delta"; Harris, "'Well, I Just Generally Bes the President of Everything.'"
3. Devine, *On Behalf*, 3.
4. Grim, "From the Yazoo Mississippi Delta," 126.
5. Grim, "From the Yazoo Mississippi Delta," 127.
6. I have read my esteemed University of Arkansas colleague Jeannie Whayne's book *Delta Empire: Lee Wilson and the Transformation of Agriculture in the New South* many times. This, in addition to her other works on Arkansas history and the Delta in particular, provided me with much-needed scaffolding as I developed an analytical framework for my study.

CHAPTER I

1. "Little Rock to Host State PTA," *Chicago Defender*, December 7, 1940, 12; "PTA Workshop Has Large Attendance: Miss Upchurch New State President," *Arkansas State Press*, November 11, 1942, 1; "State PTA Congress in Session," *Hope Star*, March 3, 1967, 7.
2. "Ila Upchurch, Jeanes teacher," http://ahc.digital-ar.org/digital/collection/p16790 coll12/id/70 (accessed October 4, 2017).
3. "News from the Field," *Arkansas State Press*, April 10, 1942, 3.
4. "Nevada County Citizens Hold Mass Meeting" *Arkansas State Press*, September 21, 1945, 1; see "Prescott," *Arkansas State Press*, November 8, 1946, 3.
5. "Prescott," *Arkansas State Press*, February 1, 1946, 8.
6. "Prescott," *Arkansas State Press*, June 28, 1946, 6.
7. Williams et al., *Jeanes Story*, 175. See "Prescott," *Arkansas State Press*, November 8, 1946, 3; "Nevada School Board Fires Supervisors," *Hope Star*, December 31, 1949, 1.
8. hooks, *Yearning*, 382.
9. The sources vacillate between references to Jeanes Supervisors or Jeanes Teachers. I prefer to use "Jeanes Supervisors," because it was the original title and more accurately describes their work in rural schools.
10. Turner, *Women and Gender*, 106.
11. Olsson, *Agrarian Crossings*, 104.
12. Olsson, *Agrarian Crossings*, 104.
13. Woyshner, *National PTA*, 59.
14. Turner, *Women and Gender*, 107, 110.
15. Anderson, *Education*, 235.
16. King and Swartz, *Afrocentric Praxis*, 88.
17. Turner, *Women and Gender*, 109.

18. Woyshner, *National PTA*, 57.

19. Caldwell, "Work," 174–75.

20. "3-Year Comparison of Budgets," *Hope Star*, January 7, 1936, 1.

21. "Helping Negro Teachers in Arkansas," *Southern Workman*, January 1913, 375–76.

22. "Negro Teachers Conference," *Daily Arkansas Gazette*, December 8, 1914, 10.

23. "Art League," *Daily Arkansas Gazette*, February 21, 1915, 14.

24. "Negro Teachers of Arkansas to Meet Here Today," *Pine Bluff Daily Graphic*, December 28, 1915, 2.

25. Scott, *Reluctant Farmer*, 122; see also Rosenberg, *4-H Harvest*, 52–53.

26. Rosenberg, *4-H Harvest*, 23.

27. "Favrot Discusses Negro School Work," *Arkansas Gazette*, July 13, 1913, 25.

28. "To Organize Negro Clubs: Black Youth Will Be Taught Culture of Corn and Tomatoes," *Daily Arkansas Gazette*, April 8, 1913, 8.

29. "Favrot Discusses Negro School Work," *Arkansas Gazette*, July 13, 1913, 25.

30. "Capitol Notes," *Arkansas Gazette*, June 29, 1913, 8.

31. Betton, "Brief History," 2; Williams et al., *Jeanes Story*, 116–17; "Negroes to Exhibit Products at Shows," *Daily Arkansas Gazette*, October 19, 1915, 4.

32. Matkin-Rawn, "Great Negro State of the Country," 1, 2.

33. "Jefferson to Get Share," *Arkansas Gazette*, July 10, 2015, 14.

34. Patterson, *History*, 44.

35. Hoffschwelle, *Rebuilding*, 67.

36. "Negro Work Progressing," *Daily Arkansas Gazette*, November 25, 1916, 12.

37. "State Now Has 107 Rosenwald Schools," *Arkansas Gazette*, February 25, 1924, 10.

38. "My Work and I," *Arkansas Gazette*, January 2, 1927, 23.

39. "Rosenwald Schools," Encyclopedia of Arkansas, https://encyclopediaofarkansas .net/entries/rosenwald-schools-2371/ (accessed July 20, 2015); Turner, *Women and Gender*, 110.

40. King and Swartz, *Afrocentric Praxis*, 90; Anderson, *Education*, 32.

41. Cutler, *Parents and Schools*, 144.

42. "Teach Negroes to Think," *Daily Arkansas Gazette*, December 31, 1914, 2.

43. Devine, *On Behalf*, 18–20.

44. Devine, *On Behalf*, 18–20.

45. "Report of Jeans [*sic*] Teacher," *Osceola Times*, December 7, 1923, 2.

46. "Negro Extension Schools for Mississippi County," *Arkansas Gazette*, February 21, 1926, 29.

47. Cooley, *To Live and Dine*, 38–39.

48. Devine, *On Behalf*, 145.

49. Littlefield, "'To Do,'" 131–32.

50. "Arkansas Jeanes Teachers," Southern Education Foundation Archives, box 66, folder 3, Archives Research Center, Atlanta University Center, Robert W. Woodruff Library, Atlanta, Georgia; Williams et al., *Jeanes Story*, 115–16.

51. Williams et al., *Jeanes Story*, 116.

52. Smith and Jackson, *Educating the Masses*, 13–14.

53. Patterson, *History*, 33.

54. Smith and Jackson, *Educating the Masses*, 13–14.

55. Patterson, *History*, 34. After Childress's death in 1958, his wife established a $500

revolving loan fund for students in his honor at Philander Smith College. See "Wife of the Late Dr. Childress Establishes Loan Fund at Philander," *Arkansas State Press*, April 3, 1958, 3.

56. "Visiting Negro Schools," *Daily Arkansas Gazette*, March 12, 1911, 14. Johnson was born in Georgia in 1877. See the 1930 United States Census.
57. "Favrot Discusses Negro School Work, *Daily Arkansas Gazette*, July 13, 1913, 21.
58. King and Swartz, *Afrocentric Praxis*, 91.
59. "Favrot Discusses Negro School Work," *Daily Arkansas Gazette*, July 13, 1913, 21.
60. "Favrot Discusses Negro School Work," *Daily Arkansas Gazette*, July 13, 1913, 21.
61. "Negroes to Exhibit at Products Show," *Daily Arkansas Gazette*, October 19, 1915, 4.
62. Hoffschwelle, *Rebuilding*, 7.
63. Favrot, "Notable Negro Exhibit," 336.
64. Summary of Reports of Mr. Leo M. Favrot, State Agent for Negro Rural Schools of Arkansas, January 1, 1916, to December 31, 1916, Southern Education Foundation Archives, box 34, folder 4, Archives Research Center, Atlanta University Center, Robert W. Woodruff Library.
65. "Negro Work Progressing," *Daily Arkansas Gazette*, November 25, 1916, 12.
66. "6588 Negroes in Industrial Classes," *Arkansas Democrat*, August 28, 1917, 6.
67. Presson, *Bulletin*, 8. Dr. James H. Dillard, was president of the Jeanes board from 1907 to 1931. See "A Guide to the Papers of the Dillard Family, 1717–1964," http://ead.lib.virginia.edu/vivaxtf/view?docId=uva-sc/viu00599.xml (accessed August 12, 2014); Turner, *Women and Gender*, 107.
68. "State Now Has 107 Rosenwald Schools," *Arkansas Gazette*, February 25, 1924, 10.
69. "State Now Has 107 Rosenwald Schools," *Arkansas Gazette*, February 25, 1924, 10.
70. "My Work and I," *Arkansas Gazette*, January 2, 1927, 23.
71. "My Work and I," *Arkansas Gazette*, January 2, 1927, 23; "State Now Has 107 Rosenwald Schools," *Arkansas Gazette*, February 25, 1924, 10.
72. McClure, *Jeanes Teachers*, 65.
73. "Ekron Negro Teacher Awarded Jeanes Prize," *Courier News*, June 9, 1930, 1.
74. "Negro Farm Bureau Unit Plans Drive for Members," *Courier News*, November 23, 1937, 2; Whayne, *Delta Empire*, 135; Snowden, *Mississippi County*, 51.
75. "Jeanes Teacher for Colored Schools," *Osceola Times*, October 19, 1923, 8.
76. "Ten Annual Mississippi County Rally and Fair Program for This Year," *Osceola Times*, August 24, 1924, 7.
77. "Mississippi County Colored Teachers Represented in State Association," *Osceola Times*, November 30, 1923, 6.
78. Edrington, *History*, 387.
79. "Wilson Colored School Will Open with Barbecue," *Osceola Times*, September 12, 1924, 8.
80. "William Louis Currie Sr. and Annie Holland Currie: Models in Education and Service," *Delta Historical Review*, Winter 2012, 6–8.
81. "Arkansas," *Chicago Defender*, August 27, 1938, 23.
82. "They Finished Social Work School," *Atlanta Daily World*, June 23, 1940, 5.
83. "Offers Scholarships to Jeanes Teachers," *Chicago Defender*, Mary 28, 1938, 4.

84. "Jeanes Teachers Study at Hampton," *Chicago Defender*, July 22, 1939, 1.

85. "County Schools Hold Standards: Efficiency Generally Maintained Despite Shortage of Funds," *Courier News*, February 4, 1932, 1.

86. "Christmas Seal Drive," *Osceola Times*, November 9, 1923, 2. Christmas Seal stamps were first issued in 1907 to raise funds to help end tuberculosis.

87. "Tuberculosis Seal Sale Being Pushed," *Courier News*, December 3, 1937, 1.

88. Cutler, *Parents and Schools*, 144.

89. "Fifty Negro Teachers at Quarterly Session," *Courier News*, May 1, 1934, 3.

90. Patterson, *History*, 62.

91. Patterson, *History*, 62.

92. "500 Negro 4-H Club Youths Hold Big Rally," *Courier News*, July 14, 1934, 2.

93. "Booklets Distributed to Negro PTA Group," *Courier News*, December 2, 1936, 6.

94. "Haraway Heads County Negro Teachers Group," *Courier News*, December 16, 1937, 6; "William Louis Currie Sr. and Annie Holland Currie: Models in Education and Service," *Delta Historical Review*, Winter 2012, 9.

95. Edrington, *History*, 387.

96. "Armorel School Wins Sweepstakes," *Courier News*, April 8, 1938, [page unknown], quoted in "William Louis Currie Sr. and Annie Holland Currie: Models in Education and Service," *Delta Historical Review*, Winter 2012, 10.

97. "Armorel Winner of Negro Meet," *Courier News*, April 4, 1938, 3.

98. Shaw, *What A Woman*, 179.

99. "Negro Jeanes Teacher Ends 17 Years' Service," *Courier News*, December 19, 1939, 8.

100. "Card of Thanks," *Courier News*, June 26, 1943, 2; Arkansas Death Index. In 1947, the Mississippi County Negro Teachers Association met at the Osceola Rosenwald School and collected money with plans to construct a new gymnasium to be named in her honor. See "Negroes Raising Funds for School Auditorium," *Courier News*, January 3, 1947, 11.

101. Reck, *4-H Story*, 138.

102. Smith, *Sick and Tired*, 2.

103. Narrative Report of Annie L. Smith, Local HD Agent, Lee County, December 1926 to June 30, 1927, RG 33, SW Region, NARA, Fort Worth, TX; Woofter, "Organization," 73.

104. Division of Negro Education, *Problems*, 21.

105. "Arkansas State, Nashville, Arkansas," *Chicago Defender*, September 29, 1934, 21; Hurt, *African American Life*, 6.

106. Division of Negro Education, *Problems*, 21.

107. Erle Chambers to Board of Managers, Arkansas College for Negroes, September 15, 1930, Florence C. Williams Papers, Small Manuscript Collections, box 49, folder 7, Arkansas State Archives, Little Rock. In 1922, Erle Chambers was the first woman elected to the Arkansas state legislature and was also a member of the Arkansas Council of the Association of Southern Women for the Prevention to Lynching. See Jones-Branch, "'Working Slowly.'"

108. Jones-Branch, "'Working Slowly.'"

109. Littlefield, "'To Do,'" 131–32.

110. "College Station," *Arkansas State Press*, January 8, 1943, 3.

111. "Educator is Dead at Age 78," *Courier-Journal*, November 27, 1962, 15.

112. "National Council of Negro Women (NCNW)," *Encyclopedia Britannica* (online), https://www.britannica.com/topic/National-Council-of-Negro-Women (accessed October 22, 2017); "Ignores Bitter Assailment of N.A.C.W. Prexy," *Pittsburgh Courier*, December 28, 1935, 8. US Congress. *General Housing Act of 1945*, 859–60. See also Tuuri, *Strategic Sisterhood*.

113. Minutes, Regional Jeanes Association, No.2, September 17, 1943, Jeanes Foundation, box 1, folder 3, Arkansas State Archives, Little Rock; application for Jeanes Teacher Aid, Mary F. Jones, 1939, Southern Education Foundation Archives, box 113, folder 11, Archives Research Center, Atlanta University Center, Robert W. Woodruff Library; Turner, *Women and Gender*, 111.

114. Program, National Jeanes Association Regional, No. 2, September 27, 1954, Jeanes Foundation, box 1, folder 3, Arkansas State Archives, Little Rock; "Ark. Teachers Close Confab at Pine Bluff," *Chicago Defender*, April 6, 1940, 7; Patterson, *History*, 86. Americans of all hues were invested in social change and educational, recreational, and health opportunities for all children. However, these concerns did not usually extend to a thorough examination of the pernicious impact of race, gender, or class. The NCCPT was the counterpart of the predominantly white National Congress of Parents and Teachers (NCPT). Founded in 1897 as the National Congress of Mothers, the NCPT, like the state and local parent-teacher associations, were largely segregated in the first half of the twentieth century. Although the NCPT considered integrating the organization in 1908, such a move would have surely alienated southern whites and impeded Black women's educational activism in their communities. The NCCPT, founded in 1926 by Black teachers, clubwomen, and school leaders, rested on a foundation established by the African Methodist Episcopal Church and the National Association of Colored Women. Both nationally and locally, African Americans were dedicated to improving access to and the quality of liberal-arts education for Black children and increasing the number of available Black teachers. While Black leaders on the whole came from the middle class, Black women in particular understood that all African Americans endured racism. Class consciousness by and large did not pose obstacles to their activism in rural Black communities. As NCCPT, NJA, and RJA members, Arkansas Jeanes Supervisors' goals were not radically different from white women in that they also employed their skills to procure much needed local, state, and organizational resources to improve educational opportunities for their children. See Cutler, *Parents and Schools*, 112–113.

115. "Maeleen Arrant, a Recent Recipient of the Lester Silbernagel Award, Reflects on Four Decades in Public Education," date unknown, possibly from the *Commercial Appeal*, Memphis, Tennessee. See also the *Arkansasyer* 10, no. 1 (May 1940): 114. In 1937, she married Adam Arrant, a postal employee, in Pine Bluff, Arkansas, in Jefferson County. See the US Register of Civil, Military, and Naval Service, 1863–1959.

116. Kilmer, *Women*, 23–24.

117. Kilmer, *Women*, 23–24.

118. Smith and Jackson, *Educating*, 129; "Workers Hold Meeting, " *Plain Dealer*, April 13, 1951, 8; 1920 United States Federal Census; interview with Maeleen Arrant, date unknown, Pine Bluff Women's Center Collection, M92–06, box 3, University of Central Arkansas Archives, Conway.

119. Smith and Jackson, *Educating*, 129.
120. US Social Security Death Index, 1935–2014.
121. Cutler, *Parents and Schools*, 10–11.
122. Woyshner, *National PTA*, 56.
123. Harlan, *Booker T. Washington*, 159; Fairclough, *Class*, 125.
124. Giddings, *When and Where*, 103.
125. Woyshner, *National PTA*, 59.
126. Program, National Jeanes Association Regional Number Two, September 18–20, 1947, Jeanes Foundation, box 1, folder 3, Arkansas State Archives, Little Rock; "Jeanes Teachers Hit High Stride in Atlanta Meet," *Atlanta Daily World*, Mary 29, 1946, 1; "Sikeston Students Take Place in Negro School Tests," *Daily Standard*, April 25, 1950, 6.
127. "National Jeanes Group Meets in Nashville," *Chicago Defender*, October 4, 947, 3.
128. "Arkansas State: Camden, Ark.," *Chicago Defender*, August 6, 1932, 19. She was part of an NAACP Baby Contest committee. Even if she was not a member, which was unlikely, her association with the organization would have been problematic.
129. "Adult Class at Blevins Close," *Hope Star*, April 16, 1964, 6.
130. "Nevada County Development Group Meets," *Hope Star*, March 4, 1969, 1.
131. "The Negro Community," *Hope Star*, August 27, 1971, 10.
132. "Ila Upchurch, Jeanes teacher," Arkansas's Multicultural Heritage, http://ahc.digital-ar.org/digital/collection/p16790coll12/id/70 (accessed October 2, 2020).

CHAPTER 2

1. US Department of Agriculture, *List of Workers*, 55; "Meeting of Regents," *Wichita Daily Eagle*, October 11, 1903, 10. Marriage license filed on December 20 and 21, 1915, Pulaski County, AR, Marriages, 1838–1999 for H. C. Ray, www.ancestry.com.
2. "Colored Teachers Meet," *Wichita Daily Eagle*, December 11, 1904, 10.
3. Holt, *Linoleum*, 4.
4. Holt, *Linoleum*, 56.
5. Scott, *Reluctant Farmer*, 208.
6. Scott, *Reluctant Farmer*, 209.
7. Scott, *Reluctant Farmer*, 206, 210.
8. Betton, "Brief History," 1; "To Organize Negro Clubs: Black Youth Will Be Taught Culture of Corn and Tomatoes," *Daily Arkansas Gazette*, April 8, 1913, 8; "Experts at Palestine," *Daily Arkansas Gazette*, July 28, 1914, 2. In 1913, Amos was invited to present evidence of his demonstration work at the Thirty-Ninth General Assembly of the Arkansas House and Senate. With the help of demonstration club members, he served the General Assembly eighty-five hens. Born of enslaved parents in Plaquemine, Louisiana between 1859 and 1861, Amos was educated in Louisiana and spent two years at New Orleans University. Amos was ordained an African Methodist Episcopal church minister, and in June 1899 he became Ashley County's postmaster. He was replaced in September 1900 by William Neathen, an African American farmer. Between 1901 and 1907, Amos founded, edited, and published a newspaper called *The Trumpet* in Montrose, Arkansas, the time during which he also established the Montrose Male and

Female Industrial and Agricultural School and traveled to Washington, DC, to
solicit funds to support his institution. He was also well-known as an orator.
Unfortunately, the school closed after a few short years. Between 1907 and 1910,
Amos changed the name of the newspaper to the *Union Trumpet*. By 1920, he
had become a high school principal. It is believed that Amos died in the late
1920s and was buried in a private cemetery in Helms, Mississippi. See Evans
and Proctor-Streeter, "Reverend Professor Ralph Amos," 8. Amos was Proctor-
Streeter's maternal great-grandfather. "Appointments of US Postmasters, 1832–
1971" and *Official Register of the United States*, 2:46, www. ancestry.com; "South
Arkansas Conference," *Daily Arkansas Gazette*, November 18, 1899, 8; "All Over
the State," *Arkansas Democrat*, July 10, 1899, 2; Lonoke County, Arkansas, 1920
Federal Census, www.ancestry.com. "A New Industrial School for the Race in
Arkansas," *Colored American*, December 5, 1903, 3.
9. Knapp, *Demonstration Work*, 6.
10. Berlage, *Farmers Helping Farmers*, 13.
11. Hurt, *American Agriculture*, 276.
12. Schultz, "Benjamin Hubert," 86; Lowe, *Baptized with Soil*, 6.
13. Jacoway, *Yankee Missionaries*, 77, 81. The Penn School was established in 1862 to
educate enslaved African Americans during the Civil War.
14. "Government Extension Agents Aid Farmers," *Chicago Defender* September 20,
1924, A4; Strausberg, *Century of Research*, 30.
15. Betton, "Brief History," 1, Box 8, file 3; Arkansas Extension Homemakers
Council, *History*, 4.
16. "Dr. Chas. H. Brough on the Southern Race Question," *Daily Arkansas Gazette*,
January 3, 1915, 33; "Charles Hillman Brough (1876–1935)," Encyclopedia of
Arkansas, https://encyclopediaofarkansas.net/entries/charles-hillman-brough-89/
(accessed January 8, 2017).
17. Hoffschwelle, "'Better Homes,'" 52.
18. Berlage, *Farmers Helping Farmers*, 19.
19. Harris, "State's Rights," 363.
20. Strausberg, *Century of Research*, 30; True, *History of Agricultural Education*,
280–81, 365.
21. Jones, "South's First Black Farm Agents," 636.
22. Hurt, *American Agriculture*, 256.
23. Daniel, "African American Farmers," 26.
24. Whayne et al., *Arkansas*, 308.
25. Payne, "'What Ain't I Been Doing?,'" 141.
26. Ward, *Home Demonstration Work*; Hoffschwelle, "'Better Homes,'" 53.
27. Whayne, "'I Have Been Through Fire.'"
28. Mather, *Who's Who of the Colored Race*, 227. Ray, a graduate of Jefferson City,
Missouri's Lincoln Institute in Jefferson City, Missouri, had also studied vocational education and dairying at Kansas Agricultural College in Manhattan and was
the director of agriculture at Langston University in Oklahoma until he moved
to Little Rock, Arkansas. See also the *Kansas State Agricultural College Catalogue,
Fifty-First Session*, 354.
29. "White Experts Aid Many Negro Farmers," *Arkansas Democrat*, February 2, 1917, 10.
30. By the 1930s, Reed, who was born in Mississippi in between 1885 and 1887, had

returned to her birth state and remained a home demonstration agent in Jackson, Mississippi, until she retired in 1953. See "Negro 4-H Club Rally is Held," *Clarion-Ledger*, May 8, 1935, 16; "66 More People Begin Retirement," *Clarion-Ledger*, July 4, 1953, 12; 1940 US Federal Census, www.ancestry.com; *Directory of County Agricultural Agents*, 2, 6, 24, 27; Work, *Negro Year Book*, 328.

31. "Colored Girls Care for Tomato Crop," *Osceola Times*, September 24, 1920, 7. Branch Normal School was opened in Pine Bluff in 1875 and was the only state supported institution to train African Americans to become educators. See Gordon, *Caste and Class*, 96.

32. "Three Day Meeting of County Agents Opens at U. Today," *Fayetteville Daily Democrat*, August 20, 1921, 1.

33. Harris, "Grace under Pressure," 207.

34. Berlage, *Farmers Helping Farmers*, 132.

35. Smith, *Sick and Tired*, 89.

36. Hogan, "History of the Agricultural Extension Service," 155.

37. Work, *Industrial Work*, 24; and Washington, *Successful Training of the Negro*, 2.

38. "Work at Tuskegee," *Inter Ocean*, May 31, 1897, 5; "Tuskegee Normal School," *Montgomery Advertiser*, May 28, 1897, 2.

39. "Along the Color Line. Mr. Theo. Baughmen, The Plaindealer's Globe Trotting Scribe Tells of Negro Advancement in Oklahoma," *Topeka Plaindealer*, April 4, 1915, 1, 8. Apparently she also owned a business 1906; see "Anniversary Aftermath: Echoes from Tuskegee Institute Memorable Silver Jubilee—Pertinent Points About People of Whom the World Wants to Hear—Episodes and Events Which Should Be Immortalized in Print," *Freeman*, May 5, 1906, 4; *Annual Register of the University of Chicago, 1914–1915*, 699; R. R. Moton, "Extension Work and the Negro," in *Silver Anniversary Cooperative Demonstration Work*, 94.

40. "Tuskegee National Alumni Meet in Annual Conclave," *Emporia Citizen*, July 1, 1932, 1.

41. Hogan, "History of the Agricultural Extension Service," 139; *Annual Catalogue of the Colored Agricultural and Normal University*; Cameron, *Second Biennial Report*, 22; also see Debra A. Reid, "Mary L. Ray (1880?-1934) Arkansas's Negro Extension Worker," in Cherisse Jones-Branch and Gary T. Edwards, eds., *Arkansas Women: Their Lives and Times* (Athens: University of Georgia Press, 2018).

42. Whayne et al., *Arkansas*, 309.

43. Jernigan, *Manual*, 3.

44. Zellar, "H. C. Ray," 433; Whayne et al., *Arkansas*, 309; Hogan, "History of the Agricultural Extension Service," 147; "Agri Extension Service Popular Through State," *Northwest Arkansas Times*, June 6, 1947, 3.

45. "Dr. Chas. H. Brough on the Southern Race Question," *Daily Arkansas Gazette*, January 3, 1915, 33; "Charles Hillman Brough (1876–1935)," Encyclopedia of Arkansas, https://encyclopediaofarkansas.net/entries/charles-hillman-brough-89/ (accessed January 8, 2017).

CHAPTER 3

1. "Elaine Massacre of 1919," Encyclopedia of Arkansas, https://encyclopediaof arkansas.net/entries/elaine-massacre-of-1919–1102/ (accessed May 29, 2016). For

more on the Elaine Massacre see Stockley, *Blood in Their Eyes*; Whitaker, *On the Laps of Gods*; and Woodruff, *American Congo*, 75.

2. "Orders of Washington, D.C., The Great Torch of Liberty"; Rogers, "Elaine Race Riots," 146; Taylor, "'We Have Just Begun,'" 272.

3. Stockley, *Blood in Their Eyes*, 131.

4. Whitaker, *On the Laps of Gods*, 1.

5. Jones-Branch, "Women and the 1919 Elaine Massacre."

6. Danbom, *Born in the Country*, 176; Cooley, *To Live and Dine*, 40.

7. Berlage, *Farmers Helping Farmers*, 13.

8. Sworakoski, "Herbert Hoover," 42.

9. "How the Negro Is Helping to Win the War," *Daily Arkansas Gazette*, May 31, 1918, 6.

10. "Advises Simpler Methods of Living: Food Administration Asks Women of Arkansas to Consider Thrift Program," *Daily Arkansas Gazette*, December 22, 1918, 42; "Home Card Campaign," *Daily Arkansas Gazette*, October 13, 1918, 5.

11. "Home Card Campaign," *Daily Arkansas Gazette*, October 13, 1918, 5.

12. Danbom, *Born in the Country*, 177.

13. Holley, *Uncle Sam's Farmers*, 134.

14. Hogan, "History of the Agricultural Extension Service," 141; H. C. Ray had to register for the draft during World War I. See "U.S., World War I Draft Registration Card, 1917–1918, for Harvey C. Ray," www.ancestry.com (accessed August 12, 2014).

15. Grim, "African American Rural Culture," 114, 128.

16. Reid, *Reaping a Greater Harvest*, 68, 72, 76–77.

17. Whayne, *Delta Empire*, 179.

18. She was the state home demonstration agent from 1917 until 1950; Hill, *Faithful to Our Tasks*, 31.

19. Betton, "Brief History," 3; Whayne et al., *Arkansas*, 309; Woodruff, *American Congo*, 146.

20. Jeannie Whayne, *Delta Empire*, 179–80; Woodruff, *American Congo*, 111; "Burned at Stake Negro Murdered Is Taken from Officers by Mob," *Nashville News*, Nashville, Tennessee, January 29, 1921, 2.

21. "Negro Farmers Meet," *Osceola Times*, February 18, 1921, 5.

22. Hogan, "History of the Agricultural Extension Service," 147, 148.

23. "Negroes Are Interested: Many Join Boys and Girls Clubs in Mississippi County," *Daily Arkansas Gazette*, May 30, 1920, 48.

24. Smith, *Sick and Tired*, 102; Winn, *Documenting Racism*, 16.

25. Smith, *Sick and Tired*, 102.

26. Winn, "Documenting Racism," 34; and *Documenting Racism*, 18–19.

27. Mercier, *Extension Work*, 6.

28. Scott, *Weapons of the Weak*, xvi–xvii.

29. "Negro Farm Agents in Annual Meeting," *Daily Arkansas Gazette*, April 27, 1921, 7; Hill, *Faithful to Our Tasks*, 31.

30. "Workers Say Negroes Profit by Instruction," *Southern Standard*, July 24, 1924, 5.

31. "Gives Outline of Extension Work: M. T. Payne Addresses Negro Farm Agents at Second Day's Session," *Daily Arkansas Gazette*, March 10, 1922, 9.

32. "Gives Outline of Extension Work," *Daily Arkansas Gazette*, March 10, 1922, 9.

33. "Farmers in Conference at Tuskegee Institute," *Chicago Defender*, February 7, 1925, 3. In 1925, H. C. and Mary Ray and a delegation of Arkansas farmers attended the Tuskegee Institute's annual farmers' conference to address educational, health, and of course agricultural concerns.
34. "Will Keep County Agents on the Job: Quorum Courts of at least 25 Counties make appropriations," *Arkansas Gazette*, October 23, 1919, 1.
35. "Demonstration Agents Retained by Pope County," *Arkansas Gazette*, November 1, 1925, 3.
36. "Will Keep County Agents on the Job: Quorum Courts of at least 25 Counties make appropriations," *Arkansas Gazette*, October 23, 1919, 1.
37. "15 More Counties Keep Farm Agents: Quorum Courts Appropriate Funds for Demonstration Work," *Arkansas Gazette*, October 24, 1919, 3.
38. "Negro Canning Clubs," *Arkansas Gazette*, June 26, 1920, 8.
39. "Quorum Court Meetings," *Arkansas Gazette*, November 15, 1927, 2.
40. "Many Win Prizes at Arkansas State Fair," *Chicago Defender*, November 22, 1924, A1; Roberts, *Pageants, Parlors, and Pretty Women*, 118.
41. Scott, *Reluctant Farmer*, 16.
42. Scott, *Reluctant Farmer*, 16 and 17.
43. Kechnie, *Organizing Rural Women*, 7.
44. "Negro Girl of 14 Is Breadmaking Winner," *Arkansas Gazette*, September 23, 1923, 25. Bessie Jones won first prize for the best loaf and rolls, second prize for muffins, and third prize for biscuits.
45. "Contest in Bread Making Held Here," *Arkansas Gazette*, May 24, 1925, 13.
46. "May 24 Programs KUOA," *Fayetteville Democrat*, May 22, 1926, 7.
47. Patterson, *History of the Arkansas Teachers Association*, 47.
48. Patterson, *History of the Arkansas Teachers Association*, 46–47.
49. Hilton, "Both in the Field," 125.
50. Cooley, *To Live and Dine*, 78.

CHAPTER 4

1. Daniel, *Deep'n as It Come*, 36, 144.
2. Arkansas Extension Homemakers Council, *History*, 325.
3. "Lauderdale County Negro Fair Proved a Decided Success," *Dallas Express*, July 16, 1921, 7.
4. "Arkansas Demonstration Agent Resigns Post," *Broad Axe*, September 10, 1927, 2. Toler was formerly an educator at Little Rock's Williams Industrial College, founded in 1893. See Patterson, *Patterson's College and School Directory*, 21.
5. "Memphis, Tenn," *Plaindealer*, August 25, 1939, 5; "State Choir Gives Christmas Concert," *Arkansas State Press*, December 24, 1948, 1; Brown, *He Built a School*, 57. Toler established the home in 1942 and was its executive director. It was also known as the Lula Toler Convalescing Home. Lula Toler died on August 17, 1958. See *Toler v. Lula Toler Convalescing Home*, 364 S.W.2d 680 (1963), www.law.justia .com (accessed July 29, 2014); "African American Firsts," *Pine Bluff Commercial*, February 18, 2013 (accessed July 29, 2014); "Former PB Residents Protest Killing," *Pine Bluff Commercial*, October 7, 2013 (accessed July 29, 2014).
6. Maples, *Farther Down the Road*, 46.

7. Holley, "Plantation Heritage," 260.

8. Roll, *Spirit of Rebellion*, 72.

9. Zellar, "H. C. Ray," 441.

10. Spencer, "Contested Terrain," 172.

11. Roll, *Spirit of Rebellion*, 72.

12. Zellar, "H. C. Ray," 442.

13. Mizelle, *Mississippi Flood of 1927*, 76, 80.

14. Daniel, *Deep'n as It Come*, 36, 144; "Smash Barleycorn, WTCU Workers Prepare to Put Rum on the Run," *Salina Evening Journal*, August 28, 1915, 1; 1906 Little Rock City Directory, www.ancestry.com (accessed June 5, 2016).

15. Narrative Report of County Local (Negro) Home Demonstration Agent, Lugenia Christmas, St. Francis County, 1927, NARA.

16. Nelson, *Rural Hygiene*, no page number.

17. Narrative Report of Annie L. Smith, Local HD Agent, Lee County, December 1926–June 30, 1927, NARA.

18. Spencer, "Contested Terrain," 172.

19. "Sins Crying to Heaven for Vengeance," *Our Colored Missions*, October 1, 1932, 148.

20. Narrative Report of County Home Demonstration Agent, Lee County, 1927, SW Region, NARA.

21. Zellar, "H. C. Ray," 442. See *Final Report of the Colored Advisory Commission*, 23.

22. "Flood Commission's Work Expanded," *Light and Heebee Jeebies*, July 23, 1927, 15.

23. Narrative Report of District Director, Negro Home Demonstration Work, 1927, RG 33, SW Region, NARA.

24. *Official Record* (USDA), May 9, 1928, 5. Ray resumed her position the following year.

25. Cooley, *To Live and Dine*, 30.

26. 1928 Annual Narrative Report, Phillips County Local HDA, RG 33, SW Region, NARA. Between 1913 and 1930, 365 school buildings had been aided by the Rosenwald Fund. See Caliver, "Rural Elementary Education," 43.

27. Hill, *Splendid Piece of Work*, 85. Symptoms of pellagra include red and scaly skin, stomach disorders, diarrhea, and depression. The United States Public Health Service conducted investigations of the disease, and two wealth northern philanthropists donated $1,500 to study pellagra. See Smith, *Sick and Tired*, 9; Whayne et al., *Arkansas*, 296.

28. Narrative Report of (Negro) County Local Home Demonstration Agent, Phillips County, 1927, NARA.

29. Special to the *New York Times*, "Coolidge Projects Inland Waterways for Flood Control," October 4, 1927, 1; Whayne et al., *Arkansas*, 314; Zellar, "H. C. Ray," 441–42; Daniel, *Deep'n as It Come*, 137, 144. H. C. Ray was appointed to a "Colored Commission" under the Flood Relief Commission by President Herbert Hoover. See "Hoover Revealed As," *Light: America's News Magazine*, March 10, 1928, 16; Hill, *Splendid Piece of Work*, 68–69; Narrative Report of Lugenia Christmas, 1927, NARA.

30. Smith, *Sick and Tired*, 88.

31. Narrative Report of Lugenia Christmas, 1927, NARA.

32. "In Memoriam: Mrs. Lugenia Bell Christmas, Local Home Demonstration

Agent, St. Francis County, 1917 to 1942," in Hill, *Splendid Piece of Work*, no page number; Narrative Report of Lugenia Christmas, 1927, NARA; "Fargo Agricultural School," Encyclopedia of Arkansas, https://encyclopediaofarkansas .net/entries/fargo-agricultural-school-2375/ (accessed July 19, 2015); Patterson, *History of the Arkansas Teachers Association*, 91. Founded in 1920 by Tuskegee graduate Floyd Brown, Fargo provided industrial education to African American students residing in rural areas and was supported by such Black organizations as the Arkansas Teachers Association, of which Brown was president from 1942 to 1944, and the Arkansas Association of Colored Women.

33. "Movable Schools Bring Modern Farm Methods to Rural Homes," *Chicago Defender*, September 20, 1924, 13; "Movable Schools," *New York Amsterdam News*, December 9, 1925, 10; Betton, "Brief History," 3–4; Ferguson, "Caught in 'No Man's Land,'" 34–37.

34. "Tells How Famous Movable School Started," *Chicago Defender*, October 12, 1940, 2; Rieff, "'Go Ahead and Do All You Can,'" 139; Zellar, "H. C. Ray," 444; Jones, "Role of Tuskegee Institute," 262–65; Smith, *Sick and Tired*, 91; Thomas Monroe Campbell, *The Movable School Goes to the Negro Farmer* (Alabama: Tuskegee Institute Press), 1936, vii.

35. Zellar, "H. C. Ray," 444. Woodard had trained at Tuskegee Institute.

36. Hogan, "History of the Agricultural Extension Service," 149; Zellar, "H. C. Ray," 444.

37. "ARKANSAS," *Chicago Defender*, July 27, 1929, 1. Lincoln School was one of the earliest schools to educate African Americans in southwest Arkansas. See "Lincoln High School," http://historicwashington.wikifoundry.com/page /Lincoln+High+School (accessed August 11, 2014).

38. "Keiser, Arkansas," *Chicago Defender*, February 8, 1930, A8.

39. "Ellison, Arkansas," *Chicago Defender*, May 30, 1931, 22.

40. Shinn, *Agricultural Instruction*. This address had previously been presented at the Negro Educational Conference in Nashville, Tennessee, on August 1, 1927, and at the Negro State Teachers Association in Little Rock, Arkansas, on November 11, 1927.

41. *Report of Special Summer Schools for Negro Extension Agents*, 1, 2, 3, and 33.

42. Narrative Report of County Home Demonstration Agent, Mary L. Stubblefield, Negro Home Demonstration Agent, October 23, 1944–November 30, 1944, NARA.

43. Narrative Report of Mary L. Stubblefield. They also attended Better Babies conferences, where they were able to discuss problems associated with childcare.

44. *Annual Report of Extension Service*, 32.

45. "Health Is Stressed," 17.

46. "Farm Conference at Fargo College," *Chicago Defender* April 9, 1932, 2. The Fargo Agricultural School was founded in 1920 and operated until 1949. See "Fargo Agricultural School," Encyclopedia of Arkansas, https://encyclopedia ofarkansas.net/entries/fargo-agricultural-school-2375/ (accessed August 19, 2013); Patterson, *History*, 91.

47. "Farmers Plan Meet Exhibit in Arkansas: Home Improvement Is Urged at Osceola Monthly Confab," *Chicago Defender*, December 25, 1937, 5.

48. *Blytheville/Mississippi County Black Culture Sesquicentennial Scrapbook*, 56. In 1922, Viola Gabashane, a Presbyterian, attended the Canadian Synodical Sabbath

School Convention in Oklahoma City, where she gave a talk on "Elementary Methods for Sunday School." See "Program of the Canadian Synodical Sabbath School Convention," *Black Dispatch*, August 22, 1922, 5. From the "The Gateway to Oklahoma History," https://gateway.okhistory.org. The school was built in 1925 and later operated as Rosenwald High School until it was integrated in 1971.

49. Lowe, *Baptized with Soil*, 2–3.
50. Hilton, "Both in the Field," 131.
51. Higginbotham, *Righteous Discontent*, 17–18.
52. Myers and Sharpless, "'Of the Least and the Most,'" 55, 65.
53. Myers and Sharpless, "'Of the Least and the Most,'" 76.
54. "ARKANSAS STATE," *Chicago Defender*, May 27, 1933, 20; *Annual Report of Extension Service*, 73.
55. "Forrest City, Arkansas," *Plaindealer*, April 27, 1934, 3. She was married to R. J. Christmas, a Presbyterian minister.
56. Highfill and Wilson, *Progress of Extension Teaching*, 13.
57. The home demonstration club in Dermott (Chicot County), Arkansas, for example, was founded in 1955. See "Dermott," *Arkansas State Press*, January 28, 1955, 2.
58. "500 Negro 4-H Club Youths Hold Big Rally," *Courier News*, July 14, 1934, 2. 4-H clubs from Osceola, San Souci, Grider, Carson, Wilson, Luxora, Burdette, Double Bridges, Hickman, Birdson, Frenchman's Bayou, Kelser, Sandy Bayou, Friendship, and Promised Land attended the rally.
59. "Negroes in 38 Counties Reached by Extension Program in 1938," 34 (page number is a guess; pages are unnumbered.)
60. "Arkansas Women Aid Better Homes Movement There," *Atlanta Daily World*, July 23, 1939, A6.
61. Wesley, *History*, 488–89.
62. "On Advancement of the Negro in State Government," September 1967, Winthrop Rockefeller Collection, RG III, box 43, folder 3. She married physician Dr. Clyde A. Lawlah, a Bessemer, Alabama native, and 1925 Morehouse College and University of Chicago Medical School graduate, in 1938. In 1956, Dr. Lawlah made history in his own right: he became the first African American physician in Arkansas to join a formerly all-white medical society when he was elected secretary-treasurer of the Jefferson County Medical Society. He practiced medicine for thirty-five years until his death in Pine Bluff in March 1968. See "Negro Named Sec'y-Treas to Integrated Med Society," *Hope Star*, January 20, 1956, 4; and "Obituaries," *Hope Star*, March 25, 1968, 10.
63. Hurt, *American Agriculture*, 287.
64. Hurt, *American Agriculture*, 288.
65. Biles, *South and the New Deal*, 43.
66. Coclanis and Simon, "Exit, Voice, and Loyalty," 200; Mitchell, *Mean Things Happening*, 42. See also Ross, *Rise and Fall*.
67. Mitchell, "Founding," 364–365.
68. Yard, "'They Don't Regard My Rights,'" 201.
69. Biegert, "Legacy of Resistance," 88–89.
70. 26th Annual Meeting of the State Home Demonstration Council, from the personal records of Annie Zachary Pike, Marvell, Arkansas.
71. "Farmers Seeking Dismissed Count: Seven Men Seek to Get Freedom of

Flogging Charges in Appeal to Court," *Kingsport Times*, May 4, 1938, 12; "Trial Under Anti-Slave Law Faced by Official in Cotton Strike Sequel," *Democrat and Chronicle*, November 24, 1936, 1; "$15,000 Asked by Flog Victim," *Des Moines Register*, August 30, 1936, 4.

72. Newspaper reports of the incident say she was between sixty and sixty-five years old, in which case she was born in the 1870s. In contrast, the 1930 census lists her as being forty-three years old and living and working on Floyd Robert's farm in Tyronza, Cross County, Arkansas.

73. "Alleged Victims of Arkansas Floggers Files Damage Suit: Another Man and Woman Also Seek $15, 000 Damages for Floggings," *Corsicana Daily Sun*, August 29, 1936, 1; "Dies as $15,000 Suit Waits Action," *Chicago Defender*, May 28, 1938, 6.

74. "Denials of the Defendants," *New York Times*, August 30, 1936, 12.

75. Mitchell, *Mean Things Happening*, 88; "Beaten by Planters," *Anniston Star*, May 17, 1938, 1.

76. "To Dismiss Actions Against Seven Planters," *Blytheville Courier*, November 8, 1938, 2.

77. "Eliza Nolden, Woman for Whom the STFU Filed a $15,000 Suit in U.S. Court, Dies," *Atlanta Daily World*, May 20, 1938, 6.

78. Hurt, *American Agriculture*, 314.

79. "Arkansans Sued Over Three Floggings," *New York Times*, August 30, 1936, 12.

80. Jones, "In Search of Jennie Booth Moton," 446.

81. Jennie Moton to E. A. Miller, Assistant to the Director, Division of Cotton, Agricultural Adjustment Administration, December 22, 1936, RNACWC, reel 10.

82. Jennie Moton to James P. Davis, Head Field Officer, AAA, November 13, 1937, RNACWC, reel 10. Incidentally, the Rays also had a daughter, named Mary Lee Ray (no relation to H. C. Ray's first wife), who later graduated from Dunbar High School in Little Rock in 1952. She graduated from Tuskegee Institute in 1956. See "Little Rock Pebbles," *Chicago Defender*, June 28, 1952, 9; "Around Dunbar," *Arkansas State Press*, April 4, 1952, 7; and "Here and There," *Arkansas State Press*, June 8, 1956, 5.

83. Albon L. Holsey, Field Officer to C. C. Randall, November 9, 1937, RNACWC, reel 10.

84. Whayne, "I Have Been through Fire," 183; Jones, "In Search of Jennie Booth Moton," 455.

85. Jones, "In Search of Jennie Booth Moton," 163; Cassa H. Lawlah, Arkansas district home demonstration agent to Jennie B. Moton, November 10, 1936, Moton Family Papers, folder 18, box 18; L. W. Dougan, "AAA Director Praises Negro Farmers for Part in War Effort," *Atlanta Daily World* December 11, 1942. Jennie Moton was also president of the National Association of Colored Women from 1937 to 1941. Jones, "In Search of Jennie Booth Moton," 446.

86. Jennie B. Moton to Cassa Lawlah, April 26, 1938, folder 18, box 18, Moton Family Papers.

87. Jones, "In Search of Jennie Booth Moton," 456.

88. Lee County Sesquicentennial Committee, *History of Lee County*, 338. Moton High School was constructed between 1926 and 1927 under Strong's direction. Its counterpart in Farmville, Virginia, was built in 1939.

89. Lee County Sesquicentennial Committee, *History of Lee County*, 338.

90. "Anna Strong (1884–1966)," Encyclopedia of Arkansas, https://encyclopediaof arkansas.net/entries/anna-strong-2734/ (accessed August 29, 2015).

91. Smith and Jackson, *Educating the Masses*, 43.

92. Lee County Sesquicentennial Committee, *History of Lee County*, 338. Strong was so well-regarded throughout Arkansas that she was awarded an honorary degree from Arkansas AM&N College in 1955 and a federated club in Hope was named in her honor. See the *Hope Star*, May 28, 1955, 6, and June 7, 1962, 4.

93. "15 Committees Working on Nat'l Education Conference," *Pittsburgh Courier*, May 5, 1934, 2.

94. "Wins Degree," *Chicago Defender*, June 4, 1938, 2; "Honorees," *Pittsburgh Courier*, June 4, 1955, 16. In 1950, the Robert R. Moton High School in Marianna, Arkansas, named its new gymnasium the A. M. P. Strong Gymnasium in her honor. She also received an honorary Doctor of Laws degree from Arkansas AM&N in 1955. See "To Dedicate New Gymnasium," *Arkansas State Press*, December 15, 1950, 6; and "231 Graduated from Negro College," *Hope Star*, May 28, 1955, 6.

95. Division of Negro Education, *Problems*; *Arkansasyer*, May 1940, 17.

96. "Anna Strong (1884–1966)," Encyclopedia of Arkansas, https://encyclopediaof arkansas.net/entries/anna-strong-2734/ (accessed August 29, 2015).

97. Report of Services Rendered by Employees, September 1–30, 1941, RNACWC, reel 10; "Anna Strong (1884–1966)," Encyclopedia of Arkansas, https:// encyclopediaofarkansas.net/entries/anna-strong-2734/ (accessed August 29, 2015).

CHAPTER 5

1. Mrs. J. B. Watson, "Girl, 16, Supervises Canning Kitchen," *Chicago Defender*, June 15, 1935, 15.

2. "Emergency Relief Association Canning Kitchens," in Wilks, *Few Events and Occurrences*, no page number.

3. Bernice V. Shepherd, Negro Home Demonstration Agent, Narrative Report of the (Woodruff) County Home Demonstration Agent, December 1, 1943 to October 31, 1944, Arkansas Annual Reports, 1917–1970, RG 33, NARA, Reel 106; Johnson, *Arkansas in Modern America*, 34.

4. Rieff, "Go Ahead and Do All You Can," 136–137; Heywood, "Home Demonstration Clubs," 253.

5. Mrs. J. Howard Crawford, President, Arkansas Council of Home Demonstration Clubs, Arkadelphia, "Home Demonstration Work in Arkansas," *Proceedings of the Arkansas Academy of Science* 4, (1951): 183, http://libinfo.uark.edu/aas /issues/1951v4/v4a26.pdf (accessed August 21, 2012). At times, Black and white home demonstration agents shared the same meeting space. The first session of the Arkansas Home Demonstration Club Council's 19th annual meeting in September 1947 was held at the predominantly African American Arkansas Baptist College in Little Rock. Fannie Mae Boone was in charge of arrangements and home demonstration agents Margaret P. Williams and Lena Eddington reported on a nutrition workshop they had attended at Hampton Institute. See "Demonstration Club Holds Two-Day Meeting," *Atlanta Daily World*, September 19, 1947, 3.

6. Lugenia B. Christmas, Local Home Demonstration Agent, Narrative Report of

174 NOTES

County Extension Workers, St. Francis County, December 1, 1935-November 30, 1936, Arkansas Annual Reports, 1917–1970, RG 33, NARA, Reel 106; "Arkansas Farmers in 16th Annual Meet," *Chicago Defender,* September 5, 1936, 15. Lawlah, born Cassa Hamilton in Hope, Arkansas, was the daughter of a public school teacher. In 1938, she married Dr. Clyde A. Lawlah, a physician, a native of Bessemer, Alabama, and a graduate of Morehouse College and the University of Chicago Medical School. See "Newlyweds Warmly Welcomed at Reception," *Chicago Defender,* April 9, 1938, 14. In 1952, she was elected president of the Arkansas Medical and Pharmaceutical Association Auxiliary. See "Little Rock Pebbles," *Chicago Defender,* June 28, 1952, 9. She was also a charter member of the I.Q. Bridge Club in Pine Bluff, Arkansas. See "Arkansas Bridge Club Fetes Its 20th Year, 72 Present," *Chicago Defender,* February 9, 1963, 13. In 1977, Lawlah was appointed to finish a term on the University of Arkansas, Pine Bluff, Board of Visitors. She was also a member of the Cotillion Federated Club in Pine Bluff and Alpha Kappa Alpha Sorority. See "Jernigan Named," *Camden News,* February 15, 1977, 3; "Local Club Members attend Regional Meeting," *Hope Star,* March 23, 1972, 5; "Annual Costume Ball," *Arkansas State Press,* April 25, 1952, 1.
7. Arkansas Extension Homemakers Council, *History,* 311; "Arkansas Farmers in 16th Annual Meet," *Chicago Defender,* September 5, 1936, 15; Hill, *Splendid Piece of Work,* 260.
8. *Official Record* (USDA), April 4, 1929, 8.
9. New York State Passenger and Crew Lists, 1917–1967, for Fannie Mae Boone, www.ancestry.com; "Arkansas Farmers in 16th Annual Meet," *Chicago Defender,* September 5, 1936, 15; "Two Agricultural Employes [*sic*] Receive Superior Awards," *Atlanta Daily World,* June 9, 1956, 1; "National Home Demonstration Agents Hold First Annual Meeting in Ark," *Daily Defender,* November 1, 1958, 15; "Photo Standalone 5 – no Title," *Atlanta Daily World,* June 12, 1956, 2. Her husband, Albert C. Boone, was principal of Burdette Negro High School in Mississippi. He died in Luxora, Arkansas, in 1951. See Sadie A. Thompson, "Little Rock Pebbles," *Chicago Defender,* December 15, 1951, 9; and "Albert C. Boone, Burdette School Principal Dies," *Blytheville Courier News,* November 24, 1951, 16. In 1956, Fannie Mae Boone received a superior service award from the USDA. She was the only home demonstration agent from Arkansas to receive such an honor. See "Marianna," *Arkansas State Press,* July 6, 1956, 7.
10. "Rural Leaders to Be Honored at 4-H Club Camp," *Atlanta Daily World,* July 22, 1960, 6; "Boone Family Boosts Burdette, Luxora," *Blytheville/Mississippi /County Black Culture Sesquicentennial Scrapbook,* 50.
11. *Blytheville/Mississippi /County Black Culture Sesquicentennial Scrapbook,* 50.
12. Lugenia B. Christmas, Local Home Demonstration Agent, Narrative Report of County Extension Workers, St. Francis County, December 1, 1935–November 30, 1936, Fort Worth, Texas, Federal Extension Service, Arkansas Annual Reports, 1917–1970, RG 33, NARA, Reel 106. In 1936, the council celebrated its fifteenth anniversary at Blout Park, located a mile outside of Forrest City.
13. Highfill and Wilson, *Progress of Extension Teaching,* 11.
14. Arkansas State Emergency Relief Administration, *Traveling Recovery Road,* 93–94.
15. Johnson, *Arkansas in Modern America,* 34; Maple, *Farther Down the Road,* 62.
16. Hilton, "Both in the Field," 125.
17. T. M. Campbell, "Home Demonstration Work among Negroes in South Has

Aided Many," *Atlanta Daily World*, February 6, 1935, 2 ; Cotton, *Lamplighters*, 53;
Walker, *All We Knew Was to Farm*, 113.

18. Reck, *4-H Story*, vii, 3.
19. Reid, *Reaping a Greater Harvest*, 63.
20. Rosenberg, *4-H Harvest*, 8.
21. Rosenberg, *4-H Harvest*, 154–55.
22. Rosenberg, *4-H Harvest*, 9, 155.
23. "Negro 4-H Clubs of County Holding Rally at Osceola," *Courier News*, July 19, 1930, 3.
24. "Arkansas State," *Chicago Defender*, July 16, 1932, 10.
25. Zellar, "H. C. Ray," 431, 433; Hogan, "History of the Agricultural Extension Service," 139; Mary L. Ray Death Certificate. Ray's funeral services were held at Bethel A.M.E. Church in Little Rock. She was survived by her husband and some cousins. See "Arkansas State," *Chicago Defender*, August 11, 1934, 21; Betton, "Brief History," 2. H. C. Ray retired in 1952.
26. "Farmers Plan Meet Exhibit in Arkansas," *Chicago Defender*, December 25, 1937, 5.
27. "Educational Exhibits at Fair Hold Interest," *Courier News*, September 22, 1949, 25. This article misidentifies the organization New Farmers of America as "Negro Farmers of America."
28. "Negro 4-H Girl Gets Award," *Camden News*, October 7, 1948, 2.
29. "Burdette Negro Girl Wins Award for 4-H Work," *Courier News*, November 28, 1950, 9.
30. "4-H Achievement Banquet," *Hope Star*, November 24, 1954, 12.
31. Higginbotham, *Righteous Discontent*, 186–87.
32. Carmen Harris, "You're Just Like Mules," 256; McKinney, "From Canning to Contraceptives."
33. Higginbotham, *Righteous Discontent*, 186–87.
34. Scott, *Domination and the Arts of Resistance*, 4.
35. Jones, *Mama Learned Us to Work*, 153.
36. Highfill and Wilson, *Progress of Extension Teaching*, 36–37.
37. Scott, *Reluctant Farmer*, 217.
38. Highfill and Wilson, *Progress of Extension Teaching*, 34–36.
39. Scott, *Reluctant Farmer*, 155; Larson, "Development of Short Courses," 33.
40. Scott, *Reluctant Farmer*, 155 and 158.
41. "25 Attend Negro Agri Short Course," *Hope Star*, August 24, 1938, 6.
42. "Short Course at Branch Normal Is Well Attended," *Pine Bluff Daily Graphic*, August 29, 1921, 6.

CHAPTER 6

1. Minutes of the Twelfth Biennial Convention of the NACW, July 12–16, 1920, Tuskegee Institute, Alabama, RNACWC, reel 1.
2. Dilliard, "Scipio A. Jones," 207.
3. "How Did Black Women in the NAACP Promote the Dyer Anti-Lynching Bill, 1918–1922," https://documents.alexanderstreet.com/c/1000636528 (accessed July 12, 2017). The NAACP's Anti-Lynching Crusaders were founded in 1922, to raise money to support the passage of the Dyer Anti-Lynching Bill. The bill was

first introduced into the House of Representatives in 1918 by Missouri congressman Leonidas Dyer. See also Anti-Lynching Crusaders, *Million Women United.*

4. "Elaine Race Massacre," Encyclopedia of Arkansas, http://www.encyclopedia
ofarkansas.net/encyclopedia/entry-detail.aspx?search=1&entryID=1102 (accessed
February 15, 2017). Minutes of the Twelfth Biennial Convention of the NACW,
RNACWC, reel 1.

5. Julia Bumry Jones, "The National Convention Held at Tuskegee," *Competitor,*
July 1920, 143–44; Minutes of the Twelfth Biennial Convention of the NACW,
RNACWC, reel 1.

6. Cooley, *To Live and Dine,* 41.

7. Rieff, "Go Ahead and Do All You Can,"138.

8. Woyshner, *National PTA,* 61.

9. "The National Association of Colored Women," *Voice of the Negro,* July 1, 1904, 311.

10. Knowles, "'It's Our Turn Now,'" 306; Bowers, *Country Life Movement,* 22.

11. Wesley, *History,* 486. Later the AACW established the Mary H. Speight Scholarship
and Loan Fund in her honor to "help need, deserving, and ambitious girls."

12. "Negro Women's Clubs' Session," *Arkansas Gazette,* June 30, 1909, 6;
"Assignments of School Teachers," *Daily Arkansas Gazette,* September 6, 1908,
12; "Many Changes in Teaching Force," *Daily Arkansas Gazette,* September 6,
1911, 1. In 1902, Speight taught at the Capitol School in Little Rock along with
Charlotte Stephens, who in 1868 became the first African American teacher hired
in the Pulaski County school system. See "High Schools," *Arkansas Democrat,*
September 15, 1902, 4, Patterson, 29, and "Charlotte Andrews Stephens,"
Encyclopedia of Arkansas, https://encyclopediaofarkansas.net/entries/charlotte
-andrews-1772/ (accessed July 18, 2016). By 1913, both women were employed
by M. W. Gibbs High School. See "Teachers Assigned to City's Schools," *Daily
Arkansas Gazette,* August 31, 1913, 12.

13. Wesley, *History,* 486.

14. "Negro Women's Clubs' Session," *Arkansas Gazette,* June 30, 1909, 6.

15. "Will Lecture to Negroes," *Arkansas Gazette,* August 6, 1911, 8.

16. "Oppose 'Birth of a Nation,'" *Arkansas Gazette,* November 6, 1917, 8.

17. See Stokes, *D. W. Griffith's "The Birth of a Nation."*

18. "Meeting of Negro Club Women Comes to Close," *Daily Arkansas Gazette,*
December 30, 1905, 10.

19. "Meeting of Negro Club Women Comes to Close," *Daily Arkansas Gazette,*
December 30, 1905, 10; and "Says Negro Women's Clubs do Good Work," *Reno-
Gazette Journal,* January 8, 1906, 1.

20. "Dr. Washington Hosts Trip to Nova Scotia," *New York Age,* August 19, 1915, 7.

21. Mather, *Who's Who,* 165; 1920 United States Federal Census, www.ancestry.com.

22. "Fisk Exercises to Open Today," *Tennessean,* June 5, 1938, 6. She and Du Bois
received alumni awards at this commencement. See also Lewis, *W. E. B. Du Bois,*
76; and W. E. B. Du Bois Papers, 1868–1963, Special Collections and University
Archives, University of Massachusetts Amherst Libraries.

23. Gordon, "Black Women in Arkansas"; Walker, "Howard School," 11.

24. 1900 United States Federal Census, www.ancestry.com.

25. "St. Paul," *Appeal,* September 14, 1912, 2; 1900 United States Federal Census,
US City Directory, Fort Smith, Arkansas, 1911, US City Directories, 1822–1994,
Provo, UT, www.ancestry.com. Josenberger's daughter's name is Ernestine in the

directory, but she is listed as Mrs. William Ernest Josenberger in the Fort Smith
City Death Record, book 3, page 155, May 30, 1919. See "Ernest J. Stevens,"
www.findagrave.com.

26. Shennette Garrett-Scott, "Grand Court Order of Calanthe of Texas, Inc.,"
https://www.tshaonline.org/handbook/entries/grand-court-order-of-calanthe
-of-texas-inc (accessed November 29, 2016); "Negro Lodge Women Meet," *Daily
Arkansas Gazette*, July 24, 1912, 7.

27. "Changes in Court of Calanthe," *Western Outlook*, January 29, 1916, no page.
Josenberger served on a committee to revise Court of Calanthe rituals and
remained the Grand Register of Deeds until 1916. In 1907, she was elected the
organization's Supreme Assistant Conductress and was the Supreme Orator of
the "colored" Knights of Pythias in the 1920s. See "Mrs. M. A. Josenberger, State
of Arkansas," *Topeka Plaindealer*, August 12, 1921, 6; "Women in Spotlight of
Colored Pythians," *Indianapolis News*, August 21, 1929, 12; "Ft. Smith, Arkansas,"
Topeka Plaindealer, April 15, 1938, 4; "Mame Stewart Josenberger," *Journal of the
Fort Smith Historical Society*, September 2016, 4.

28. "Negro Undertaker Dead," *Arkansas Democrat*, September 30, 1909, 8; "Last Will
and Testament of W. E. Josenberger," June 16, 1909, www.ancestry.com (accessed
January 4, 2017). See also Hamilton, *Booker T. Washington*, 135. This was also the
year she joined St. Augustine's Episcopal Church in Fort Smith.

29. "National Negro Business League," Library of Congress (online), http://memory
.loc.gov:8081/ammem/amrlhtml/dtnegbus.html (accessed December 5, 2016).

30. Gordon, *Caste and Class*, 78.

31. US City Directory, 1910, US City Directories, 1822–1994, Provo, UT, www
.ancestry.com.

32. Based upon images shared by Fort Smith Museum of History, on loan from Mr.
Herbert Norwood.

33. "Real Estate Transfers," *Daily Arkansas Gazette*, December 4, 1913, 12.

34. "Seeing Fort Smith, Arkansaw: The Negroes and Their Wealth Engaged in All
Sorts of Business," *Freeman*, March 14, 1914, 7; "Ft. Smith, Arkansas. Beautiful
Southern City, the Home of Many Reputable, Enterprising Colored Citizens,"
Topeka Plaindealer, September 22, 1916, 2; "Fine Program Rendered by Popular
Club," *Chicago Defender*, August 25, 1931, 6.

35. "Mrs. Mame Stewart Josenberger, A.B.," *National Cyclopedia*, 99; Inflation
Calculator, in2013dollars.com (accessed November 25, 2018).

36. "Praise Booker T. Washington," *Great Bend Tribune*, August 17, 1916, 5.

37. "Negro Women to Meet in Brooklyn Tomorrow," *Brooklyn Daily Eagle*,
August 23, 1908, 41.

38. "The N.A. of C.W.C. Very Successful Meet—Woman Suffrage Endorsed—
Presentations—Several," *Cleveland Gazette*, August 14, 1914, 2.

39. "Georgia Representative Gives Review of Great National Club Women's Meet
in Fort Worth by Mrs. W. A. Scott Atlanta, Ga.," *Capitol Plaindealer*, August 6,
1937, 2; Gordon, "Black Women in Arkansas," 30–31; "Partisan Politics Enters
Ranks of the N.A.C.W.," *Chicago Defender*, August 7, 1937, 17.

40. Higginbotham, "In Politics to Stay," 200.

41. "LHSAA Inducts Three to Hall of Honor," *Lincoln Echo*, October 2006, front
page; "Club Women to Hold Biennial Meeting in July," *New York Amsterdam
News*, June 18, 1930, 9.

42. Harley and Terborg-Penn, *African American Woman*, 104. The association memo-
    rialized Douglass's home in Cedar Hill, Anacostia, in Washington, DC.
43. "Douglass Memorial Ass'n To Increase Its Membership," *Pittsburgh Courier*,
    April 18, 1942, 9.
44. "Ft. Smith, Arkansas. Beautiful Southern City, the Home of Many Reputable,
    Enterprising Colored Citizens," *Topeka Plaindealer*, September 22, 1916, 2.
45. "Colored Women Hold Three Day Session in Washington of World International
    Council," *New York Age*, August 18, 1923, 5; Ramdani, "Afro-American Women
    Activists," 7, 8; "International Council Holds Public Meeting: Women of
    Darker Races Make First Appearance After Four Years' Work," *Chicago Defender*,
    August 16, 1924, 10.
46. "Mame Steward [*sic*] Josenberger," www.findagrave.com (accessed December 5,
    2016).
47. "Better Homes Schools (For Colored Women) and Arkansas Committee for
    Better Homes in America and Better Homes Department Arkansas Federation
    of Colored Women's Clubs Cooperating," *National Notes*, January 28–29,
    1930; "A Glimpse of the 1930 Convention, Hot Springs, Ark.," *National Notes*,
    September 1, 1930, 6; "A Significant Meeting," *National Notes*, December 1, 1930,
    8; "Better Homes Stressed at Women's Meetings," *Plaindealer*, July 25, 1930, 1;
    "National Association of Women Hold Biennial Meet," *Chicago Defender*, July 26,
    1930, 6.
48. Hutchison, "American Housing," 6. *The Delineator* was a woman's magazine
    owned by the Butterick Publishing Company. Altman, "Modernity, Gender, and
    Consumption."
49. "Better Homes Schools (For Colored Women) and Arkansas Committee for
    Better Homes in America and Better Homes Department Arkansas Federation
    of Colored Women's Clubs Cooperating," *National Notes*, January 28–29,
    1930; "A Glimpse of the 1930 Convention, Hot Springs, Ark.," *National Notes*,
    September 1, 1930, 6; "A Significant Meeting," *National Notes*, December 1, 1930,
    8; "Better Homes Stressed at Women's Meetings," *Plaindealer*, July 25, 1930,
    1; "National Association of Women Hold Biennial Meet," *Chicago Defender*,
    July 26, 1930, 6. The Arkansas Association of Colored Women was organized in
    1905. See "Activities of State Units of National Association of Colored Women,
    Inc.," *Chicago Defender*, May 29, 1937, 15.
50. Lillian McDermott to Jessie Daniel Ames, October 16, 1931, ASWPL Papers,
    reel 1.
51. Erle Chambers to Jessie Daniel Ames, August 6, 1931, ASWPL Papers, reel 5.
52. "Fourth Annual Christian Conference for Colored Women," Philander Smith
    College, Little Rock, Arkansas, June 21–27, 1930, Porter Family Papers, 1902–
    1996, box 8, folder 9.
53. "Colored Teachers Close Institute," *Camden News*, June 20, 1930, 9.
54. "Colored Homes Much Improved," *Camden News*, May 12, 1930, 2.
55. "Better Homes Campaign," *Camden News*, May 18, 1932, 2.
56. "Report of Jeanes Agent in Ouachita Shows Fine Achievements Are Result and
    Colored Residents Enthusiastic," *Camden News*, November 22, 1930, 4.
57. "Report of Jeanes Agent," *Camden News*, November 22, 1930, 4.
58. Hoffschwelle, *Rebuilding the Rural Southern Community*, 137–38.
59. Hoffschwelle, *Rebuilding the Rural Southern Community*, 11.

60. Mitchell, *Righteous Propagation*, 142.

61. Mitchell, *Righteous Propagation*, 148.

62. Narrative Report of County Extension Workers, St. Francis County, Lugenia B. Christmas, Local Home Demonstration Agent, December 1, 1932–November 11, 1933, RG 33, NARA.

63. "Arkansas Women Aid Better Homes Movement There," *Atlanta Daily World*, July 23, 1939, A6.

64. "Elected Chairman of Better Homes Drive," *Arkansas State Press*, February 5, 1943, 3; "Down Our Way," *Arkansas State Press*, January 7, 1944, 8.

65. Cash, *African American Women*, 46.

66. "From the Field: Arkansas," *National Notes*, September 1, 1930, 8.

67. Cash, *African American Women*, 46.

68. "From the Field: Arkansas," *National Notes*, September 1, 1930, 8.

69. "Governor Favors Reform School for Negroes," *Arkansas Democrat*, November 5, 1910, 9.

70. "Endorses Negro School," *Arkansas Gazette*, July 21, 1915, 5.

71. "Donate Site for School: Federation of Colored Women's Clubs Wants Industrial Institute for Boys," *Arkansas Gazette*, January 1, 1917, 8. There was at least one such institution, the Mountain Valley Industrial School and Home for Negro Boys just north of Argenta in North Little Rock. See "Argenta News," *Daily Arkansas Gazette*, June 16, 1908, 12; Williams, *African American Religion*, 141.

72. "Boys' Industrial School and Its Value to the State," *Arkansas Gazette*, December 22, 1918, 11.

73. "Negro Boys Industrial School Fire of 1959," and "Wrightsville," Encyclopedia of Arkansas, https://encyclopediaofarkansas.net/entries/negro-boys-industrial -school-fire-of-1959-5500/ and https://encyclopediaofarkansas.net/entries /wrightsville-pulaski-county-977/ (accessed July 21, 2016). It was relocated to Wrightsville in Pulaski County in 1931.

74. "Plan School for Delinquent Girls," *Daily Arkansas Gazette*, October 17, 1915, 6.

75. Cahn, *Sexual Reckonings*, 6, 7.

76. Brown, *He Built a School*, 7 and 8.

77. Brown, *He Built a School*, 7 and 8.

78. "Adkins Pledges Greater Economy in Improvements," *Hope Star*, January 12, 1943, 1.

79. "Fargo Agricultural School," Encyclopedia of Arkansas, https://encyclopediaof arkansas.net/entries/fargo-agricultural-school-2375/ (accessed July 19, 2015).

80. "Senate Completes Warren Aid Bill: Budget Group Favors Raising Some Appropriations," *Hope Star*, January 21, 1949, 1, 3.

81. "McMath Names Board," *Hope Star*, May 21, 1949, 6.

82. "Training Schools Plan Accepted by Harris," *El Dorado Times*, June 21, 1968, 1.

CHAPTER 7

1. "Hold Annual Farm Meet in Fargo, Ark.," *Chicago Defender*, February 8, 1941, 12.

2. "Hold Annual Farm Meet in Fargo, Ark.," *Chicago Defender*, February 8, 1941, 12.

3. "Arkansas Women Stage 'Cotton Dress' Revue," *Atlanta Daily World*, June 10, 1940, 2; Hogan, "History of the Agricultural Extension Service," 227, 232.

4. Frances Sampson, "Arkansas Club Women to Care for Convicted Girl," *Atlanta*

Daily World, June 24, 1939, 1; "Arkansas' 35th Session Makes Fine Display," *Chicago Defender*, July 2, 1938, 17; Brown, *He Built a School*, 4.

5. "McGehee Observes Better Homes Week," *Arkansas State Press*, November 9, 1941, 6.

6. Rebecca Stiles Taylor, "Activities of Women's National, Organizations," *Chicago Defender*, February 17, 1940, 18.

7. "Negroes Establish New Club Center," *Courier News*, August 27, 1946, 7. The Blytheville Social Art Club was founded by Mrs. Jimmie Moddest Robinson.

8. *Blytheville/Mississippi County Black Culture Sesquicentennial Scrapbook*, 4; "Blytheville Compress Founded in 1938: Has 52,000 Bale Capacity," *Courier News*, October 10, 1950, 2.

9. *Blytheville/Mississippi County Black Culture Sesquicentennial Scrapbook*, 4.

10. "Buy A Chance on a Bale of Cotton," Sponsored by the B.S.A. and R.B. Clubs, October 1945. Raffle ticket courtesy of Dr. Anes Wiley Abraham, Blytheville, Arkansas.

11. "Open House of the Club Center, Royal Brotherhood and Federated Women's Clubs," Blytheville, Arkansas, August 25, 1946. Flyer courtesy of Dr. Anes Wiley Abraham, Blytheville, Arkansas.

12. "Wiley committed to education," *Courier News*, June 30, 1993, 10. Interview with Dr. Anes Wiley Abraham, September 27, 2017, Blytheville, Arkansas. Dr. Abraham was also the first Black woman doctor to practice medicine in Mississippi County.

13. *The Lion of 1930, Published by the Students of the Fourth Year Class, Arkansas State College*, yearbook courtesy of Dr. Anes Wiley Abraham.

14. Wiley, "Matlocks of Princeton," 50–51. Courtesy of Wiley's daughter, Dr. Anes Wiley Abraham of Blytheville, Arkansas.

15. "Wileys: A Closer Look," "Fire: The Blaze is Ruled Accidental," *Courier News*, May 4, 2007, 3.

16. Wiley, "Matlocks of Princeton," 51. Courtesy of Dr. Anes Abraham. In 1950, Wiley became the principal of Blytheville's segregated Elm Street Elementary School. When she became pregnant with her son William Robert Wiley in 1951, she had to give up her job, as was the custom of the time for women. But she returned to the Blytheville school system several years later and taught mathematics and French for four years. She was then appointed supervisor of the colored elementary schools in the Blytheville district.

After the US Supreme Court's 1954 ruling on *Brown v. Board of Education of Topeka, Kansas* declared segregated schools unconstitutional, Wiley was asked to resign her position as a school supervisor to teach elementary school music. She recalled, "I had my Master's degree in Administration from the University of Arkansas and was not a music major; however, the new assignment gave me more time to spend with my children." Additionally, she remained an active member of the Blytheville Social and Art Club, which in May 1955 was selected by the *Woman's Home Companion* as one of the "250 Honor Clubs of America." Wiley taught music until she retired in 1971. In 1975, she was elected AACW president. She helped parents register their children for the daycare center the AACW supported. As AACW president, home and community uplift informed Wiley's and Black clubwomen's activist agenda. In her address to the AACW's seventy-fifth annual convention, held in Blytheville in 1980, Wiley stressed, "Home, mother, and child face many challenges. We must let them know we care. Caring and sharing is the only way we will see the kind of world our founders dreamed it could be." She died in Blytheville in 2007 at age 97. See "The Woman's Home Companion Presents Second Annual Awards to America's Honor Women's Clubs and Clubwomen," *Woman's Home Companion*, May 1955, 34–35; "Negroes Buy Building for Youth Center," *Courier News*, June 4, 1946, 18; "The Arkansas Association of Women, Youth, and Young Adults Clubs, Inc., A Brief History," from Mrs. Linda A. Murray, current president, July 2015 (special thanks to Dr. Herman Strickland for allowing me to copy this); application for Jeanes Teacher Aid, Alena Erby Wiley, Southern Education Foundation Archives, box 117, folder 1; "Haraway Heads County Negro Teachers Group," *Courier News*, December 16, 1937, 6; *Blytheville/Mississippi County Black Culture Sesquicentennial Scrapbook*, 8 and 9; Alena E. Wiley, US Social Security Death Index, 1935–2014; "Wileys: A Closer Look," "Fire: The Blaze is Ruled Accidental," *Courier News*, May 4, 2007, 3.

17. Narrative Report of Mildred S. Davis, County Home Demonstration Agent, Monroe County, December 1, 1943–November 30, 1944, RG 33, NARA.

18. Narrative Report of the County Home Demonstration Agent, St. Francis County, Jennie B. Wright, Negro Home Demonstration Agent, December 1, 1943–November 30, 1944, RG 33, NARA; Patton, "Surviving the System," 12.

19. Narrative Report of Jennie B. Wright, NARA.

20. Maples, *Farther Down the Road*, 63.

21. "Dixie Sleeps Well, Due to U.S. Mattress Projects," *Chicago Defender*, February 21, 1942, 6; Narrative Report of Mildred S. Davis, NARA, Reel 104; Maples, *Farther Down the Road*, 63.

22. Woods and Nash, interview in *Behind the Veil*.

23. Berlage, *Farmers Helping Farmers*, 152.

24. Arkansas Extension Homemakers Council, *History*, 328.

25. Narrative Report of Mary L. Stubblefield, Negro Home Demonstration Agent, October 23, 1944–November 30, 1944. RG 33, NARA.

26. Narrative Report of Jennie B. Wright, NARA.

27. Narrative Report of Mary L. Stubblefield, NARA.

28. "Hookworms are blood-sucking parasites that enter between the toes of bare feet and live in the intestines, where female hookworms produce eggs that pass out in the feces and hatch in the soil." Between 1910 and 1915, a hookworm eradication campaign was sponsored with a $1 million from the Rockefeller Foundation. The program called for the eradication of hookworms through the introduction of sanitary privies or toilets and wearing shoes. See Smith, *Sick and Tired*, 9; *Educational Bulletin on Hookworm Disease*. Hookworms had been largely eradicated in Arkansas by 1914, but clearly the issue still concerned home demonstration agents, who worked with some populations that still lacked outside toilets in the 1940s.

29. Narrative Report of Jennie B. Wright, NARA.

30. Narrative Report of Jennie B. Wright, NARA. Lincoln High School was founded in 1921. See Patton, "Surviving the System," 7.

31. Narrative Report of Jennie B. Wright, NARA.

32. "PTA New Column," *Arkansas State Press*, April 10, 1942, 3.

33. Woods and Nash, interview in *Behind the Veil*. They also made sheets, pillow cases, and face towels out of flour sacks.
34. Roberts, *Pageants, Parlors, and Pretty Women*, 11.
35. "Conway County Home Demonstration News," *Arkansas State Press*, December 25, 1925, 4.
36. Narrative Report of Mary L. Stubblefield, NARA.
37. Narrative Report of Mary L. Stubblefield, NARA.
38. Narrative Report Jennie B. Wright, NARA.
39. Glave, "Rural African American Women," 38.
40. Brown, *He Built a School*, 57.
41. Mary P. Gaines, Negro Home Demonstration Agent to Presidents and Garden Leaders of Hill Lake Home Demonstration Club, September 19, 1941, Carl E. Bailey Papers, Series 4, Box 30, Folder 1.
42. "Negro Farmer Confab Slated for Arkansas," *Chicago Defender*, July 4, 1942, 5; "Negro Farmers Part in Victory Drive to be Thrashed Out Soon," *Atlanta Daily World*, July 6, 1942, 5; "800 Attend AAA Meets in Arkansas," *Atlanta Daily World*, July 22, 1942, 2. It was also known as the "Food for Victory Campaign."
43. "Farm Leaders Set for Conference," *Arkansas State Press*, June 26, 1942, 1.
44. "Farm Leaders Set for Conference," *Arkansas State Press*, June 26, 1942, 1.
45. "Negro Farmer Confab Slated for Arkansas," *Chicago Defender*, July 4, 1942, 5; "Negro Farmers Part in Victory Drive to be Thrashed Out Soon," *Atlanta Daily World*, July 6, 1942, 5; "800 Attend AAA Meets in Arkansas," *Atlanta Daily World*, July 22, 1942, 2.
46. Brunner, *Rural America*, 87.
47. Narrative Report of County Home Demonstration Agent, Union County, Marguerite P. Williams, Negro Home Demonstration Agent, December 1, 1941–November 30, 1942, RG 33, NARA.
48. Narrative Report of Marguerite P. Williams, NARA.
49. "Only Saboteurs Neglect Their Victory Gardens," *Arkansas State Press*, June 19, 1942, 5.
50. "Negros to Hole Meat Exhibition," *Courier News*, March 13, 1942, 6. KLCN is also known as Arkansas's oldest radio station.
51. "Farm Agents Hold 3 Day Conference," *Arkansas State Press*, January 29, 1943, 3.
52. J. E. Clayton to Walter White, April 17, 1943, Papers of the NAACP, Part 13.
53. Narrative Report of Mildred S. Davis, NARA; Narrative Report of Marguerite P. Williams, NARA.
54. Narrative Report of Marguerite P. Williams, NARA.
55. Narrative Report of Marguerite P. Williams, NARA.
56. Whayne, "Segregated Farm Program," 436; Woodruff, *American Congo*, 146; Lena H. Eddington, Negro Home Demonstration Agent, Report of the (Poinsett) County Home Demonstration Agent, December 1, 1943–October 11, 1944, Arkansas Annual Reports, 1917–1970, RG 33, NARA, Fort Worth Texas Reel 104.
57. Rieff, "Revitalizing Southern Homes," 136.
58. "Yearbook, 1944–1945, Negro Home Demonstration Clubs of St. Francis County," Narrative Report of Jennie B. Wright, NARA.
59. Webb, "By the Sweat of the Brow," 338; Charles Morrow Wilson, Editorial Correspondence, "Arkansas Moves to Guard Future," *New York Time*, February 15,

1931, 56; "Arkansas Farmers Win," *Atlanta Constitution*, November 1, 1931, 4C; Earle E. Griggs, "Backbone and Spareribs," *Atlanta Constitution*, November 1, 1931, 5C; photograph of Lena H. Eddington, *Arkansas State Press*, June 4, 1954, 1. In 1954, Eddington was the Pulaski County home demonstration agent.

60. Harris, *Grace under Pressure*, 217; June L. Rhue, "Arkansas H-D Agent Finds Meals Balanced(2)," *Chicago Defender*, October 6, 1951, 10; Brunner, *Rural America*, 87; Johnson, *Arkansas in Modern America*, 34.

61. Coclanis and Simon, "Exit, Voice, and Loyalty," 194, 196.

62. Kirk, *Redefining the Color Line*, 7.

63. "2000 Negroes at Hope Station: 31 Counties Represented at Negro Visiting Day," *Hope Star*, June 28, 1941, 1.

64. "News: The People's Column," *Arkansas State Press*, December 5, 1941, 2.

65. Kinkead, *Farm*, 184.

66. James H. Purdy Jr., "Farmers Win Live-at-Home County Prizes," *Chicago Defender*, December 20, 1941, 9; "Arkansas Family Wins Inter-State Farm Award," *Chicago Defender*, December 30, 1944, 8.

67. "Live-at-Home Competition in 3 States," *Chicago Defender*, March 11, 1939, 7.

68. "4-H Club Winners Announced from Phillips County," *Arkansas State Press*, November 14, 1947, 8.

69. "On the Agricultural Front with the U.S. Department of Agriculture," "T. R. Betton, Movable School Farm Agent," *Arkansas State Press*, April 13, 1945, 3.

70. "County Agents Given New Appointments," *Arkansas State Press*, July 12, 1946, 1.

71. Division of Negro Education, *Problems*, 4.

72. Hegarty, *Victory Girls*, 30.

73. Hegarty, *Victory Girls*, 30.

74. "PTA Aids VD Campaign," *Chicago Defender*, December 2, 1944, 3; "Ohio Congressman Urges Continued Fight on Prostitution by National Organizations," *Cincinnati Enquirer*, Cincinnati, Ohio, March 18, 1946, 2.

75. "Parent and Teacher Organization Endorses National Venereal Disease Program," *New York Age*, December 16, 1944, 12; "National Congress of CPT Pledges Full Co-operation in V.D. Campaign Says Eastern Arkansas Leader," *Arkansas State Press*, December 1, 1944, 1; Social Protection Division, FSA, *Meet Your Enemy*; "Women's Advisory Social Protection Committee Membership Announced," National Events, *Journal of Social Hygiene*, November 1943, 541.

76. "We Fight, Theme of PTA Group," *Arkansas State Press*, November 5, 1943, 7: "Fifteenth Annual Session of the A.C.C.P.T. (Arkansas Congress of Colored Parents and Teachers)," *Arkansas State Press*, November 19, 1943, 3.

77. "Negroes' Health Programs Cited: Harrison High School Here Wins Award for Fifth Straight Year," *Courier News*, March 17, 1949, 14. Built in 1927, Harrison High School was formerly known as the Blytheville Rosenwald School, which then only went up to the tenth grade. Named for Afro-Canadian actor Richard B. Harrison, who played the role of De Lawd in the 1929 Marc Connelly play *The Green Pastures*, one of the first all-Black casts on Broadway, the high school housed all grades until 1950, when it became Elm Street Elementary School. Former Jeanes Supervisor Alena Erby Wiley was its first principal. Also in 1949, Harrison High School's health club won a certificate of merit for its achievements during National Negro Health Week. See Snowden, *Mississippi County*, 86;

"Richard B. Harrison, 1864–1935," http://www.blackpast.org/aah/harrison
-richard-b-1864–1935 (accessed July 21, 2016); "148 Elm Street Students Cited
for Attendance," *Courier News*, April 24, 1951, 19. "National Negro Health Week
Awards, Year 1949," *National Negro Health News*, July–September 1949, 2.
78. Whayne, "'I Have Been Through Fire,'" 187.
79. Hoffschwelle, "Better Homes on Better Farms," 53.
80. Zellar, "H. C. Ray," 429, 434.

CHAPTER 8

1. "Leoda Berry Gammon," http://www.findagrave.com/memorial/108544416
   /leoda-gammon; "Personals," *Negro Spokesman*, March 7, 1941, 3; Narrative
   Report of (Desha) County Agent and Assistant Home Demonstration Agent for
   Negro Work, December 1, 1954–November 30, 1955, RG 33, NARA.
2. "Home Demonstration Agent," *Pittsburgh Courier*, October 29, 1938, 7.
3. "PTA Workshop Has Large Attendance: Miss Upchurch New State President,"
   Arkansas State Press, November 11, 1942, 1.
4. Arkansas Extension Homemakers Council, *History*, 317; Narrative Report of
   Assistant County Agent and Assistant Home Demonstration Agent for Negro
   Work, Crittenden County, December 1, 1954–November 30, 1955, RG 33, NARA.
5. Like many middle-class Black women, Berry-Gammon was also involved in Jack
   and Jill, Inc., a mother's club formed in 1938 by African American women, was
   secretary of the Keys of Sunshine Federated Club in Marion, founded in 1951 and
   affiliated with the Arkansas Association of Colored Women, and Alpha Kappa
   Alpha Sorority Inc. The Keys of Sunshine Club also included home demonstration agents Levada Parker Mason and Iola B. Rhone who would later become
   an officer in the National Negro Home Demonstration Agents' Association.
   "Leoda Berry Gammon," http://www.findagrave.com/memorial/108544416
   /leoda-gammon; "NAACP Branches Hold Fiery Session—'To "Scalp" President'
   Pine Bluff Branch Urges Withdrawal From Region," *Arkansas State Press*,
   February 4, 1949, 8; "Marion," *Arkansas State Press*, July 7, 1951, 3; "Marion
   Federated Club Organized," *Arkansas State Press*, February 9, 1951, 6.
6. Jones-Branch, "Farming Women," 125.
7. Danbom, *Born in the Country*, 183–84.
8. Campbell, *Farm Bureau*, 24.
9. "Negro Farm Bureau Unit Plans Drive for Members," *Courier News*,
   November 23, 1937, 2.
10. Born in Marion in 1904 or 1906, Gammon was the son of sharecroppers and a
    1931 Arkansas AM&N College graduate, which he had attended with Mississippi
    County Jeanes Supervisor Alena Erby Wiley. Gammon began his career as an
    educator in at the Fitzhugh School in Woodruff County, a position he retained
    until 1935, after which he worked for the Resettlement Administration, the fore-
    runner of the Farmers Home Administration. Gammon remained the Negro
    Division's president until the organization was integrated into the ARFBF in
    1966. "Eleventh Negro Farm Bureau Convention Held," *Hope Star*, November 29,
    1958, 6; "Arkansas Farmers Organize at A.M. and N. College," *Arkansas State
    Press*, January 23, 1948, 1; "Planter Prospers, Points The Way for Others,"

Commercial Appeal, September 8, 1968, 34; "Hold Rural School Confab at Fisk U.," *Plaindealer*, May 17, 1935, 8.

11. Narrative Report of the Assistant County Agent and Assistant Home Demonstration Agent for Negro Work, Crittenden County, December 1, 1954–November 30, 1955, RG 33, NARA.

12. "Program, Eleventh Annual Convention Negro Division, Arkansas Farm Bureau Federation, November 24th and 25th, 1958," Arkansas Council on Human Relations Papers, box 25, folder 269.

13. "FB Negro Division Re-elects Gammon; Approves 7 Program Recommendations," *Farm Bureau Press*, January 1959: 7.

14. "Egg Law," *Farm Bureau Press*, June 1959, 5.

15. "The Origin and History of the Rural Life Conference," personal collection of Harry Linton. See also "Dr. Sellers J. Parker," Arkansas Agriculture Hall of Fame, https://www.arkansasaghalloffame.org/members/member/parker-dr-sellers-j/ (accessed July 17, 2019).

16. "UAPB School of Agriculture, Fisheries, and Human Sciences," Facebook, www.facebook.com (accessed January 6, 2017). Parker, who had been born in Wabash, Arkansas (Phillips County), in 1911, was a 1939 AM&N graduate who earned a PhD from Cornell University in 1949. After teaching vocational agriculture in Cleveland, Arkansas (Conway County), and organizing the state's first Black agricultural association, Parker returned to AM&N as a professor of horticulture. In 1962, he was appointed the first dean of AM&N's Division of Agricultural and Technology. Dr. Parker retired in 1982, and in 1984 became the first recipient of the George Washington Carver Public Service Hall of Fame Award. He died in 1987. See "Dr. Sellers J. Parkier," https://www.arkansasaghalloffame.org/members/member/parker-dr-sellers-j/ (accessed January 6, 2017). The award is given annually to individuals affiliated with or who have worked with 1890 land-grant institutions over a career and who exemplify Dr. Carver's public service philosophy and leadership qualities. See https://www.farmfoundation.org/projects/the-george-washington-carver-public-service-hall-of-fame-award-296-d1/; and "A Brief History of the George Washington Carver Public Service Hall of Fame Award, Professional Agricultural Workers Conference, Tuskegee University," http://pawc.info/the-hall/ (accessed January 6, 2017).

17. "Foto; Members; Planning," *Arkansas State Press*, January 1, 1956, 1; "Bridging Generations: UAPB's 60th Rural Life Conference sustains path to agricultural future," *Pine Bluff Commercial* (online), March 4, 2016, http://www.pbcommercial.com/news/local/bridging-generations-uapb-s-60th-rural-life-conference-sustains-path-agricultural-future (accessed January 6, 2017).

18. "6th Annual Rural Life Confab Held At State College," *Arkansas State Press*, January 31, 1958, 7.

19. "6th Annual Rural Life Confab," *Arkansas State Press*, January 31, 1958, 7.

20. "Farm Bureau Federation Here Mon.–Tues," *Arkansas State Press*, November 21, 1958, 3.

21. "Negro Division's Meetings Stressed Machine Training and Leader Development," *Farm Bureau Press*, April 1963, 6.

22. "Negro Division Convention Sets Program for New Year," *Farm Bureau Press*, January 1961: 6.

23. "Opportunities for Economic Advancement Explored at Negro Division's Convention," *Farm Bureau Press*, February 1964, 6.

24. Eden, *Growing Arkansas*, 6, 33; "Arkansas Farm Bureau Federation," Encyclopedia of Arkansas, https://encyclopediaofarkansas.net/entries /arkansas-farm-bureau-federation-4155/.

25. Hajdik, "'Bovine Glamour Girl,'" 487.

26. Roberts, *Pageants, Parlors, and Pretty Women*, 106–109, 150.

27. Roberts, *Pageants, Parlors, and Pretty Women*, 152–53; see also the Venson Cotton Makers Jubilee Collection.

28. Venson Jubilee Collection finding aid; Hajdik, "'Bovine Glamour Girl,'" 487. A native Memphian, Ethyl Venson was its first queen and also served as its first director from 1970 to 1985.

29. Roberts, *Pageants, Parlors, and Pretty Women*, 154. In 1957, the Harrison High School band participated in the Cotton Makers Jubilee Parade. See "Of Interest to Colored People," *Courier News*, May 27, 1957, 3.

30. "Harrison School Children Attend Cotton Carnival," *Courier News*, May 14, 1948, 6.

31. "Top Students Vie for Coveted Title, 'Spirit of Cotton,'" *Arkansas State Press*, March 6, 1953, 1.

32. "Negroes to Choose Own Bathing Beauties," *Courier News*, May 6, 1940, 6.

33. Daisy Bates Papers finding aid; "Daisy Lee Gatson Bates," Encyclopedia of Arkansas, https://encyclopediaofarkansas.net/entries/daisy-lee-gatson-bates-591/ (accessed October 17, 2016).

34. "Bettye Johnson Named in Contest by JBC to Compete in 'Spirit of Cotton' Contest," *Arkansas State Press*, April 3, 1950, 1; "Spirit of Cotton Calls on Agri Secretary," *Arkansas State Press*, April 14, 1950, 1.

35. "'Spirit of Cotton' Comes to Little Rock Sunday," *Arkansas State Press*, April 21, 1950, 1; "When the 'Spirit of Cotton' Comes to Little Rock," *Arkansas State Press*, April 28, 1950, 1.

36. "51 Spirit of Cotton Sweeps Washington in Triumphant Tour," *Pittsburgh Courier*, April 7, 1951, 2; Venson Jubilee Collection, box 1, series 1, folder 9; "Spirit of Cotton Appears with Arthur Godfrey; On Breakfast Club April 11th," *Arkansas State Press*, April 6, 1950, 1.

37. "National Designer Praises 'The Spirit' on Her Fabulous Cotton Wardrobe," *Arkansas State Press*, April 13, 1950, 7.

38. "Local Girl Take Second Place in 'Spirit Contest,'" *Arkansas State Press*, March 7, 1952, 1.

39. "Spirit of Cotton Gets Warm Reception in Nation's Capital," *Arkansas State Press*, April 18, 1952, 1; "Entertained by the Arkansas Club," *Arkansas State Press*, May 2, 1952, 1; Jubilee Collection, box 1, series 1, folder 10; "Right Around Us," *Arkansas State Press*, May 23, 1952, 5.

40. "Spirit of Cotton Makers Jubilee Gets Check," *Arkansas State Press*, May 11, 1956, 1.

41. Roberts, *Pageants, Parlors, and Pretty Women*, 156.

42. "Cotton Carnival, The Cotton Makers Jubilee, and Carnival Memphis," WKNO (website), http://wknofm.org/post/cotton-carnival-cotton-makers-jubilee-and -carnival-memphis (accessed September 25, 2016).

CHAPTER 9

1. "Woodruff Co.," *Arkansas State Press*, February 10, 1950, 3.

2. "LaFayette H.D. Club Meeting," *Camden News*, January 18, 1950, 1.

3. "Faulkner County Extension News," *Arkansas State Press*, March 10, 1950, 7

4. Narrative Report of Negro agents, Lee County, December 1, 1949–October 20, 1950, RG 33, NARA.

5. Narrative Report of Negro agents, Cross County, December 1, 1949–November 30, 1950, NARA.

6. Narrative Report of Negro agents, Little River County, February 16, 1950–November 30, 1950, NARA.

7. Narrative Report of Carreather F. Banks, Assistant Home Demonstration Agent for Negro Work, St. Francis County, December 1, 1950–November 30, 1951, RG 33, NARA.

8. Narrative Report of Negro agents, Union County, December 1, 1953–November 30, 1954, RG 33, NARA.

9. Narrative Report of Negro agents, Union County, NARA.

10. Narrative Report of Negro agents, Lafayette County, December 1, 1953–November 30, 1954, RG 33, NARA.

11. The cypress "knees" are the part of the tree that lies above water. See, "Lake Village," *Arkansas State Press*, February 2, 1955, 4.

12. Hadwiger and Cochran, "Rural Telephones in the United States," 222, 230. The REA had been established by President Franklin Roosevelt through Executive Order 7037 on May 11, 1935, as part of an unemployment relief program. Congress passed the REA as a bill making it a government agency exactly one year later. In July 1939, it became a part of the USDA. See *Brief History of Rural Electric and Telephone Programs*, 1.

13. "Dermott," *Arkansas State Press*, March 2, 1955, 4. According to one source, Black families in Lee County had telephones as early as 1925. See Highfill and Wilson, *Progress*, 10; Grim, "From the Yazoo Mississippi Delta," 128; Kline, *Consumers in the Country*, 53.

14. "New Telephone Construction in Rural Areas Here," *Marvell Messenger*, August 13, 1965, front page.

15. "250 Arkansas Farm Families Lift Themselves by Their Own Bootstraps," *Arkansas State Press*, July 31, 1959, 7.

16. "Cash Crops Help Small Ark. Farmer make Good Living," *Chicago Defender*, December 22, 1956, 10; Hurt, *American Agriculture*, 293.

17. Kline, *Consumers in the Country*, 2–3.

18. Eden, *Growing Arkansas*, 10.

19. Whayne et al., *Arkansas: A Concise History*, 278.

20. Kline, *Consumers in the Country*, 3.

21. Jellison, *Entitled to Power*, 3.

22. Whayne et al., *Arkansas*, 329 and 331.

23. "Levada Parker," 1940 United States Federal Census, ancestry.com (accessed July 6, 2016).

24. Fisk University Rosenwald Fund Card File Database, http://rosenwald.fisk.edu/ (accessed July 28, 2015).

25. Smith, *Educating the Masses*, 212.

26. Cloke, "Conceptualizing Rurality," 18.

27. "New Park for Lewisville Negroes," *Lafayette County Democrat*, date and page unknown; "Lewisville Negro Home Demonstration Club Dedication Program," Narrative County Agent and Assistant Home Demonstration Agent for Negro Work, Lafayette County, December 1, 1953–November 30, 1954, RG 33, NARA.

28. Narrative Report of Negro agents, LaFayette County, December 1, 1953–November 30, 1954; Narrative Report of Assistant County Agent and Assistant Home Demonstration Agent for Negro Work, Chicot County, December 1, 1963, to November 30, 1964, RG 33, NARA.

29. Narrative Report of Negro agents, Pulaski County, December 1, 1949–November 30, 1950, RG 33, NARA.

30. Narrative Report of Negro agents, Lee County, December 1, 1949–October 20, 1950, RG 33, NARA.

31. Betton, "Brief History," 5.

32. Narrative Report of Negro agents, Lonoke County, December 1, 1953–November 30, 1954, RG 33, NARA; Sixteenth Annual Meeting of the Arkansas Negro State Home Demonstration Council, September 11–12, 1952, Twenty-Third Annual Meeting of the Arkansas Negro State Home Demonstration Council, September 2–4, 1959, Twenty-Fifth Annual Meeting of the Arkansas Negro State Home Demonstration Council, August 30-September 1961, box 8, file 3, UACESR.

33. Annual Conference of Negro Extension Agents, National Baptist Hotel, Hot Springs, Arkansas, December 6–8, 1960, box 8, file 4, UACESR.

34. In-Service Training Conference, County Extension Personnel for Negro Work, National Baptist Hotel, April 18–20, 1962, box 8, file 3, UACESR; "Arkansas Club Women Break Ground for New Center," *Pittsburgh Courier*, December 8, 1962, 10.

35. Betton, "Brief History," 1.

36. Maples, *Farther Down the Road*, 59, 61. Born impoverished in Mount Ida, Arkansas (Montgomery County), in 1907, Charles Austin Vines began his career with the Arkansas Extension Service in 1934 as an assistant county agent in St. Francis County. He became associate director in 1952 and then director in 1959. Vines worked for the extension service until 1976 and died in 2001.

37. C. A. Vines, Associate Director of Extension to Mrs. Elveria Heard, February 6, 1957, box 8, file 3, UACESR.

38. P. V. Kepner, Deputy Administrator, USDA to C. A. Vines, Associate Director of Extension, Little Rock, January 25, 1957, box 8, file 3, UACESR.

39. 1940 US Federal Census, www.ancestry.com.

40. Mrs. Elveria Heard, Home Demonstration Council President, to Dr. John Tyler Caldwell, President, University of Arkansas, December 19, 1956, box 8, file 3, UACESR.

41. "4-H'er Makes Good," *Tribune*, [date unknown], 1950, page unknown.

42. P. V. Kepner, USDA Deputy Administrator, to Elveria Heard, January 25, 1957, box 8, file 3, UACESR.

43. Smith, *Sick and Tired*, 2.

44. Smith, *Sick and Tired*, 102.

45. "Arkansas Town Takes A New Lease on Life," *Chicago Defender*, February 6, 1960, 15.

46. "Housekeeping Context Set for Residents of Ivory Heights," *Camden News*, March 29, 1963, front page.

47. "Arkansas Town Takes A New Lease on Life," *Chicago Defender*, February 6, 1960, 15.

48. "Arkansas Town Takes A New Lease on Life," *Chicago Defender*, February 6, 1960, 15; "Negro Health Week Movement Terminated," *Atlanta Daily World*, February 20, 1951, 1.

49. Reid, *Reaping*, 63; Brown, "National Negro Health Week Movement," 553; "National Negro Health Week to Be Observed," 457; Beardsley, *History of Neglect*, 102.

50. "Health Week is Factor in Race Relations," *National Notes*, April 1, 1926, 10.

51. Smith, *Sick and Tired*, 33; Beardsley, *History of Neglect*, 103.

52. Smith, *Sick and Tired*, 13. The Tuskegee program was actually based on a Black health program begun two years earlier by the Negro Organization Society of Virginia. See Beardsley, *History of Neglect*, 102; and Smith, *Sick and Tired*, 36.

53. "Negroes Observe Health Week," *Southern Standard*, April 5, 1923, 1.

54. "150 Negroes Examined at Clinic Last Week," *Courier News*, April 7, 1930, 1.

55. Smith, *Sick and Tired*, 34.

56. "Negro Observe 'Health Week,'" *Camden News*, April 10, 1930, 1.

57. "Colored FERA Work in County," *Camden News*, July 8, 1935, 3.

58. "Faulkner County Extension News," *Arkansas State Press*, March 10, 1950, 7. Mastitis is an infection of the breast tissue. "Upchurch," *Arkansas State Press*, February 2, 1954, 6; "Lake Village," *Arkansas State Press*, June 10, 1955, 3.

59. Quoted in Rodrique, "Black Community," 147–48.

60. Mrs. C. S. Smith from Ashley County, Mrs. Bessie Corrothers from Bradley County, Mrs. Alena Erby Wiley from Mississippi County, and Miss Ila D. Upchurch from Nevada County. DNSPPFA, December 1, 1942.

61. "State HD Council Hold 17th Annual Meeting at ABC (Arkansas Baptist College)," *Arkansas State Press*, September 25, 1953, 1.

62. Narrative Report of Negro agents, Union County, December 1, 1953–November 30, 1954, RG 33, NARA.

63. Narrative Report of Negro agents, Lafayette County, December 1, 1953–November 30, 1954, RG 33, NARA.

CHAPTER 10

1. "Listen Here, Mr. Editor!," *Arkansas State Press*, January 1, 1949, 4.

2. Handy, *We Witness*, xii.

3. Handy, *We Witness*, xiii.

4. Lowe, *Baptized with Soil*, 3.

5. Lowe, *Baptized with Soil*, 3.

6. "Guide to the Home Missions Council of North America Records," Presbyterian Historical Society, www.history.pc.usa.org.

7. Handy, *We Witness Together*, xii.

8. Year: *1940*; Census Place: *Pine Bluff, Jefferson, Arkansas*; Roll: *m-t0627–00146*; Page: *9B*; Enumeration District: *35–53*.

9. "Mrs. O. G. Dawson (Ethel B.)—Pine Bluff" in Kilmer, *Women of the Arkansas Delta*, 7.

10. Interview, Mrs. O. G. (Ethel B.) Dawson, 1976, Box 2, Pine Bluff Women's Center Collection.

11. Interview, Mrs. O. G. (Ethel B.) Dawson, 1976, Box 2, Pine Bluff Women's Center Collection.

12. Vesely-Flad, *Racial Purity and Dangerous Bodies*, 64. See also Blackmon, *Slavery by Another Name*.

13. Year: *1940*; Census Place: *Pine Bluff, Jefferson, Arkansas*; Roll: *m-t0627–00146*; Page: *9B*; Enumeration District: *35–53*, ancestry.com. *Arkansas, County Marriages Index, 1837–1957* [database on-line].

14. *Arkansasyer*, May 1940, 114.

15. *Arkansas Educational Directory, 1944–1945*; *Arkansasyer*, May 1941, 23.

16. Interview, Mrs. O. G. (Ethel B.) Dawson, 1976, Box 2, Pine Bluff Women's Center Collection.

17. Interview, Mrs. O. G. (Ethel B.) Dawson, 1976, Box 2, Pine Bluff Women's Center Collection.

18. Interview, Mrs. O. G. (Ethel B.) Dawson, 1976, Box 2, Pine Bluff Women's Center Collection.

19. "Church Leaders Discuss Basis for Making Brotherhood Work," *Pittsburgh Courier*, April 26, 1947, 12; "Jackson, Tennessee," *Plaindealer*, February 14, 1947, 9.

20. "Jackson, Tennessee," *Plaindealer*, February 14, 1947, 9. Founded in 1944, the school trained ministers and religious workers for the Colored Methodist Church, later renamed the Christian Methodist Church. See "The History of the Phillips School of Theology," Phillips School of Theology, http://www.phillipsschoolof theology.org/pst-history.

21. The UCCW's purpose was to "united church women in their allegiance to their Lord and Savior, Jesus Christ, through a program looking to their integration into the total life and work of the church, and to the building of a world Christian community." See Jones, "'How Shall I Sing the Lord's Song?,'" 132–33.

22. Jones, "'How Shall I Sing the Lord's Song?,'" 132–33.

23. Jones, "'How Shall I Sing the Lord's Song?,'" 134–35.

24. "United Church Women Call for End of Army Jim Crow: More Than One Hundred Negro Women Attend Sessions," *Atlanta Daily World*, November 25, 1948, 1; "Negro Women Active in United Council Assembly," Claude A. Barnett Papers.

25. "The History of Phillips Theology School," Phillips School of Theology, http:// www.phillipsschooloftheology.org/pst-history.

26. "Philips Theology School Offers Mid-Term Session," *Plaindealer*, December 26, 1947, 7.

27. "Regional Conference," *Negro Star*, March 5, 1948, 1. Lowe, *Baptized with Soil*, 48.

28. "Gould," *Arkansas State Press*, September 10, 1948, 8.

29. "Nearly $1,800 For March of Dimes Is Negroes' Record," *Arkansas State Press*, March 3, 1949, 4.

30. "What are the Branches Doing," *Crisis*, June 1950, 385; "Pine Bluff NAACP Executive Committee," *Arkansas State Press*, May 12, 1950, 1; "Pine Bluff NAACP Elects New Officers, Pushes Membership Drive," April 28, 1950, Papers of the NAACP, Part 25.

31. "Pine Bluff," *Arkansas State Press*, March 17, 1950, 3; Felton, *These My Brethren*.

32. "Down Our Way," *Arkansas State Press*, June 22, 1951, 6.

33. "Right Around Us," *Arkansas State Press*, March 28, 1952, 5.

34. "Pine Bluff," *Arkansas State Press*, December 19, 1952, 6; John Kirk, "Facilitating Change: The Arkansas Council on Human Relations, 1954–1964," 1, http://plaza.ufl.edu/wardb/Kirk.doc. "Arkansas Council on Human Relations (ACHR)," Encyclopedia of Arkansas, https://encyclopediaofarkansas.net/entries/arkansas-council-on-human-relations-2959/.

35. Egerton, *Speak Now*, 311–12.

36. Johnson, *Arkansas in Modern America*, 123; John Kirk, "Facilitating Change," http://www.encyclopediaofarkansas.net/encyclopedia/entry-detail.aspx?search=1&entryID=2959; "Arkansas Organizes Council on Human Relations," *Arkansas State Press*, December 10, 1954, 6; "Organized in '54," *Arkansas Gazette*, January 4, 1954, front page.

37. Castro, "Mexican Braceros," 29.

38. Castro, "Mexican Braceros," 39.

39. ACHR Log June 6–24, 1955, Southern Regional Council Papers, 1944–1968, Series IV, State Councils on Human Relations, Reel 141.

40. Alexander, *Arkansas Plantation*, 79, 86.

41. Lowe, *Baptized with Soil*, 48–49; Daniel, *Breaking the Land*, 178 and 179.

42. Ethel B. Dawson to Reverend Don F. Pielstick, January 20, 1951, Group 7, Box 8, Folder 9, NCCDHM.

43. Flyer about the Rural Life Meeting at Arkansas Agricultural, Mechanical, and Normal College, 1951, Group 7, Box 8, Folder 9, NCCDHM.

44. "Bishop Wilkes Announces District Meeting," *Arkansas State Press*, August 8, 1952, 2.

45. Ethel B. Dawson, General Summary Report for December 1953, Group 7, Box 8, Folder 9, NCCDHM.

46. Ethel B. Dawson, Correspondence, April 2, 1954, Group 7, Box 8, Folder 9, NCCDHM.

47. "Rest Rooms Asked for the Colored," *Pine Bluff Commercial*, November 12, 1954, no page; Interview, Mrs. O. G. (Ethel B.) Dawson, 1976, Box 2, Pine Bluff Women's Center Collection.

48. "City Council," *Pine Bluff Commercial*, November 16, 1954, 1 and 11.

49. Handy, *We Witness Together*, 101.

50. "Rural Life Conference at Gould First Baptist Church Slated Friday," *Pine Bluff Commercial*, May 6, 1954, no page.

51. "Rural Life Conference at Gould First Baptist Church Slated Friday," *Pine Bluff Commercial*, May 6, 1954, no page.

52. Ethel B. Dawson, General Summary Report for August 1955, Group 7, Box 8, Folder 9, NCCDHM.

53. Ethel B. Dawson, General Summary Report for November 1955, Group 7, Box 8, Folder 9, NCCDHM.

54. Ethel B. Dawson, Progressive Women's Voters Association, 1953, Group 7, Box 8, Folder 9, NCCDHM.

55. Ethel B. Dawson, Progressive Women's Voters Association, 1953, Group 7, Box 8, Folder 9, NCCDHM.

56. "Mrs. O. G. Dawson (Ethel B.)—Pine Bluff," in Kilmer, *Women of the Arkansas Delta*, 7.

57. "Negroes Run in Arkansas," *Student Voice*, September 23, 1964, 1.

58. Wallach and Kirk, *ARSNICK*, 61; "Ezekiel Candler Gathings," Encyclopedia of Arkansas, https://encyclopediaofarkansas.net/entries/ezekiel-candler-took-gathings-4397/.

59. Interview, Mrs. O. G. (Ethel B.) Dawson, 1976, Box 2, Pine Bluff Women's Center Collection.

CHAPTER II

1. 1958 El Dorado, Arkansas City Directory, and Arkansas County Marriages Index, 1837–1957, www.ancestry.com (accessed December 4, 2014).

2. Smith and Jackson, *Educating the Masses*, 163; "Arkansas Colored Women Hold Annual Meeting in Madison," *Arkansas State Press*, June 15, 1956, 4; "Social and Art Club Gives Program: Theme 'Night and Day,'" *Arkansas State Press*, May 14, 1954, 5. In 1952, she became president of the Business and Professional Women's Circle of First Baptist Church in El Dorado. See "El Dorado," *Arkansas State Press*, March 21, 1952, 5.

3. Smith and Jackson, *Educating the Masses*, 163.

4. Reeves, *History*, 5.

5. Reid, *Reaping*, 160.

6. "Agricultural Association Elects 1946 Officers," *Chicago Defender*, January 19, 1946, 13; 1940 US Federal Census, El Dorado, Union County, www.ancestry.com (accessed December 4, 2014).

7. "Model Farming Project Grows," *Pittsburgh Courier*, November 16, 1946, 2; "Negro Community Ends 5 Yr Improvement Plan," *New York Age*, November 23, 1946, 9; Arkansas Extension Homemakers Council, *History*, 346.

8. "National Negro Home Demonstration Agents' Association (NNHDAA), 1957–1965," National Extension Assoc. of Family and Consumer Services, http://www.neafcs.org/content.asp?pageID=2087 (accessed April 2, 2012).

9. "Study Needs of Rural Families," *Chicago Defender*, November 15, 1958, 21.

10. "NNHDAA Mulls Topic 'Readjustment for Better Living' at Annual Meeting," *Arkansas State Press*, October 24, 1958, 16.

11. "National Negro H.D. Meeting in Jackson," *Camden News*, October 15, 1959, 13; "Negro HD Agents form National Group Here," *Clarion-Ledger*, May 2, 1957, 3.

12. Narrative Report of All County Extension Agents, Columbia County, December 1, 1964– November 30, 1965, RG 33, NARA.

13. Daniel, *Dispossession*, 1.

14. National Extension Association of Family and Consumer Sciences, http://www.neafcs.org/content.asp?pageID=2087 (accessed April 3, 2012); Daniel, *Dispossession*, 54.

15. Daniel, *Dispossession*, 166.

16. "Extension Titles Are Changed," *Hope Star*, December 10, 1966, front page; Warren, *Official History*, 44. In 1993, the Council changed its name to the National Association for Family and Community Education.

17. "1965 County Budget," *El Dorado Times*, January 2, 1965, 3.

18. "Quorum County Sets Expenses," *Hope Star*, November 23, 1966, front page.

19. Reid, *Reaping*, 181.

20. Daniel, *Dispossession*, 212.

21. Bolsterli, *Things*, 10.

22. "Cotton Plant Academy," Encyclopedia of Arkansas, https://encyclopediaof arkansas.net/entries/cotton-plant-academy-6548/ (accessed June 29, 2016).

23. "Swift Memorial College," *Tennessee Encyclopedia of History and Culture* (online), http://tennesseeencyclopedia.net/entry.php?rec=1682 (accessed June 29, 2016).

24. LaVerne Williams Feaster, "One of Its Kind in America: State Leader 4-H," 12, Hazel Jordon Papers, box 1, folder 1.

25. Feaster, "One of Its Kind in America," 13.

26. Feaster, "One of Its Kind in America," 13.

27. Feaster, "One of Its Kind in America."

28. Interview with Carreather Banks Perry. She died in July 2016.

29. "Resident Chosen as Extension Agent," *El Dorado News-Times*, March 2, 1975, 3; Year: *1940*; Census Place: *Little Rock, Pulaski, Arkansas*; Roll: *m-t0627–00168*; Page: *3A*; Enumeration District: *60–68A*, www.ancestry.com.

30. "Mrs. Lillie Mae Doss," *Hope Star*, June 25, 1975, 2.

31. US, Social Security Applications and Claims Index, 1936–2007, ancestry.com.

32. Narrative Report of All County Extension Agents, Cross County, December 1, 1964–November 30, 1965, NARA.

33. Feaster, "One of Its Kind in America," 14.

34. Feaster, "One of Its Kind in America"; "LaVerne Williams-Feaster," *Arkansas-Democrat Gazette*, May 31, 2013, 6B. Feaster died on May 27, 2013. Smith and Jackson, *Educating the Masses*, 164.

35. "LaVerne Williams Feaster," *Arkansas-Democrat Gazette*, May 31, 2013, 6B.

36. Feaster, "One of Its Kind in America."

CHAPTER 12

1. Interview with Annie R. Zachary, Pine Bluff Women's Center Collection, M92–06, box 3.

2. Kilmer, *Women of the Arkansas Delta*, 30.

3. Matkin-Rawn, "'Great Negro State of the Country,'" 5.

4. "Phillips County," Encyclopedia of Arkansas, https://encyclopediaofarkansas.net /entries/phillips-county-797/.

5. "Phillips County," Encyclopedia of Arkansas, https://encyclopediaofarkansas.net /entries/phillips-county-797/.

6. 1940 United States Federal Census, www.ancestry.com; interview with Annie Zackary Pike, July 2016.

7. Interview with Annie Zachary Pike, July 2016.

8. Department of the Interior, Bureau of Education, *Negro Education*, 123.

9. "Consolidated White River Academy," Encyclopedia of Arkansas, https:// encyclopediaofarkansas.net/entries/consolidated-white-river-academy-5351/ (accessed June 10, 2016).

10. "Homer G. Phillips Hospital (1937–1979)," Black Past, http://www.blackpast .org/aah/homer-g-phillips-hospital-1937-1979 (accessed July 21, 2016); "Four

Suspects Held Upon Inquiry of a Slaying, Homer Phillips, Dead Man, Shot Down Thursday in St. Louis," *Sedalia Democrat*, June 19, 1931, 1; "Phillips' Slayers Identified," *Pittsburgh Courier*, June 27, 1931, 17.

11. Cleve Zachary was born in Marvell, Arkansas, in 1886. See, US World War I Draft Registration Cards, 1917–1918, ancestry.com.

12. "Annie R. Zachary For State Senate, Dist. 34," Tom Dillard Black Arkansiana Collection, series 1, box 16, folder 36; "Annie Zachary," Republican Party State Headquarters Collection, 1964–1984, box 12, folder 30.

13. *Arkansas Gazette*, December 12, 1959; and *Commercial Appeal*, December 12, 1959. See also "Annie R. Zachary for State Senate, Dist. 34," in Tom Dillard Black Arkansiana Collection, series 1, box 16, folder 36; and "Annie Zachary," in Republican Party State Headquarters Collection, 1964–1984, box 12, folder 30.

14. Berlage, *Farmers Helping Farmers*, 13.

15. Kilmer, *Women of the Arkansas Delta*, 30; interview with Annie R. Zachary.

16. Kilmer, *Women of the Arkansas Delta*, 30; interview with Annie R. Zachary.

17. Schackel, *Working the Land*, 32; Chafe, *Paradox of Change*, 154–72.

18. Osterud, "Land Identity," 73–87.

19. Jellison, *Entitled to Power*, xxi and 15.

20. Kilmer, *Women of the Arkansas Delta*, 30; Berlage, *Farmers Helping Farmers*, 35.

21. Kilmer, *Women of the Arkansas Delta*, 30; Berlage, *Farmers Helping Farmers*, 35.

22. Kilmer, *Women of the Arkansas Delta*, 30; Berlage, *Farmers Helping Farmers*, 35; interview with Annie R. Zachary.

23. Walker, "Shifting Boundaries," 81.

24. Kilmer, *Women of the Arkansas Delta*, 30.

25. Kilmer, *Women of the Arkansas Delta*, 30.

26. Interview with Annie R. Zachary.

27. "Colored News," *Marvell Messenger*, October 25, 1963, 2.

28. "Former Welfare Director Amazed at GOP Charges," *Camden News*, July 13, 1967, 1.

29. Reck, *4-H Story*, vii, 3. "4-H Activity Held at Lake View," *Marvell Messenger*, April 30, 1965, page unmarked. The extent to which segregated 4-H clubs helped young Black people has been woefully underexplored in scholarship on this topic with the one exception being Gabriel Rosenberg's 2016 study, *The 4-H Harvest: Sexuality and the State in Rural America*.

30. "Phillips County Fair to Open on September 16," *Marvell Messenger*, September 13, 1963, 1.

31. "Banquet Held for Negro 4-H Leaders," *Marvell Messenger*, February 5, 1965, 7.

32. Interview with Annie R. Zachary.

33. Narrative Report of All County Extension Agents, Phillips County, December 1, 1964–November 30, 1965, NARA.

34. "Colored News," *Marvel Messenger*, October 25, 1963, 2.

35. "Arkansas to Entertain National Home Demonstration Council," *Northwest Arkansas Times*, October 16, 1963, 8; "Home Demonstration Council Changes Name; Tells Officers," *Northwest Arkansas Times*, October 25, 1963, 6.

36. Interview with Annie R. Zachary; "Mrs. Gardner HD Club Hostess," *Wellington Leader*, November 21, 1963, 6.

37. "Negro Home Demonstration Group Merges with Whites at Meeting," *Sentinel Record*, August 31, 1965, 3.

38. LaVerne Williams Feaster, "One of Its Kind in America: State Leader 4-H," 13, Hazel Jordon Papers, box 1, folder 1.
39. "Arkansas Extension Homemakers Council's annual held in Little Rock, Arkansas, October 5–7, 1966," in Arkansas Extension Homemakers Council Papers.
40. "Arkansas Extension Homemakers Council's annual meeting held at Henderson State College, August 13–16, 1968," in Arkansas Extension Homemakers Council Papers.
41. Interview with Annie R. Zachary.
42. Finley, "Crossing the White Line," 119 and 121.
43. Interview with Annie Zachary Pike, July 2016; Rigueur, *Loneliness*, 2.
44. Interview with Annie R. Zachary, Pine Bluff Women's Center Collection; Kirk, "Southern Road," 176–77.
45. Johnson, *Arkansas in Modern America*, 166.
46. Interview with Annie R. Zachary, Pine Bluff Women's Center Collection.
47. Arkansas Association of Colored Women's Clubs to Winthrop Rockefeller, October 27, 1966, Winthrop Rockefeller Collection, III, box 162, folder 2. Like many Black home demonstration clubwomen, Ms. Annie was a member of the Marvell district twenty-two PTA, Marvell NAACP (chartered in 1948), chaired the county teachers' day program for over forty years, and served as the assistant secretary, and program chairman of the local affiliate of the AACW. See "NAACP Organized in 45 States," *Arkansas State Press*, June 25, 1948, 8.
48. Kirk, "Southern Road," 187.
49. Finley, "Crossing the White Line," 128.
50. "Former Welfare Director Amazed at GOP Charges," *Camden News*, July 13, 1967, 1; Kilmer, *Women of the Arkansas Delta*, 30; "Negro Named to Welfare Board," *Northwest Arkansas Times*, April 29, 1967, 6.
51. Johnson, *Arkansas in Modern America*, 167.
52. Kirk, "Southern Road," 177.
53. Kirk, "Southern Road," 188.
54. Interview with Annie R. Zachary, Pine Bluff Women's Center Collection.
55. Interview with Annie R. Zachary.
56. Interview with Annie R. Zachary.
57. "Moss Denies Welfare Group Gave Him $3000," *Northwest Arkansas Times*, July 13, 1967, 11.
58. "Moss Denies Welfare Group Gave Him $3000," *Northwest Arkansas Times*, July 13, 1967, 11.
59. "Blaylock, State Welfare Board Renew Clash," *Northwest Arkansas Times*, August 19, 1967, 14.
60. "GOP Leader Wants Inquiry," *Commercial Appeal Little Rock Bureau*, September 19, 1972, page unknown.
61. Center for the American Woman and Politics, *Women in Public Office*, 29.
62. Memorandum, October 7, 1970, Winthrop Rockefeller Collection, III, box 136, folder 13; Rogerline Johnson to Winthrop Rockefeller, July 12, 1970, Winthrop Rockefeller Collection, III, box 205, folder 5.
63. Daniel, *Dispossession*, 1; see *Equal Opportunity in Farm Programs*.
64. Daniel, *Dispossession*, 1–2, 4–5, 217–218.
65. "Field Report," March 24, 1970, Winthrop Rockefeller Collection, III, box 172, folder 6.

66. Annie R. Zachary to Clifford Hardin, Secretary of Agriculture, October 1, 1970, Winthrop Rockefeller Collection, RG III, box 136, file 13.

67. "Conference Meet," *Arkansas Outlook*, October 1968, 3.

68. "Toward A National Policy," 160.

69. "Senior Citizens," *Arkansas Outlook*, March 1972, 4–6.

70. "Arkansas Council on Human Relations," Encyclopedia of Arkansas, https:// encyclopediaofarkansas.net/entries/arkansas-council-on-human-relations-2959/; John A. Kirk, "Facilitating Change: The Arkansas Council on Human Relations," http://plaza.ufl.edu/wardb/Kirk.doc (accessed September 16, 2016).

71. "Marvell Water Assoc. to meet with DUSCO," *Courier Index*, December 4, 1975, 1C.

72. Memorandum, October 7, 1970, Winthrop Rockefeller Collection, III, box 136, folder 13.

73. Author's copy of Ms. Annie's delegate badge. See also Moore, *Defeat of Black Power*, 1.

74. "Ticker Tape U.S.A.," *Jet Magazine*, September 7, 1972, 11; "Arkansas Delegates Bask Serenely, Miles from Uproar of Convention," *Arkansas Gazette*, August 22, 1972, 7A.

75. "Temporary Roll of Delegates and Alternate Delegates to Republican National Convention, Miami Beach, Florida, August 21, 1972," Winthrop Rockefeller Collection, IV, box 268, file 5.

76. "43 File for 36 GOP Delegate Posts," *Arkansas Gazette*, June 16, 1972, 4A; "Arkansan Appointed to GOP Committee," *Arkansas Gazette*, July 27, 1972, page unknown.

77. "State's GOP Delegation 'Most Representative" in History," *Arkansas Outlook*, August 1972, front page and 2; *Official Program, 30th Republican National Convention*, 89; "Delegate Battle for GOP?," *Arkansas Democrat*, July 9, 1972, page number unknown.

78. Rymph, *Republican Women*, 68.

79. "Mrs. Nixon and Daughters Hear Speech by Phillips County Delegate," *Helena, Arkansas Daily World*, August 23, 1972, page unknown.

80. "Arkansas Delegates Bask Serenely, Miles from Uproar of Convention," *Arkansas Gazette*, August 22, 1972, 7A.

81. "Women Must Work Together," *Florida Today*, August 22, 1972, 1D; "Mrs. Nixon and Daughters Hear Speech by Phillips County Delegate," *Helena, Arkansas Daily World*, August 23, 1972, page unknown.

82. "State GOP Roasts National Democrats," *Commercial Appeal Little Rock Bureau*, September 17, 1972, page unknown; "15 Delegates from Arkansas Support Nixon," *Arkansas Gazette*, July 30, 1972, page unknown.

83. Interview with Annie R. Zachary.

84. "1972 General Election Results," *Arkansas Outlook*, December 1972, 5.

85. Kilmer, *Women of the Arkansas Delta*, 30.

86. "Grand Jury Indicts Senator," *Hope Star*, September 15, 1972, 1.

87. "Sen. Anderson Resigns Post," *Camden News*, May 12, 1973, 1. Ms. Annie's loss was also the source of controversy among African American students at the University of Arkansas at Pine Bluff after its chancellor, Dr. Lawrence A. Davis endorsed the incumbent Joe Lee Anderson. The students, led by the Student

Government Association president, boycotted and demanded that Davis and three faculty members resign. Davis was further threatened by Black leaders who promised that he would be "removed from power" at the college. See "Chancellor of UAPB Tells of Conspiracy," *Northwest Arkansas Times*, December 6, 1972, 17.

88. "State Minority Republicans Elect Officers," *Arkansas Outlook*, July 1972, front page.

89. "State GOP Committee Members Listed as Meeting Draws Near," *Arkansas Outlook*, November 1974.

90. "Central Arkansas," and "Progress Through the Arkansas Federation of Young Republicans," *Arkansas Outlook*, October 1971, 6 and 8.

91. "Youth Day at Winrock," *Arkansas Outlook*, October 1971, 8.

92. Mr. Cleve died in 1973. In 1977, Ms. Annie married Lester Pike from Postelle, a small Black community also located in Phillips County.

93. "Helena," *Courier Index*, December 22, 1977, 6; Schultz, *Tri-Faith America*, 30–32.

94. "Governor Appoints Pike to State Tobacco Control Board," newspaper name and date unknown. Interview with Annie R. Zachary, Pine Bluff Women's Center Collection; Lester Pike died in 1997.

95. "AEA Convention Begins," *Northwest Arkansas Times*, October 10, 1985, 19; Smith and Jackson, *Educating the Masses*, 92; interview with Annie R. Zachary, Pine Bluff Women's Center Collection.

96. Interview with Annie Zachary Pike, July 2016.

97. Amber Hardin, Scheduler, Office of the Lieutenant Governor to Annie Pike, March 12, 2002. Letter is in Ms. Annie's possession. The daughter of Lithuanian immigrants, she was born Jievute Paulekiute. Paul died from a blood disorder in 2006. Barbara died in 2008. See "Barbara Sears Rockefeller, Actress with a Famous Divorce Settlement, Dies at 91," *New York Times*, May 21, 2008, https://www.nytimes.com/2008/05/21/nyregion/21rockefeller.html (accessed December 6, 2019).

98. State of Arkansas Office of the Lieutenant Governor to Pleasant Grove Missionary Baptist Church, August 18, 2002, photocopy in the author's possession; "Annie Ruth Zachary Pike, Citizen of the Year, Sphinx Temple, # 25, October 2007," photocopy in the author's possession.

CONCLUSION

1. Devine, *On Behalf of the Family Farm*, 142.

BIBLIOGRAPHY

PRIMARY SOURCES

Websites

"C. P. Williams to Marguerite Pearson, September 30. 1939," Arkansas County
    Marriages Index, 1837–1957, www.ancestry.com.
"Ernest J. Stevens," https://www.findagrave.com/memorial/7801960/ernest-j.-stevens.
"H. C. Ray to Mary Lee McCrary, December 20 and 21, 1915," Pulaski County
    Marriages Index, 1838–1999, www.ancestry.com.
"Last Will and Testament of W. E. Josenberger," June 16, 1909, www.ancestry.com.
"1958 El Dorado, Arkansas City Directory, www.ancestry.com.
"Leoda Berry Gammon," http://www.findagrave.com/memorial/108544416
    /leoda-gammon.
"Ralph Amos," U.S. Appointments of U.S. Postmasters, 1832–1971, volume 98, 9,
    www.ancestry.com.
Toler v. Lula Toler Convalescing Home, 364 S. W. 2nd 680 (1963), www.law.justia.com.
US City Directory, 1910, www.ancestry.com.
US Federal Census, www.ancestry.com.
US Social Security Applications and Claims Index, 1936–2007, www.ancestry.com.
US Social Security Death Index, 1935–2014, www.ancestry.com.
US World War I Draft Registration Card, 1917–18 for Harvey C. Ray, www.ancestry
    .com.
US World War I Draft Registration Card, 1917–18 for Grover Cleveland Zachary,
    www.ancestry.com.

Manuscript Archives

Abraham, Dr. Anes Wiley. Personal Collection. Blytheville, AR.
Arkansas Council on Human Relations Papers. University of Arkansas Libraries
    Special Collections. Fayetteville, Arkansas.
Arkansas Extension Homemakers Council Papers. Arkansas State Archives. Little
    Rock, Arkansas.
Association of Southern Women for the Prevention of Lynching (ASWPL) Papers,
    Sanford, NC: Microfilming of America, 1983.
Claude A. Barnett Papers: The Associated Negro Press, 1918–67, Part 1: Associated
    Negro Press New Releases, 1928–64, Series B: 1945–55, Chicago Historical
    Society, IL.
Daisy Bates Papers. University of Arkansas Libraries Special Collections. Fayetteville,
    Arkansas.
Division of Negro Service, Planned Parenthood Federation of America (DNSPPFA).
    Florence Rose Papers, Sophia Smith Collection. Northampton, Massachusetts.

Federal Extension Service Records, RG 33. National Archives and Records Administration. Fort Worth, TX (NARA).

Florence C. Williams Papers. Arkansas State Archives. Little Rock, AR.

Hazel Jordon Papers. University of Arkansas Libraries Special Collections. Fayetteville, AR.

Herbert Norwood Collection. Fort Smith Museum of History, AR.

Jeanes Foundation Papers. Arkansas State Archives. Little Rock, AR.

Linton, Harry. Personal collection. University of Arkansas at Pine Bluff Museum. Pine Bluff, AR.

Moton Family Papers. Library of Congress. Washington, DC.

National Council of Churches of Christ, Division of Home Missions, 1950–64 (NCCDHM). Presbyterian Historical Society. Philadelphia, PA.

Papers of the NAACP, Part 13: NAACP and Labor, Series A: Subject Files on Labor Conditions and Employment Discrimination, 1940–55, Library of Congress, Washington, DC.

Papers of the NAACP, Part 25: Branch Department Files, Series A: Regional Files and Special Report, 1941–55, Group II, Series C, Branch Department Files, Regional Offices, Library of Congress, Washington, DC.

Pike, Annie Zachary. Personal collection. Marvell, AR.

Pine Bluff Women's Center Collection. University of Central Arkansas Archives. Conway, AR.

Porter Family Papers, 1902–96. Center for Arkansas History and Culture. University of Arkansas at Little Rock.

Records of the National Association of Colored Women's Clubs, 1895–1992 (RNACWC), University of Memphis Libraries.

Republican Party State Headquarters Collection. Center for Arkansas History and Culture. University of Arkansas at Little Rock.

Southern Education Foundation Archives. Archives Research Center, Atlanta University Center, Robert W. Woodruff Library, Atlanta, GA.

Southern Regional Council Papers, 1944–68, Atlanta, GA.

Tom Dillard Black Arkansiana Collection. Butler Center for Arkansas Studies. Little Rock, AR.

University of Arkansas Cooperative Extension Service Records, 1914–88 (UACESR). University of Arkansas Libraries Special Collections. Fayetteville, AR.

Upchurch, Ila. Jeanes Teacher Project Records. Arkansas State Archives. Little Rock, AR.

Venson, Dr. R. Q. and Ethyl H. Cotton Makers Jubilee Collection. Memphis and Shelby County Room, Memphis/Shelby County Public Library and Information Center. Memphis, Tennessee.

W. E. B. Du Bois Papers, 1868–1963, Special Collections and University Archives, University of Massachusetts Amherst Libraries.

Winthrop Rockefeller Collection, 1912–73. Center for Arkansas History and Culture. University of Arkansas at Little Rock.

Newspapers and Periodicals

Anniston Star (AL)
Appeal (Saint Paul, MN)
Arkansas Democrat (Little Rock)
Arkansas Gazette (Little Rock)
Arkansas Outlook
Arkansas State Press (Little Rock)
Arkansasyer (Pine Bluff)
Atlanta Constitution
Atlanta Daily World
Black Dispatch (Oklahoma City, OK)
Broad Axe (Chicago, IL)
Brooklyn Daily Eagle (New York)
Camden News (Arkansas)
Capitol Plaindealer (Topeka, KS)
Chicago Daily Defender
Chicago Defender
Cincinnati Enquirer
Clarion-Ledger (Jackson, MS)
Cleveland Gazette (Ohio)
Colored American (Washington, DC)
Commercial Appeal (Memphis, TN)
Commercial Appeal, Little Rock Bureau (Memphis, TN)
Competitor (Pittsburgh, PA)
Corsicana Daily Sun (TX)
Courier Index (Marianna, AR)
Courier-Journal (Louisville, KY)
Courier News (Blytheville, AR)
Daily Arkansas Gazette (Little Rock)
Daily Standard (Sikeston, MO)
Dallas Express (Texas)
Democrat and Chronicle (Rochester, NY)
Des Moines Register (IA)
El Dorado Times (AR)
Emporia Citizen (KS)
Farm Bureau Press: Official Publication of the Arkansas Farm Bureau Federation
Fayetteville Democrat (AR)
Freeman (Indianapolis, IN)
Great Bend Tribune (KS)
Helena, Arkansas Daily World
Hope Star (AR)
Indianapolis News (IN)
Inter Ocean (Chicago, IL)
Jet Magazine
Journal of the Fort Smith Historical Society (AR)
Kingsport Times (TN)
Lafayette County Democrat (Lewisville, AR)

Light and Heebee Jeebies (Chicago, IL)
Light: America's News Magazine (Chicago, IL)
Lincoln Echo (Fort Smith, AR)
Marvell Messenger (AR)
Montgomery Advertiser (AL)
Nashville News (TN)
National Negro Health News
National Notes: Official Organ of the National Association of Colored Women (Kansas City, MO)
Negro Spokesman (Pine Bluff, AR)
Negro Star (Wichita, KS)
New York Age
New York Amsterdam News
New York Times
Northwest Arkansas Times (Fayetteville, AR)
Official Record (United States Department of Agriculture) (Washington, DC)
Osceola Times (AR)
Our Colored Missions (New York, NY)
Pine Bluff Commercial (AR)
Pine Bluff Daily Graphic (AR)
Pittsburgh Courier (PA)
Plaindealer (Kansas City, KS)
Reno-Gazette Journal (NV)
Salina Evening Journal (KS)
Sedalia Democrat (MO)
Sentinel Record (Hot Springs, AR)
Southern Standard (Arkadelphia, AR)
Southern Workman (Hampton Institute, VA)
Student Voice (Atlanta, GA)
Tennessean (Nashville, TN)
Topeka Plaindealer (KS)
Tribune (Marked Tree, AR)
Wellington Leader (TX)
Western Outlook (Oakland, CA)
Wichita Daily Eagle (KS)
Woman's Home Companion

Articles, Pamphlets, Journals, and Books

Annual Catalogue of the Colored Agricultural and Normal University. Langston, OK: n.p., 1911.
Annual Register of the University of Chicago, 1914–1915. Chicago: University of Chicago Press, 1914.
Annual Report of Extension Service. College of Agriculture, University of Arkansas, Extension Circular No. 391, January 1937.

Anti-Lynching Crusaders. *A Million Women United to Suppress Lynching.* Buffalo, NY: n.p., 1922. Available online at: https://catalog.hathitrust.org/Record/102393691.

Arkansas Educational Directory, 1944–1945. Little Rock: State Department of Education, 1945.

Arkansas State Emergency Relief Administration. *Traveling Recovery Road: The Story of Relief, Work-Relief, and Rehabilitation in Arkansas, August 30, 1932 to November 15, 1936.* Little Rock: Emergency Relief Administration, 1936.

Betton, T. R. "A Brief History of Agricultural Extension Work Among Negroes in Arkansas." N.p., 1962. University of Arkansas Cooperative Extension Service Records, 1914–88.

Bradley, Gladyce H. "Some Health Education Implications of the Physical Examinations of Negroes in World War II." *Journal of Negro Education* 16, no. 2 (Spring 1947): 148–54.

Campbell, Thomas Monroe. *The Movable School Goes to the Negro Farmer.* Alabama: Tuskegee Institute Press, 1936.

Department of the Interior, Bureau of Education. *Negro Education: A Study of the Private and Higher Schools for Colored People in the United States* 2, no. 39. Washington, DC: US Government Printing Office, 1917.

Directory of County Agricultural Agents, Farm Bureaus, Home Demonstrators, and Boys' and Girls' Clubs in the United States and Canada List of the Agricultural Representatives, Directors of Women's Institutes and Secretaries of Federal and Provincial Wide Agricultural Organizations. Cambridge, MA: William Grant Wilson, 1920.

Division of Negro Education. *Problems of Negro Health in Arkansas: A Preliminary Study.* Little Rock: State Department of Education, 1939.

Educational Bulletin on Hookworm Disease and Rural Sanitation Issue by the Arkansas State Board of Health. Little Rock: Arkansas State Board of Health, 1914.

Equal Opportunity in Farm Programs: An Appraisal of Services Rendered by Agencies of the United States Department of Agriculture; a Report, Washington, DC: US Government Printing Office, 1965.

Favrot, Leo M. "A Notable Negro Exhibit." *Southern Workman* 44 (June 1915): 335–42.

The Final Report of the Colored Advisory Commission Appointed to Cooperate with the American National Red Cross and the President's Committee on Relief Work in the Mississippi Valley Flood Disaster of 1927. Washington, DC: American Red Cross, 1929.

Felton, Ralph A. *These My Brethren: A Study of 570 Negro Churches and 1,542 Negro Homes in the Rural South.* Madison: Drew Theological Seminary, 1950.

"Health Is Stressed as Primary Asset of Arkansas Rural Families." *Annual Report of the Extension Service.* University of Arkansas College of Agriculture, U.S. Department of Agriculture, Cooperating: December 1, 1938, to November 30, 1939. Circular No. 420, 1940.

Highfill, J. V., and M. C. Wilson. *Progress of Extension Teaching in Lee and Hot Springs Counties, Arkansas.* Circular No. 397, June 1937. Fayetteville: Extension Service, College of Agriculture, University of Arkansas.

Jernigan, W. J. *A Manual on Boys' and Girls' Agricultural Club Work: Designed Especially for Rural Teachers.* Little Rock: H. G. Pugh, 1920.

Jones, Julia Bumry. "The National Convention Held at Tuskegee." *The Competitor* 2, no. 1 (August-September 1920): 142–48.

Kansas State Agricultural College Catalogue, Fifty-First Session, 1913–1914. Topeka: Kansas State Printing Office, 1914.

Knapp, S. A. *Demonstration Work in Cooperation with Southern Farmers, U.S. Department of Agriculture Farmers' Bulletin 319.* Washington, DC: US Government Printing Office, 1908.

Mather, Frank Lincoln. *Who's Who of the Colored Race: A General Biographical Dictionary of Men and Women of African Descent.* Chicago: n.p., 1915.

Mercier, W. B. *Extension Work Among Negroes, 1920.* Circular 190. Washington, DC: US Government Printing Office, 1921.

"Mrs. Mame Stewart Josenberger, A.B." *The National Cyclopedia of the Colored Race.* Montgomery: National Publishing Company, 1919, 99.

"The National Association of Colored Women." *Voice of the Negro* 1, no. 7 (July 1904): 310–11.

"Negroes in 38 Counties Reached by Extension Program in 1938." *Annual Report of the Extension Service,* College of Agriculture, Fayetteville: University of Arkansas, Agriculture Extension Service, Circular No. 418, December 1, 1937 to November 30, 1938.

Nelson, Martin. *Rural Hygiene.* Circular No. 31. Fayetteville: University of Arkansas Agricultural Experiment Station and College of Agriculture, 1914.

Official Program, 30th Republican National Convention, Miami, Florida, August 1972. New York: Franklin/Rapid/Dart Organization, Inc., 1972.

Official Register of the United States, Containing a List of the Officers and Employees of the Civil, Naval, and Military Service, Together with a List of Vessels Belonging to the United States, July 1, 1903. Volume 2. Washington, DC: US Government Printing Office, 1903.

"Orders of Washington, D.C., The Great Torch of Liberty," Casefile 10218–372; Investigation of the Race Riot, Elaine, Arkansas, 1919 Federal Surveillance of Afro-Americans (1917–25): The First World War, the Red Scare, and the Garvey Movement, National Archives, Washington, DC.

Patterson, Homer L. *Patterson's College and School Directory of the United States and Canada.* Chicago: American Education Company, 1914.

Payne, M. T. *Value of Agricultural Extension Service to Farmers of Arkansas, Some Results of the World of the County Farm Agents, County Home Demonstration Agents, and Members of the Boys and Girls Agricultural and Home Economics Clubs for the Year of 1920.* Circular No. 102. Fayetteville: Extension Division, College of Agriculture, University of Arkansas, 1921.

Presson, J. A. *Bulletin: State of Arkansas Department of Education, Annual Report of Educational Activities in Negro Schools, June 30, 1920.*

Report of Special Summer Schools for Negro Extension Agents. Washington, DC: Office of Cooperative Extension Work, August 1930.

Shinn, E. H. *Agricultural Instruction: A Means of Establishing Better Racial Relations in Southern Communities.* Federal Extension Service Circular 68. Washington, DC: US Department of Agriculture, 1928.

Silver Anniversary Cooperative Demonstration Work, 1903–1928, Proceedings of the Anniversary Meeting Held at Houston, Texas, February 5th, 6th, and 7th, 1929.

College Station, TX: Extension Service, Agricultural and Technical College of Texas, 1929.

"Sins Crying to Heaven for Vengeance." *Our Colored Missions* 18, no. 10 (October 1932): 148–49.

Social Protection Division, Office of Community War Services, Federal Security Agency. *Meet Your Enemy, Venereal Disease.* Washington, DC: US Government Printing Office, 1944.

US Congress. Senate. Committee on Banking and Currency. *General Housing Act of 1945: Hearings before the Committee on Banking and Currency, United States Senate, Seventy-ninth Congress, First Session, on S. 1592, A Bill to Establish a National Housing Policy and Provide for Its Execution.* Washington: Government Printing Office, 1945.

US Department of Agriculture. *List of Workers in Subjects Pertaining to Agriculture and Home Economics in the U.S. Department of Agriculture and in the State Agricultural Colleges and Experiments Stations.* Washington, DC: US Government Printing Office, 1914.

Ward, Florence A. *Home Demonstration Work Under the Smith-Lever Act, 1914–1924.* Circular No. 43. Washington, DC: US Department of Agriculture, 1929.

Washington, Booker T. *The Successful Training of the Negro.* New York: Doubleday, 1903.

Work, Monroe N. *Industrial Work of Tuskegee Graduates and Former Students During the Year 1910.* Tuskegee, AL: Institute Press, 1911.

———. *Negro Year Book: An Annual Encyclopedia of the Negro, 1921–1922.* Tuskegee, AL: Negro Year Book Publishing Company, 1922.

Woofter, T. J., Jr. "Organization of Rural Negroes for Public Health." *Proceedings of the National Conference of Social Work*, 1923, 72–75.

Interviews

Dawson, Mrs. O. G. (Ethel B.) Pine Bluff Women's Center Collection, University of Central Arkansas Archives, 1976.

Perry, Carreather Banks. Telephone interview with author. Forrest City, Arkansas, January 26, 2015.

Woods, Delores Twillie, Thelma Woods Nash. Interviewed by Mausiki S. Scales, Forrest City (Ark.), July 19, 1995. In *Behind the Veil: Documenting African-American Life in the Jim Crow South Digital Collection*, John Hope Franklin Research Center, Duke University Libraries, Durham, NC.

Zachary, Annie R. Pine Bluff Women's Center Collection, University of Central Arkansas Archives, 1976.

Zachary Pike, Annie. Interview with author. Marvell, Arkansas, July 14, 2016.

SECONDARY SOURCES

Alexander, Donald Crichton. *The Arkansas Plantation, 1920–1942.* New Haven: Yale University Press, 1943.

Anderson, James D. *The Education of Blacks in the South, 1860–1935.* Chapel Hill: University of North Carolina Press, 1988.

Arkansas Extension Homemakers Council. *History of Home Demonstration Work in Arkansas, 1914–1965: Extension Homemaker Work, 1966–1975.* 1978. Arkansas Extension Homemakers Council Papers.

Altman, Karen Elizabeth. "Modernity, Gender, and Consumption: Public Discourses on Women and the Home." PhD diss., University of Iowa, 1987.

Beardsley, Edward H. *A History of Neglect: Health Care for Blacks and Mill Workers in the Twentieth Century South.* Knoxville: University of Tennessee Press, 1987.

Berlage, Nancy. *Farmers Helping Farmers: The Rise of the Farm and Home Bureaus, 1914–1935.* Baton Rouge: Louisiana State University Press, 2016.

Bernhard, Virginia, Betty Brandon, Theda Purdue, and Elizabeth Turner, eds. *Southern Women: Hidden Histories of Women in the New South.* Columbia: University of Missouri Press, 1994.

Biegert, M. Langley. "Legacy of Resistance: Uncovering the History of Collective Action by Black Agricultural Workers in Central East Arkansas from the 1860s to the 1930s." *Journal of Social History* 32, no. 1 (Autumn 1998): 73–99.

Biles, Roger. *The South and the New Deal.* Lexington: University of Kentucky Press, 1994.

Blackmon, Douglas A. *Slavery by Another Name: The Re-Enslavement of Black Americans from the Civil War to World War II.* New York: Anchor, 2009.

Blytheville/Mississippi County Black Culture Sesquicentennial Scrapbook. Blytheville, AR: n.p., 1986.

Bolsterli, Margaret Jones. *Things You Need to Hear: Collected Memories of Growing Up in Arkansas, 1890–1980.* Fayetteville: University of Arkansas Press, 2012.

Bowers, William L. *The Country Life Movement in America, 1900–1920.* Port Washington, NY: Kennikat Press, 1974.

A Brief History of Rural Electric and Telephone Reforms. Washington, DC: United States Department of Agriculture, 1986.

Brown, D. Clayton. *Electricity for Rural America: The Fight for REA.* Westport, CT: Greenwood Press, 1980.

Brown, Floyd. *He Built a School with Two Dollars and Eighty-Five Cents: Floyd Brown, Founder, Fargo Agricultural School, Arkansas: His Friends Tell the Story in This Book.* Fargo, AR: n.p., 1956.

Brown, Roscoe C. "The National Negro Health Week Movement." *Journal of Negro Education* 6, no. 3 (July 1937): 553–64.

Browne, Hugh A. "A Brief History of McRae Memorial Sanatorium." *Journal of the National Medical Association* 54, no. 4 (July 1962): 517–19.

Brunner, Edmund de Schweinitz. *Rural America and the Extension Service.* Menasha, WI: George Banta Publishing Company, 1949.

Cahn, Susan K. *Sexual Reckonings: Southern Girls in a Troubling Age.* Cambridge: Harvard University Press, 2007.

Caldwell, B. C. "The Work of Jeanes and Slater Funds." *Annals of the American Academy of Political and Social Sciences* 49, The Negro's Progress in Fifty Years (September 1913): 173–76.

Caliver, Ambrose, Senior Specialist in the Education of Negroes, US Office of Education. *Rural Elementary Education Among Negroes Under Jeanes Supervising Teachers.* Bulletin no. 5. Washington, DC: United States Government Printing Office, 1933.

Cameron, E. D. State Superintendent of Public Instruction. *Second Biennial Report, Department of Public Instruction, State of Oklahoma*. Guthrie, Oklahoma, 1908.

Campbell, Christiana McFadyen. *The Farm Bureau and the New Deal: A Study of the Making of National Farm Policy, 1933–1940*. Urbana: University of Illinois Press, 1962.

Cash, Floris Barnett. *African American Women and Social Action: The Clubwomen and Volunteerism from Jim Crow to the New Deal, 1896–1936*. Westport, CT: Greenwood Press, 2001.

Castro J. Justin. "Mexican Braceros and Arkansas Cotton: Agricultural Labor and Civil Rights in the Post World War II South." *Arkansas Historical Quarterly* 75, no. 1 (Spring 2016): 27–46.

Center for the American Woman and Politics. *Women in Public Office: A Biographical Directory and Statistical Analysis*. Metuchen, NJ: Scarecrow Press, 1978.

Chafe, William H. *The Paradox of Change: American Women in the 20th Century*. New York: Oxford University Press, 1991.

Cloke, Paul. "Conceptualizing Rurality." In *Handbook of Rural Studies*, edited by Paul Cloke, Terry Marsden, and Patrick H. Mooney, 18–28. London: Sage Publications, 2006.

Coclanis, Peter, and Bryant Simon. "Exit, Voice, and Loyalty: African American Strategies for Day to Day Existence/Resistance in the Early Twentieth Century South." In *African American Life in the Rural South, 1900–1950*, edited by R. Douglas Hurt, 189–209. Columbia: University of Missouri Press, 2003.

Coddington, James W. *Hospital and Health Services in Arkansas*. Fayetteville: University of Arkansas, Bureau of Research, 1947.

Cooley, Angela Jill. *To Live and Dine in Dixie: The Evolution of Urban Food Culture in the Jim Crow South*. Athens: University of Georgia Press, 2015.

Cotton, Barbara R. *The Lamplighters: Black Farm and Home Demonstration Agents in Florida, 1915–1965*. Tallahassee: United States Department of Agriculture; Florida Agricultural and Mechanical University, 1982.

Cutler, William W., III. *Parents and Schools: The 150 Year Struggle for Control in American Education*. Chicago: University of Chicago Press, 2000.

Danbom, David. *Born in the Country: A History of Rural America*. Baltimore: Johns Hopkins University Press, 2006.

Daniel, Pete. "African American Farmers and Civil Rights." *Journal of Southern History* 73, no. 1 (February 2007): 3–38.

———. *Breaking the Land: The Transformation of Cotton, Tobacco, and Rice Culture since 1880*. Urbana: University of Illinois Press, 1985.

———. *Deep'n as It Come: The 1927 Mississippi River Flood*. Fayetteville: University of Arkansas Press, 1996.

———. *Dispossession: Discrimination Against African American Farmers in the Age of Civil Rights*. Chapel Hill: University of North Carolina Press, 2013.

Devine, Jenny Barker. *On Behalf of the Family Farm: Iowa Farm Women's Activism since 1945*. Iowa City: University of Iowa Press, 2013.

Dillard, Tom. "Scipio A. Jones." *Arkansas Historical Quarterly* 31, no. 3 (Autumn 1972): 201–219.

Eden, Randall. *Growing Arkansas: Farm's Role in Arkansas History*. Little Rock: Publishing Concepts, 2003.

Edrington, Mabel. *History of Mississippi County, Arkansas, 1962.* Ocala, FL: Ocala Star Banner, 1962.

Egerton, John. *Speak Now Against the Day: The Generation Before the Civil Rights Movement in the South.* Chapel Hill: University of North Carolina Press, 1994.

Evans, Derryl and LaVerne Proctor-Streeter. "Reverend Professor Ralph Amos." *Arkansas Family Historian* 44, no.1 (March 2006): 4–11.

Fairclough, Adam. *A Class of Their Own: Black Teachers in the Segregated South.* New York: Belknap Press, 2007.

Ferguson, Karen J. "Caught in 'No Man's Land': The Negro Cooperative Demonstration Service and the Ideology of Booker T. Washington, 1900–1918." *Agricultural History* 72, no. 1, (Winter 1998): 33–54.

Finley, Randy. "Crossing the White Line: SNCC in Three Delta Towns, 1963–1967." *Arkansas Historical Quarterly* 65, no. 2 (Summer 2006): 116–37.

Giddings, Paula. *When and Where I Enter: The Impact of Black Women on Race and Sex in America.* New York: Quill, 1984.

Glave, Dianne D. "Rural African American Women, Gardening, and Progressive Reform in the South." In *To Love the Wind and the Rain: African Americans and Environmental History*, edited by Dianne D. Glave and Mark Stoll, 37–50. Pittsburgh: University of Pittsburgh Press, 2006.

Gordon, Fon Louise. "Black Women in Arkansas." *Pulaski County Historical Review* 35 (Summer 1987): 26–37.

———. *Caste and Class: The Black Experience in Arkansas, 1880–1920.* Athens: University of Georgia Press, 1995.

Grim, Valerie. "African American Rural Culture, 1900–1950." In Hurt, *African American*, 108–28.

———. "From the Yazoo Mississippi Delta to the Urban Communities of the Midwest: Conversations with Rural African American Women." *Frontiers: A Journal of Women Studies* 22, no. 1 (2001): 126–44.

Hadwiger, Don F., and Clay Cochran. "Rural Telephones in the United States." *Agricultural History* 58, no. 3 (July 1984): 221–38.

Hajdik, Anna Thompson. "A 'Bovine Glamour Girl': Borden Milk, Elsie the Cow, and the Convergence of Technology Animals, and Gender at the 1939 New York World's Fair." *Agricultural History* 88, no. 4 (Fall 2014): 470–90.

Hamilton, Kenneth M. *Booker T. Washington in American History.* Champaign: University of Illinois Press, 2017.

Handy, Robert T. *We Witness Together: A History of Cooperative Home Missions.* New York: Friendship Press, 1956.

Haney, Wava G., and Jane B. Knowles, eds. *Women and Farming: Changing Roles, Changing Structures.* Boulder: Westview Press, 1988.

Harlan, Louis, R. *Booker T. Washington: The Wizard of Tuskegee, 1901–1915.* New York: Oxford University Press, 1983.

Harley, Sharon, and Rosalyn Terborg-Penn. *The African American Woman: Struggles and Images.* Baltimore: Black Classic Press, 1997.

Harris, Carmen. "Grace under Pressure: The Black Home Extension Service in South Carolina 1919–1966." In *Rethinking Home Economics: Women and the History of a Profession*, edited by Sarah Stage and Virginia B. Vincenti, 203–228. Ithaca: Cornell University Press, 1997.

———. "State's Rights, Federal Bureaucrats, and Segregated 4-H Camps in the United

States, 1927–1969." *Journal of African American History* 93, no. 3 (Summer 2008): 362–88.

———. "'Well I Just Generally Bes the President of Everything': Rural Black Women's Empowerment through South Carolina Home Demonstration Activities." *Black Women, Gender, and Families* 3, no.1 (Spring 2009): 91–112.

———. "You're Just Like Mules, You Don't Know Your Own Strength: Rural South Carolina Black and the Emergence of the Civil Rights Struggle." In Reid and Bennett, *Beyond Forty Acres*, 254–270.

Hegarty, Marilyn E. *Victory Girls, Khaki-Wackies, and Patriotutes: The Regulation of Female Sexuality During World War II.* New York: New York University Press, 2008.

Heywood, Eunice. "Home Demonstration Clubs and Council." In *The Cooperative Extension Service*, edited by H. C. Sanders, 251–60. Englewood Cliffs, NJ: Prentice-Hall, 1966.

Higginbotham, Evelyn Brooks. "In Politics to Stay: Black Women Leaders and Party Politics in the 1920s." In *Women, Politics, and Change*, edited by Louise Tilly and Patricia Gurin, 199–220. New York: Russell Sage Foundation, 1992.

———. *Righteous Discontent: The Women's Movement in the Black Baptist Church, 1880–1920.* Cambridge: Harvard University Press, 1994.

Hill, Elizabeth Griffin. *Faithful to Our Tasks: Arkansas's Women and the Great War.* Little Rock: Butler Center Books, 2017.

———. *A Splendid Piece of Work: One Hundred Years of Arkansas' Home Demonstration and Extension Homemakers Clubs.* CreateSpace Independent Publishing Platform, 2012.

Hilton, Kathleen C. "Both in the Field, Each with a Plow: Race and Gender in USDA Policy, 1907–1929." In Bernhard et al., *Southern Women*, 114–33.

Hoffschwelle, Mary S. "'Better Homes on Better Farms': Domestic Reform in Rural Tennessee." *Frontiers: A Journal of Women Studies* 22, no. 1 (2001): 51–73.

———. *Rebuilding the Rural Southern Community: Reformers, Schools, and Homes in Tennessee, 1900–1930.* Knoxville: University of Tennessee Press, 1998.

Hogan, Mena. "A History of the Agricultural Extension Service in Arkansas." Master's thesis, University of Arkansas, 1940.

Holley, Donald. "The Plantation Heritage: Agriculture in the Arkansas Delta." In Whayne and Gatewood, *Arkansas Delta*, 238–77.

———. *Uncle Sam's Farmers: The New Deal Communities in the Lower Mississippi Valley.* Urbana: University of Illinois Press, 1975.

Holt, Marilyn Irvin. *Linoleum, Better Babies, and the Modern Farm Woman, 1890–1930.* Lincoln: University of Nebraska Press, 1995.

hooks, bell. *Yearning: Race, Gender, and Cultural Politics.* Boston: South End Press, 1990.

Hurt, R. Douglas, ed. *African American Life in the Rural South, 1900–1950.* Columbia: University of Missouri Press, 2000.

———. *American Agriculture: A Brief History.* West Lafayette: Purdue University Press, 2002.

Hutchinson, Janet Anne. "American Housing, Gender, and the Better Homes Movement, 1922–1935." PhD diss., University of Delaware, 1989.

Jacoway, Elizabeth. *Yankee Missionaries in the South: The Penn School Experiment.* Baton Rouge: Louisiana State University Press, 1980.

Jellison, Katherine. *Entitled to Power: Farm Women and Technology, 1913–1963*. Chapel Hill: University of North Carolina Press, 1993.

Johnson, Ben F., III. *Arkansas in Modern America, 1930–1999*. Fayetteville: University of Arkansas Press, 2000.

Jones, Allen W. "The South's First Black Farm Agents." *Agricultural History* 50, no. 4 (October 1976): 636–644.

Jones, Allen W. "The Role of Tuskegee Institute in the Education of Black Farmers." *Journal of Negro History* 60 (April 1975): 252–67.

Jones, Cherisse R. "'How Shall I Sing the Lord's Song?' United Church Women Confront Racial Issues in South Carolina, 1940s–1960s." In *Throwing Off the Cloak of Privilege: White Southern Women Activists in the Civil Rights Era*, edited by Gail A. Murray, 131–52. Gainesville: University Press of Florida, 2004.

Jones, Lu Ann. "In Search of Jennie Booth Moton, Field Agent, AAA." *Agricultural History* 72, no. 2 (Spring 1998): 446–58.

———. *Mama Learned Us to Work: Farm Women in the New South*. Chapel Hill: University of North Carolina Press, 2002.

Jones-Branch, Cherisse. *Crossing the Line: Women's Interracial Activism in South Carolina during and after World War II*. Gainesville: University Press of Florida, 2014.

———. "Farming Women and the State in North America." *Journal of Women's History* 31, no. 3 (Fall 2019): 124–28.

———. "Women and the 1919 Elaine Massacre." In *The Elaine Massacre and Arkansas: A Century of Atrocity and Resistance, 1819–1919*, edited by Guy Lancaster, 176–99. Little Rock: Butler Center Books, 2018.

———. "'Working Slowly but Surely and Quietly': The Arkansas Council of the Association of Southern Women for the Prevention of Lynching, 1930–1941." In *Bullets and Fire: Case Studies of Lynching in Arkansas from Slavery to the 1930s*, edited by Guy Lancaster, 223–237. Fayetteville: University of Arkansas Press, 2017.

Kechnie, Margaret C. *Organizing Rural Women: The Federated Women's Institutes of Ontario, 1897–1919*. Montreal: McGill-Queens's University Press, 2003.

Kilmer, Rebecca. *Women of the Arkansas Delta: The Pine Bluff Women's Center, Inc.* Pine Bluff: Pine Bluff Women's Center, 1976.

King, Joyce E., and Ellen E. Swartz. *The Afrocentric Praxis of Teaching for Freedom: Connecting Culture to Learning*. New York: Routledge, 2016.

Kinkead, Joyce. *Farm: A Multi-Modal Reader*. Southlake, TX: Fountainhead Press, 2014.

Kirk, John. "Facilitating Change: The Arkansas Council on Human Relations, 1954–1964," http://plaza.ufl.edu/wardb/Kirk.doc.

———. *Redefining the Color Line: Black Activism in Little Rock, Arkansas, 1940–1970*. Gainesville: University Press of Florida, 2002.

———. "A Southern Road Less Traveled: The 1966 Gubernatorial Election and (Winthrop)Rockefeller Republicanism in Arkansas." In *Painting Dixie Red: When, Where, Why, and How the South Became Republican*, edited by Glenn Feldman, 172–98. Gainesville: University Press of Florida, 2011.

Kline, Ronald R. *Consumers in the Country: Technology and Social Change in Rural America*. Baltimore: Johns Hopkins University Press, 2000.

Knowles, Jane B. "It's Our Turn Now: Rural American Women Speak Out, 1900–1920." In Haney and Knowles, *Women and Farming*, 303–18.

Larson, Vernon C. "The Development of Short Courses at the Land Grant Institutions." *Agricultural History* 31, no. 2 (April 1957): 31–35.

Lee County Sesquicentennial Committee. *History of Lee County, Arkansas*. Dallas: Curtis Media Corporation, 1987.

Lewis, David Levering. *W. E. B. Du Bois: Biography of a Race, 1868–1919*. New York: Henry Holt and Company, 1993.

Littlefield, Valinda. "'To Do the Next Needed Thing': Jeanes Teachers in the Southern United States, 1908–1934." In *Telling Women's Lives: Narrative Inquiries in the History of Women's Education*, edited by Kathleen Weiler and Sue Middleton, 130–146. Buckingham: Open University Press, 1999.

Lowe, Kevin M. *Baptized with Soil: Christian Agrarians and the Crusade for Rural America*. New York: Oxford University Press, 2016.

Maples, C. Richard. *Farther Down the Road: The History of the University of Arkansas Cooperative Extension Service*. Little Rock: University of Arkansas Division of Agriculture, 2007.

Matkin-Rawn, Story. "The Great Negro State of the Country: Arkansas's Reconstruction and the Other Great Migration." *Arkansas Historical Quarterly* 52, no. 1 (Spring 2013): 101–26.

Mayberry, B. D. *The Role of Tuskegee University in the Origin, Growth, and Development of the Negro Cooperative Extension System, 1881–1990*. Tuskegee: Tuskegee University Cooperative Extension Program, 1989.

McClure, Phyllis. *Jeanes Teachers: A View into Black Education in the Jim Crow South*. Charleston, SC: BookSurge Publishing, 2009.

McKinney, Amy L. "From Canning to Contraceptives: Cooperative Extension Service Home Demonstration Clubs and Rural Montana Women in the Post-World War II Era." *Montana: The Magazine of Western History* 16, no. 3 (Autumn 2011): 57–70, 95–96.

Mitchell, H. L. "The Founding and Early History of the Southern Tenant Farmers Union." *Arkansas Historical Quarterly* 32, no. 4 (Winter 1973): 342–69.

———. *Mean Things Happening in This Land: The Life and Times of H. L. Mitchell, Cofounder of the Southern Tenant Farmers Union*. Montclair, NJ: Allanheld Osmun Publishers, 1979.

Mitchell, Michele. *Righteous Propagation: African Americans and the Politics of Racial Destiny after Reconstruction*. Chapel Hill: University of North Carolina Press, 2004.

Mizelle, Richard M. *The Mississippi Flood of 1927 in the African American Imagination*. Minneapolis: The University of Minnesota Press, 2014.

Moore, Leonard. *The Defeat of Black Power: Civil Rights and the National Black Political Convention of 1972*. Baton Rouge: Louisiana State University Press, 2018.

Myers, Lois E., and Rebecca Sharpless. "'Of the Least and the Most': The African American Rural Church." In Hurt, *African American Life*, 54–80.

"National Negro Health Week to Be Observed April 1 to 8, 1928." *Public Health Reports* 43, no. 8 (February 24, 1928): 457–58.

Olsson, Tore C. *Agrarian Crossings: Reformers and the Remaking of the US and Mexican Countryside*. Princeton: Princeton University Press, 2017.

Osterud, Nancy Gray. "Land, Identity, and Agency in the Oral Autobiographies of
    Farm Women." In Haney and Knowles, *Women and Farming*, 73–87.

Patterson, Thomas. *History of the Arkansas Teachers Association*. Washington, DC:
    National Education Association, 1981.

Patton, Adell, Jr. "Surviving the System: Pioneering Principals in a Segregated School,
    Lincoln High School, Forrest City, Arkansas." *Arkansas Review: A Journal of
    Delta Studies* 42, no. 1 (April 2011): 3–21.

Payne, Elizabeth Anne. "'What Ain't I Been Doing?': Historical Reflections on
    Women and the Arkansas Delta." In Whayne and Gatewood, *Arkansas Delta*,
    128–49.

Ramdani, Fatma. "Afro-American Women Activists as True Negotiators in the
    International Arena, 1893–1945." *European Journal of American Studies* 10, no. 1
    (2015): 1–15. https://journals.openedition.org/ejas/10646.

Reck, Franklin M. *The 4-H Story: A History of 4-H Club Work*. Ames: Iowa
    State College Press, 1951.

Reeves, Maxine E. *The History of the National Extension of Home Economists, 1933–1975*.
    Phoenix: National Association of Extension Home Economists, 1976.

Reid, Debra A. *Reaping a Greater Harvest: African Americans, the Extension Service, and
    Rural Reform in Jim Crow Texas*. College Station: Texas A & M University Press,
    2007.

Reid, Debra A., and Evan P. Bennett, eds. *Beyond Forty Acres and a Mule: African
    American Landowning Families since Reconstruction*. Gainesville: University Press
    of Florida, 2012.

Reid, Debra A. "Mary L. Ray (1880?–1934) Arkansas's Negro Extension Worker." In
    Cherisse Jones-Branch and Gary T. Edwards, eds., *Arkansas Women: Their Lives
    and Times*, 237–61. Athens: University of Georgia Press, 2018.

Richardson, Harry V. *Dark Glory: A Picture of the Church among Negroes in the Rural
    South*. New York: Friendship Press, 1947.

Rieff, Lynne. "Go Ahead and Do All You Can: Southern Progressives and Alabama
    Home Demonstration Clubs, 1914–1940." In Bernhard et al., *Southern Women*,
    134–52.

———. "Revitalizing Southern Homes: Rural Women, the Professionalization of
    Home Demonstration Work, and the Limits of Reform, 1917–1945." In *Women,
    Family, and Faith: Rural Southern Women in the Twentieth Century South*, edited
    by Rebecca Sharpless and Melissa Walker, 135–65. Columbia: University of
    Missouri Press, 2006.

Rigueur, Leah Wright. *The Loneliness of the Black Republican: Pragmatic Politics and the
    Pursuit of Power*. Princeton: Princeton University Press, 2014.

Roberts, Blain. *Pageants, Parlors, and Pretty Women: Race and Beauty in the Twentieth-
    Century South*. Chapel Hill: University of North Carolina Press, 2014.

Rodrique, Jessie M. "The Black Community and the Birth Control Movement."
    In *Passion and Power: Sexuality in History*, edited by Kathy Peiss and Christina
    Simmons, 138–56. Philadelphia: Temple University Press, 1989.

Rogers, O. A., Jr. "The Elaine Race Riots of 1919." *Arkansas Historical Quarterly* 19
    (Summer 1960): 142–50.

Roll, Jarod. *Spirit of Rebellion: Labor and Religion in the New Cotton South*. Urbana:
    University of Illinois Press, 2010.

Rosenberg, Gabriel N. *The 4-H Harvest: Sexuality and the State in Rural America.* Philadelphia: University of Pennsylvania Press, 2015.

Ross, James D., Jr. *The Rise and Fall of the Southern Tenant Farmers Union in Arkansas.* Knoxville: University of Tennessee Press, 2018.

Rymph, Catherine E. *Republican Women: Feminism and Conservatism from Suffrage Through the Rise of the New Right.* Chapel Hill: University of North Carolina Press, 2006.

Schackel, Sandra K. *Working the Land: The Stories of Ranch and Farm Women in the Modern American West.* Lawrence: University of Kansas Press, 2011.

Schultz, Kevin. *Tri-Faith America: How Catholics and Jews Held Postwar America to Its Protestant Promise.* New York: Oxford University Press, 2011.

Schultz, Mark. "Benjamin Hubert and the Association for the Advancement of Negro Country Life." In Reid and Bennett, *Beyond Forty Acres,* 83–105. Scott, James C. *Domination and the Arts of Resistance: Hidden Transcripts.* New Haven: Yale University Press, 1990.

———. *Weapons of the Weak: Everyday Forms of Peasant Resistance.* New Haven: Yale University Press, 1985.

Scott, Roy V. *The Reluctant Farmer: The Rise of Agricultural Extension to 1914.* Urbana: University of Illinois Press, 1970.

Shaw, Stephanie J. *What a Woman Ought to Be and to Do: Black Professional Women Workers During the Jim Crow Era.* Chicago: University of Chicago Press, 1996.

Smith, C. Calvin, and Linda Walls Jackson. *Educating the Masses: The Unfolding History of Black School Administrators in Arkansas, 1900–2000.* Fayetteville: University of Arkansas Press, 2003.

Smith, Susan L. *Sick and Tired of Being Sick and Tired: Black Women's Health Activism in America, 1890–1950.* Philadelphia: University of Pennsylvania Press, 1995.

Snowden, Deanna. *Mississippi County, Arkansas: Appreciating the Past, Anticipating the Future.* Little Rock: Mississippi County Community College Foundation, 1986.

Spencer, Robyn. "Contested Terrain: The Mississippi Flood of 1927 and the Struggle to Control Black Labor." *Journal of Negro History* 79, no. 2 (Spring 1994): 170–81.

Stockley, Griff. *Blood in Their Eyes: The Elaine Race Massacres of 1919.* Fayetteville: University of Arkansas, 2001.

Stokes, Melvyn. *D. W. Griffith's "The Birth of a Nation": A History of "The Most Controversial Motion Picture of All Time."* New York: Oxford University Press, 2008.

Strausberg, Stephen. F. *A Century of Research: A Centennial History of the Arkansas Agricultural Experiment Station.* Fayetteville: Arkansas Agricultural Experiment Station, University of Arkansas, 1989.

Swinn, E. H. *Agricultural Instruction: A Means of Establishing Better Racial Relations in Southern Communities.* Extension Service Circular 68. Washington, DC: United States Department of Agriculture, 1928.

Sworakoski, Witold S. "Herbert Hoover, Launching the American Food Administration, 1917." In *Herbert Hoover: The Great War and Its Aftermath, 1914–1923,* edited by Lawrence E. Gelfand, 40–61. Iowa City: University of Iowa Press, 1979.

Taylor, Kieran. "'We Have Just Begun': Black Organizing and White Response in the

Arkansas Delta, 1919." *Arkansas Historical Quarterly* 58, no. 3 (Autumn 1999): 264–84.

"Toward a National Policy." *Proceedings of the 1971 White House Conference on Aging, November 28-December 2.* Final Report, volume 1. Washington, DC: US Government Printing Office, 1971.

True, Alfred Charles. *A History of Agricultural Education in the United States, 1785–1925.* New York: Arno Press, 1969.

Turner, Elizabeth Hayes. *Women and Gender in the New South.* Wheeling, Ill.: Harlad Davidson, 2009.

Tuuri, Rebecca. *Strategic Sisterhood: The National Council of Negro Women in the Black Freedom Movement.* Chapel Hill: University of North Carolina Press, 2018.

Vesely-Flad, Rima. *Racial Purity and Dangerous Bodies: Moral Pollution, Black Lives, and the Struggle for Justice.* Minneapolis: Augsburg Fortress Publishers, 2018.

Walker, Anna, E. "Howard School." *Journal of the Fort Smith Historical Society* 9, no. 1 (April 1985): 11–13.

Walker, Melissa. *All We Knew Was to Farm: Rural Women in the Upcountry South, 1919–1941.* Baltimore: Johns Hopkins University Press, 2000.

———. "Shifting Boundaries: Race Relations in the Rural Jim Crow South." In Hurt, *African American Life,* 81–107.

Wallach, Jennifer Jensen, and John A. Kirk. *ARSNICK: The Student Nonviolent Coordinating Committee in Arkansas.* Fayetteville: University of Arkansas Press, 2011.

Warren, Charline J., ed. *An Official History of the National Extension Homemakers Council, Inc., 1930–1990.* Burlington, KY: National Extension Homemakers Council, 1991.

Webb, Pamela. "By the Sweat of the Brow: The Back-to-the-Land Movement in Depression Arkansas." *Arkansas Historical Quarterly* 42, no. 4 (Winter 1983): 332–45.

Wesley, Charles Harris. *The History of the National Association of Colored Women's Clubs, A Legacy of Service.* Washington, DC: National Association of Colored Women's Clubs, 1984.

Whayne, Jeannie. *Delta Empire: Lee Wilson and the Transformation of Agriculture in the New South.* Baton Rouge: Louisiana State University Press, 2016.

———. "'I Have Been through Fire': Black Agricultural Extension Agents and the Politics of Negotiation." In Hurt, *African American Life,* 152–88.

———. "The Segregated Farm Program in Poinsett County, Arkansas." *The Mississippi Quarterly,* no. 45 (1992): 421–38.

Whayne, Jeannie M., Thomas A. DeBlack, George Sabo III, and Morris S. Arnold. *Arkansas: A Concise History.* Fayetteville: University of Arkansas Press, 2019.

Whayne, Jeannie M., Thomas A. DeBlack, George Sabo III, and Morris S. Arnold. *Arkansas: A Narrative History.* Fayetteville: University of Arkansas Press, 2013.

Whayne, Jeannie M., and Willard B. Gatewood, eds. *The Arkansas Delta: Land of Paradox.* Fayetteville: University of Arkansas Press, 1993.

Whitaker, Robert. *On the Laps of Gods: The Red Summer of 1919 and the Struggle for Justice that Remade a Nation.* New York: Crown, 2008.

Wiley, Alena. "The Matlocks of Princeton, Seven Generations, 1864–1994." *Delta Historical Review,* Summer 1994, 48–56.

Wilks, Henry, A. *A Few Events and Occurrences in the History of Brinkley, Arkansas and Surrounding Towns and Communities of the Central Delta through 1935*. Brinkley: n.p., 1997.

Williams, Johnny E. *African American Religion and the Civil Rights Movement in Arkansas*. Jackson: University Press of Mississippi, 2003.

Williams, Mildred M., Kara Vaughn, and NASC Interim History Writing Committee. *The Jeanes Story: A Chapter in the History of American Education, 1908–1968*. Atlanta: Southern Education Foundation, 1979.

Winn, J. Emmett. *Documenting Racism: African Americans in the U.S. Department of Agriculture Documentaries, 1921–1942*. New York: Continuum, 2012.

———. "Documenting Racism in an Agricultural Extension Film." *Film & History* 38, no. 1 (Spring 2008): 33–43.

Woodruff, Nan. *American Congo: The African American Freedom Struggle in the Delta*. Chapel Hill: University of North Carolina Press, 2003.

Woyshner, Christine A. *The National PTA, Race, and Civic Engagement, 1897–1970*. Columbus: Ohio State University Press, 2009.

Yard, Alexander. "'They Don't Regard My Rights at All': Arkansas Farm Workers, Economic Modernization, and the Southern Tenant Farmers Union." *Arkansas Historical Quarterly* 47, no. 3 (Autumn 1988): 201–29.

Zellar, Gary. "H. C. Ray and Racial Politics in the Arkansas American Extension Service Program in Arkansas, 1915–1929." *Agricultural History* 72, no. 2 (Spring 1999): 429–45.

INDEX

Italicized page numbers refer to illustrations.

Abraham, Anes Wiley, 180n12
Adkins, Homer, 83
Agnew, Judy, 151
Agricultural Adjustment Administration
(AAA), 59–64, 92
Allen, C. E., 87–88
Alpha Kappa Alpha Sorority, 174n6,
184n5
American County Life Association, 33
American Farm Bureau Federation
(AFBF), 100
American Red Cross, 23–24, 52–55,
94, 116
American Society for Horticultural
Science, 33
American Teachers Association, 24
Amos, Ralph, 33, 164n8
Anderson, Joe Lee, 152, 196n87
Anderson, W. F., 56
Ankrum, Henrietta, 52
Arkansas Agricultural Cooperative
Extension Service (AACES): and
cooperation with multiple organi-
zations, 11, 12, 19, 66, 100 (*see also*
individual organizations); creation
of, 34; desegregation of, 133–35;
on food security and preservation
during World War II, 92; funding
for, 35; segregation of, 37, 131; state
agricultural extension services, creation of, 13; and training programs
for agents, 12, 15–16. *See also* farm
agents; home demonstration agents;
home demonstration clubs; *individual home demonstration agents*
Arkansas Association of Colored
Women (AACW): and Better
Homes Movement, 78–81; goals and

focus of, 75, 81, 180n16; industrial
education, support of, 170n32;
industrial homes for girls, 74–75,
81–83; and multi-organization
memberships and cooperation with,
11, 63, 74, 87, 135, 184n5; political
involvement of, 81–83, 145–46; on
racial violence, 73; and respectability politics, 74, 75, 78
Arkansas Association of Public Welfare
Workers, 147
Arkansas Colored Teachers Association
(ACTA), 12, 15–17, 20, 26, 63,
96–97, 116–17
Arkansas Congress of Colored Parents
and Teachers (ACCPT), 9, 21, 22,
90, 96–97
Arkansas Council of Home Demon-
stration Clubs, 133; Black women,
exclusion from, 66
Arkansas Council of the Association
of Southern Women for the
Prevention to Lynching, 162n107
Arkansas Council on Human Relations
(ACHR), 59, 123–24, 150
Arkansas Department of Education
(ADE), 12, 19, 26, 63, 117
Arkansas Department of Health, 118
Arkansas Division of Negro Education, 64
Arkansas Economic Development
Advisory Council, 148
Arkansas Education Association (AEA),
26, 153
Arkansas Extension Homemakers
Council (AEHC), 133, 135, 143–44
Arkansas Farm Bureau Federation
(ARFBF), 143; Negro Division,
99–103, 105–6, 158

CHERISSE JONES-BRANCH is the James and Wanda Lee Vaughn Endowed Professor of History at Arkansas State University, where she is dean of the graduate school. She is the author of *Crossing the Line: Women and Interracial Activism in South Carolina during and after World War II* and the coeditor of *Arkansas Women: Their Lives and Times*.